D0712190

HAMMERING HANK

HAMMERING HANK

How the Media Made Henry Aaron

MARK STEWART
and MIKE KENNEDY

THE LYONS PRESS
Guilford, Connecticut
An imprint of The Globe Pequot Press

The Lyons Press is an imprint of The Globe Pequot Press.

10 9 8 7 6 5 4 3 2 1

Printed in the United States of America

Designed by Sheryl P. Kober

ISBN-13: 978-1-59228-930-1
ISBN-10: 1-59228-930-4

Library of Congress Cataloging-in-Publication Data is available on file.

CONTENTS

PREFACE

THE MOMENT YOU PICKED UP THIS BOOK, YOU probably noticed a thinly masked double meaning to its title. Aside from the fact that "Hammerin' Hank" is probably Henry Aaron's most recognizable nickname, it seemed an increasingly appropriate title as our research and writing progressed. When we set out to explore his career, we did so with the goal of holding "a mirror to the mirror" that the media held up to him. We suspected that the popular image of Aaron was incomplete and occasionally misleading. What we found only convinced us of this.

The treatment Aaron received in the media, at first glance, seemed no better or worse than that experienced by any other ball player. Indeed, baseball writers appeared nearly unanimous in their praise of Aaron. As our files grew inches thick, however, we began to notice an interesting theme. Aaron quite clearly was not "any other ballplayer" and media praise, though typically effusive, tended to damn him at the same time. Rarely were his qualities discussed in the popular press without allusions to his shortcomings, either real, imagined, or contrived.

Was this done in the name of balanced baseball reporting? Occasionally it was; many of the observations made regarding Aaron were either well-founded or at least supported by facts. Yet just as often the criticisms took the form of character bashing—thinly veiled stabs at Aaron's personality (or alleged lack thereof) that were said to diminish his performance on the field. The better the writer, the more subtly this was done. By all accounts, Aaron was unfailingly pleasant. Yet he seemed to rub a lot of people in the press the wrong way.

Over a quarter century or so, as Aaron's status within the game metamorphosed from country bumpkin to tenured star to grand old man, the nature of these slights changed, too. But they were always there, always coloring the public's perception. That being said, Aaron may well have served as the perfect accomplice. For most of his career he was content to let the press print whatever it wanted. He even played along sometimes, just to get the reporters out of his hair.

Eventually, we became convinced that, by the time fans began to recognize Aaron's greatness and celebrate his remarkable achievements, they did not have a clear picture of who he was, nor did they understand what his accomplishments really meant.

Perhaps this is why Aaron chose to set the record straight with *I Had a Hammer*, his 1991 autobiography. The book was snapped up by the public and Aaron was roundly hailed for his forthrightness in recounting the indignities visited upon him as a young African-American in 1950s America, and later for using the book as a platform to criticize baseball's power structure (of which he is now an important part). His more inquisitive fans, however, were disappointed in *I Had a Hammer*. Aaron gave them a peek into his world, but it was not the intimate one they craved.

Although this book counts among its primary sources *I Had a Hammer*, it goes after something different. When we started this project we believed that, somewhere between the reams of printed information produced on Aaron during his career and the post-career reflections of Aaron (and those who played with and against him), lay a more balanced and thought-provoking story. Our quest was to write a biography that explored this compelling "middle ground." In *Hammering Hank*, we believe we did just that.

The creative process began with three separate research jobs. The first (and most enjoyable) involved locating every major magazine article we could find on Aaron—particularly those published in sports magazines. These pieces typically offered more perspective and expertise than the newspaper profiles and columns we read, and as such provided a better "snapshot" of where Aaron was in relation to his world. They ran the gamut from top-line publications such as *Sport* and *Sports Illustrated* to more pedestrian offerings, including *Baseball Digest*, the *Sporting News,* and the pulp sports magazines of the 1950s, '60s and early '70s.

The second research job involved acquiring, reading, and comparing the numerous books written about Aaron. Most were aimed at a rather low common denominator, but each had a point to make and provided some information on Aaron that the others did not. The third part of the job required us to dig up articles and books mentioning Aaron in the 25 years after his career ended, as well as watching the documentaries produced to honor him 25 years after breaking Babe Ruth's career home run mark.

Interestingly, we found that the farther away we got from 1974, the cloudier the information became. Much of what we read and saw bordered on revisionist history. Some of the information presented as fact was just wrong. From a decade of interviewing athletes past and present in a number of sports, we knew that—although they may recall some things in astonishing detail—they can be astonishingly unreliable when asked about other things. They also tend to embellish and condense when it suits their needs. So we were extremely careful when separating fact from fiction.

Once all the research was done, we charted a course to reach a place other authors seem to have sailed right by—one where readers might gain new perspectives on one of the most elusive and enigmatic sports figures of our time.

Using a chronological framework to build the story of Henry Aaron's life, we were constantly evaluating our data to present a balanced and informative view of who he was and how the world perceived him. Luckily, since so much of baseball is recorded in numbers, the good and bad information was relatively easy to sort out. When we encountered two pieces of contradictory "observational" information, we presented both sides of the story. We have been fans long enough, have collaborated on enough research and writing projects, and have access to enough good information to trust our instincts and make a judgment call. In these instances, we invite you to do the same.

It certainly did not hurt that, at our fingertips, we had access to a privately owned sports research library that includes almost every bit of significant baseball writing—catalogued and uncatalogued—on Aaron from the 1950s to date. From this same collection came many of the images used in this book. We felt there was no better way to illustrate a life defined by the media than to use examples of how Aaron was presented in the media. In that respect, one might say that what you see reproduced in these pages—from cards to coloring books—is a sampling of the "ultimate" Aaron collection.

Of course, for most of Aaron's career, his feats and foibles were chronicled in baseball and general sports publications. As it became increasingly clear that he would break Ruth's record, he was recast as an object of reverence by more mainstream media outlets, including the weekly news magazines, large-circulation newspapers and, of course, television. During these pivotal years, when Aaron achieved iconic status, it could be effectively argued that he made the media as much as the media made him. A lot of the competition-driven hype and invasiveness we see in sports reporting today began with the intense scrutiny and appalling media crush Aaron endured in 1973 and 1974. Understandably, it is a part of the Aaron legacy that is almost always overlooked whenever the media sums up his impact on American sports.

In the end, we were quite satisfied with our work. Through exhaustive research and a highly selective (and, yes, incredibly painful) editing process, we sculpted a mountain of information into a final form that we think is comprehensive enough for the baseball scholar yet still very digestible for the casual fan. Where interpretation is called for, we chose to lay out the facts and present outside opinions as evenhandedly as we could; the rule of thumb we followed throughout was to step back and allow readers to draw their own conclusions. That being said, it should also be stated that on many points, no one will ever nail Aaron down.

You might wonder as you read: Why didn't they speak to Aaron himself? This is a fair question, and the answer in many ways illustrates the central theme of this book. We contacted Aaron and his representatives at the beginning of this journey, and again at its conclusion. He chose not to participate, which is certainly his right. Perhaps he was tired of telling his story, or didn't see this project as being worth his time. Maybe, too, he still distrusts writers. The fact that we were able to assemble a comprehensive, multilayered portrait of Aaron without his assistance is testimony to the fact that he and the media will be forever and inextricably linked.

Hammering Hank, however, is more than a study of how the media shaped Henry Aaron. It is, first and foremost, the story of a baseball life. That being said, it also is a look at a life affected more than most others by events outside of baseball. Long before Aaron became part of the national landscape, he was a reflection of it. And try as he might to shut out the world around him, the forces of that world—with all their complexities and indignities and randomness—were always very much a part of him.

INTRODUCTION

ON APRIL 8, 1999, AT TURNER FIELD IN ATLANTA, Major League Baseball celebrated the 25th anniversary of Henry Aaron's 715th home run, which propelled him past Babe Ruth to the top of the game's all-time home run list. Those expecting to recapture the spark of that long-ago moment may have felt a letdown. The ceremony, while touching and heartfelt, was a made-for-television event that featured stock-footage clips of Aaron and a few neatly crafted tomes recited in Aaron's honor. In retrospect, there may have been no tribute more fitting, for the Aaron with whom we have become comfortable is, after all, a creation of the media.

On that evening in 1999 baseball again got a fleeting look at the home run king, acknowledging the cheers, his eyes moist. Fans added this image to everything they know of him and what little they know of him. His is a portrait 50 years in the making which, in truth, is no more than a highly detailed caricature, exquisitely embellished yet somehow still lacking in substance.

Flash back to Cincinnati, to Opening Day of the 1974 baseball season. It was an afternoon that had an uneasy feel to it. Killer tornadoes, the worst in two generations, had ravaged Ohio, Kentucky, and Indiana just days before. Entire neighborhoods were reduced to kindling. More than a hundred people had perished and more were still missing. Thousands were homeless. Damages reached $1 billion. This grim scene fit perfectly within a larger tableau of the United States circa 1974—namely that of a nation being torn up by forces that were difficult to anticipate or comprehend, and impossible to control.

The supreme self-confidence of the post-World War II years had given way to national self-loathing. President Nixon was on the ropes. Trust had become a commodity bartered by politicians and businessmen, and a profoundly devalued one at that. As political activism embraced the use of violence, terrorism was no longer something that happened to someone in another part of the world. It could happen to you, or someone you knew. No one really felt safe anymore.

OPEC had imposed an oil embargo, and Americans were lining up for hours to fill their gas tanks. The Vietnam War remained a painful part of the national consciousness, and its devastating aftereffects were just starting to surface. Drug use was tightening its grip on society. Organized crime was being romanticized by films such as *The Godfather*. Ethnic pride surged, which only magnified the deep racial divisions that existed in the country. Morality was no longer a given, it was a flash point. The divorce rate had doubled in 10 years, and as conservative groups tried to keep *Deep Throat* out of the movie houses and *Playboy* and *Penthouse* off the magazine racks, the development of pornography into a thriving industry suggested to many that the sexual revolution had gone too far. And, perhaps worst of all, few appreciated just how bad disco music was. All joking aside, the country seemed to be crumbling at its very foundation, and storms far more devastating than those which had passed through the Midwest still loomed on the horizon.

Standing far too close for his liking to the eye of this maelstrom was Henry Aaron, the 40-year-old cleanup hitter of the Atlanta Braves. During the past two decades, he had maintained a low profile, speaking out occasionally on controversial topics when the mood struck him, but mostly being a terrific ballplayer who held his tongue and went about his business without much fanfare. By the spring of 1974, however, the media swirl around Aaron had elevated him to an unfamiliar and uncomfortable new role. The country needed a savior and, like it or not, he was the perfect candidate.

Twenty years earlier, almost to the day, Cincinnati's public address announcer spoke Aaron's name into the microphone for the first time in a major league ballpark. Save for a few extra pounds, Aaron the veteran did not look too different from Aaron the rookie. When his name was called again in the top of the first inning—more than 25,000 innings later—the slugger strode as casually as ever to the plate. His gait was still sleepy, his countenance still unaffected. As had been noted numerous times over Aaron's long and illustrious career, it was impossible to tell if he was the executioner or the man about to lay his head on the chopping block. He continued his ritual in the batter's box as the noise level began to rise at Riverfront Stadium.

Tom Seaver tried to capture the essence of a confrontation with Aaron in his 1974 book, *How I Would Pitch to Babe Ruth*, recalling the first time he faced the slugger as a rookie with the Mets in 1967. "As he approached the plate, I knew so well what his every action would be," Seaver wrote, "how he'd put on his batting helmet with both hands, how he'd carry his bat, how he'd walk, what the statement on his face would be—that I deliberately turned away from him and stared out to the outfield."

Seaver was not the only big leaguer who experienced hero worship in the presence of Aaron. Johnny Bench, the man squatting behind the plate, felt the same way. A year or so earlier, Bench had asked Aaron to autograph a picture of the two. The shot showed Aaron sliding safely under a tag being applied by Bench, then still in his 20s. The slugger, happy to oblige the young backstop, wrote: To John—Try to stay the hell out of my way!

Few had been able to do so during Aaron's career. He loved the game of baseball, his passion cultivated as a child on the sandlots in and around Mobile, Alabama. That fire intensified as he matured, his resolve strengthened by the bigotry and racism that first sought to keep him from playing professionally and then made sure he understood his "place" as he ascended the game's heights. Aaron performed throughout his career as if he were in a constant fight for acceptance. On the field, he needed to prove that he belonged. Off it, he wanted to live on his own terms. This was one of the things that made Aaron such an enigma.

For years, the media criticized him for playing with all the enthusiasm of an accountant on tax day, an observation that fans were quick to embrace. He rarely showed emotion. When he did, he displayed no more than the slightest of smiles or the mildest of grimaces. "He is one of the coolest, calmest guys I've ever known," Bench said a few months before Opening Day in 1974. "When he walks to the plate, it's just unbelievable. He does his thing in quiet. The thought of his being pressured by anything, even as he nears the record, is—well, I just can't imagine it."

So, on this day in Cincinnati, why should anything about Aaron have changed?

Because everything else around him had. For two decades, he had toiled in a strange sort of obscurity. He produced one superlative season after another and made the All-Star team every year, yet he never did anything so astonishing or provocative as to suggest that he might one day lay claim to baseball's most sacred record and eclipse the game's most cherished icon. Now one long fly ball separated him from a piece of Babe Ruth's all-time home run record.

Ever since the 1971 season, when Aaron clouted 47 home runs at the age of 37 and put himself within reasonable range of the Babe, the two had been under the statistical microscope. Baseball had several years to prepare for the "big moment" and in its infinite wisdom had used that time inviting comparisons between the two. This thrust Aaron into the unenviable position of having to justify his career and prove that he was a better hitter, or player, or person than Ruth, when the only relevant measure of Aaron was that soon he would have hit more baseballs out of more ballparks than anyone who ever played in the majors. When Aaron finished the 1973 season with 713 home runs—one short of the record—he realized how much soon could seem like a lifetime away.

Speculation about the coming season began immediately after Aaron's last swings against the Astros in Atlanta that fall. He was badgered all winter long. A furor over when and where he might attempt to hit numbers 714 and 715 erupted in spring training. And all the while, hate mail arrived in such abundance that Aaron eventually stopped caring.

Excusing the obvious cliché, it could easily be said that Aaron's short walk from the on-deck circle to the batter's box on Opening Day in 1974 represented a much longer and exceedingly more meaningful journey. The difference now was that the media was there to chronicle every one of Aaron's movements, gestures, and thoughts—no matter how insignificant. And, almost without exception, they were finally on his side.

What could be more ironic? Aaron and the press had long tolerated a forced, often clumsy relationship with one another that left both parties largely unfulfilled. Aaron never trusted the media, nor did he quite appreciate its power in shaping popular culture. The media, tired of trying to penetrate layers of humility and self-pity—and totally missing his talent for deadpan humor—possessed an equally inept understanding of Aaron. But their lots were cast. Aaron needed the media if he was to gain the respect demanded by his remarkable career, and the media needed him because his story sold newspapers and boosted ratings.

Jack Billingham, the Cincinnati starter that day, allowed two of the first three Braves he faced to reach base. With one man out and two men on, he stared in at Bench for a sign. Billingham did not care who was up. He was not going to start the season by walking the bases loaded. Aaron knew it, and Billingham knew he knew it. A nice fat strike was on its way. In a cat-and-mouse game from which few hurlers escaped Aaron's clutches, Billingham was already dead. He went into the stretch, took a deep breath, then rocked and fired.

CHAPTER ONE:

FROM 'BAMA TO THE BIGS

THAT HENRY AARON HIT EVEN ONE BASEBALL OUT of a major league ballpark—forgetting for a moment that he hammered 755 in a career that spanned 23 seasons—is remarkable in its own right. Consider that he grew up learning to hit against pitchers who hurled softballs and bottle tops, not baseballs. Consider that he received no formal coaching until after he signed his first professional contract, and that he continued to bat cross-handed after that. Consider that he was ignored by professional scouts who were quick to overlook a skinny black kid from the South. Consider that he was harassed almost every step of the way by white fans who rooted for him to fail simply because of the color of his skin.

No, nothing in Aaron's formative years suggested he would ever set foot in a big league stadium . . . unless he managed to scrape together enough money to buy a ticket to a game. Nothing, that is, except for a steely resolve that told him he was destined for greatness. Indeed, from an early age, Aaron was convinced he would attain stardom on the baseball diamond. And as he grew older, the boy who was nicknamed "The Man" because he dreamed so big, became even more determined to rise above the poverty and racism that marked his childhood.

"Like the innate perfection of his swing, the baseball beginnings of Hank Aaron are hard to explain with precision." So wrote Roger Kahn in the September 1959 issue of *Sport*. Kahn had been assigned to chronicle Aaron's rise to the majors. He soon discovered, however, that details of the slugger's early life were not easy to come by.

"Sports editors in Mobile have pretty much given up trying to get a consistent portrait of Aaron as a young man," Kahn admitted in the story. "'Every time we start the thing,' one of them says, 'we find a couple of things that don't add up. No one has ever been able to put the whole thing together.'"

To a certain extent, this remains the case today. Despite all the books (including *I Had a Hammer*) and magazines and documentaries that have profiled Aaron, piecing together a complete picture of his childhood is still a difficult task. This is in part due to the fact that Aaron's earliest years are documented only by the memories of friends and family. A story told by one often contradicts an account by another.

Some of the facts, however, are incontrovertible. No one disputes that Henry Louis Aaron was born in Mobile, Alabama on February 5, 1934, (the day before Babe Ruth turned 39). The second of Herbert and Estella Aaron's nine children, he weighed just 2¼ pounds at birth.

Just as clear is the fact that Aaron grew up amidst some of the worst conditions the South has ever seen. As the authors of *Alabama: The History of a Deep South State* wrote, "The decade of the 1930s went by lots of names, but all stood for trouble. In fact, Alabamians born during the first third of the twentieth century would live through the most severe depression and the bloodiest war in the history of the world. They were a tough generation and lived in trying times. The world would never quite be the same again. Neither would Alabama." Nor would Aaron, for that matter.

For the first seven years of his life, Aaron lived in a black district of Mobile called Down the Bay. "There was no bay in sight and nobody knew why the area was called that," wrote George Vecsey in 1972 in *The Sports Immortals*. Vecsey's assessment was not completely accurate. Mobile, which lies near the Mississippi border in the southern part of the state, is actually a port city located on Mobile Bay, which is fed by the Tensaw River and Mobile River. As a boy, Aaron fished in both.

Like most minority communities in the South in the 1930s, Down the Bay was rundown and dreary—the kind of place where it is difficult to imagine a child hoping for much more than his next meal, let alone a bright future. The rest of Alabama was hardly better. Employment sagged across the state, the loss of jobs hitting those in industry the hardest. Homelessness was epidemic. It was not unusual to see entire families among the thousands living under tents at campsites set up by the Alabama Transient Bureau. Illness and illiteracy plagued the state as well. The Board of Health, for instance, operated clinics in only 14 of 67 counties. Meanwhile, some 200,000 farmers and industrial workers could neither read nor write.

The plight of the negroes was especially desperate. Segregation, and beyond that Alabama's racial divide, limited the economic and cultural opportunities for black families. Government officials, some of whom did little to hide their ties to the Ku Klux Klan, resisted calls for change.

Yet, somehow, Aaron found hope. From a young age, in fact, he appeared determined to escape his oppressive surroundings. Aaron found solace in baseball. The sport fascinated him for many reasons, most notably the importance it placed on self-reliance. "The thing I liked about baseball was that it gave me an opportunity to be one-on-one with the competition," he told Pat Summerall in his book, *Sports in America*. "Baseball to me was a way of getting away from some of the outside pressure."

Aaron's intense love of baseball continued to develop as he grew older. This was something his mother, Estella, could not understand. In the late '30s, Jackie Robinson was still years from breaking the color barrier in the major leagues, and many blacks, especially those in the deep South, had little reason to believe such a day would ever come. Estella pushed her son to pursue more lofty goals. Whenever Aaron told his mother that he dreamed of playing in the big leagues, she scoffed and discouraged such thoughts.

"She wanted me to go to college, get an education, and come back home and be either a schoolteacher or whatever else was available for blacks at the time," Aaron recalled in Summerall's book. If her son was going to play any sport, Estella most assuredly would have chosen football, for even in the depths of the Depression, success on the gridiron could lead to a free college education.

Herbert Aaron shared his wife's views, though not as adamantly. He did not like the idea of any of his children wasting time chasing a dream that held so little promise. By the same token, he did seem to possess a better sense of his son's deep commitment to baseball. Commitment, in any form, was a trait for which Herbert had great respect. This was because the elder Aaron had grown accustomed to struggling for the things he wanted. As he put it in *Chasing the Dream*, an award-winning video that chronicled his son's life, he had "worked the hard road" his entire life. Herbert's résumé bears him out. His first job was picking cotton, until he was promoted to plowing it. After that he labored long days in a salt mill. Finally, he landed a job as a boilermaker's assistant with the Alabama Dry Dock and Shipbuilding Company, where he remained for 29 years. During this time, he also ran the Black Cat Inn, a tavern that catered exclusively to people of color.

Aaron's father knew little about baseball, and had even less time to impart his limited knowledge of the sport. This is not to say, however, that Aaron did not enjoy the benefits of good genetics. His uncle, Bubba Underwood, one of Estella's brothers, played in the Negro leagues and for some time was considered the top ballplayer in Mobile. He helped introduce Aaron to baseball, though not without a price. In *Chasing the Dream*, Uncle Bubba admitted that he used to make young Hank stroke his head 100 times before he would get off the couch and play catch.

Aaron's younger sister, Gloria, starred in track and softball in high school. Aaron's younger brother, Tommie, played professional baseball into his early '30s and was a versatile bench player and pinch hitter for the Braves for seven seasons. According to Aaron in *I Had a Hammer*, Tommie (born in 1939) was "the football star in the family." By all accounts, Aaron was not a bad gridder either. For a long time, in fact, it seemed as if football might be his ticket out of Alabama. Though he weighed only 160 pounds, Aaron had the speed, moves, and power to attract the attention of colleges throughout the South. Florida A&M reportedly considered offering the flashy tailback a full scholarship.

Baseball, however, was by far Aaron's best sport. This was the case despite the fact that no one outside his family offered anything substantial in the way of advice or training. For the most part, Aaron was very much on his own. "I don't think I really ever had a professional teacher to teach me anything about baseball," he told Summerall. "My father did the best he could with me as a baseball player. But I think I learned myself, by going out in the backyard, throwing the old broken tin caps up in the air, and swinging at them."

Though he did not teach his son how to hit a curve or field a grounder, Herbert Aaron nonetheless proved a strong role model. In *Chasing the Dream*, Aaron commented that years of watching his father labor long and hard for his family taught him the value of patience and respect. These were traits the young man would later emulate, sometimes to his detriment but ultimately to his benefit.

America's entry into World War II took the edge off of the hard times in Mobile, which became something of a boomtown thanks to a surge in the shipbuilding business. Where once jobs were like hen's teeth, suddenly workers were needed in round-the-clock shifts. Twenty liberty ships and 102 tankers were constructed in Mobile during the war, and something on the order of 3,000 vessels were repaired. The port city's population swelled to 125,000 in 1943 as shipworkers streamed in from all over the South.

Good work and steady income enabled a handful of families to flee the increasingly congested slums of Down the Bay. In 1942, the Aarons moved to the neighboring community of Toulminville. The rural hamlet offered many advantages. Foremost was room for the kids to run free. Herbert, who was working for a shipbuilding concern called ADDSCO, purchased two lots, then hired a team of carpenters to build a six-room home. In all, the house cost the Aarons slightly more than $200.

"When the walls and roof were up, we moved in, and that was it—no rent or mortgage, it was ours," Aaron remembered in *I Had a Hammer*. "We were a proud family, because the way we saw it, the only people who owned their own homes were rich folks and the Aarons."

Not surprisingly, Aaron encountered problems whenever he wandered back into his old neighborhood. The children who lived in Down the Bay looked down on families like the Aarons for leaving. "It wasn't white to black," Aaron told Vecsey about this odd brand of prejudice. "It was black to black. The Down the Bay kids just thought they were better than we were."

For a dose of racial prejudice, Aaron did not need to look far. Mobile's wartime boom was not met enthusiastically by all of its residents. White workers, in particular, were upset by both the growth of the black population and the competition for jobs created by this increase. In May of 1943, riots broke out at ADDSCO when the Fair Employment Practices Commission forced the company to promote a dozen black welders. African-American employees, including Herbert Aaron, required armed escorts to and from work to ensure their safety. As was his manner, the elder Aaron remained outwardly placid. He reacted the same a year later when black troops faced off against white military police at nearby Brookley Field, a facility built by the Army Air Corps, and in 1947, when the KKK marched in Toulminville.

Despite its racial turbulence, the Aaron boys felt fortunate to live in Toulminville. In *I Had a Hammer*, the family's move was described as a "big break," especially in baseball terms. "I might have made it as a ballplayer if I had grown up in Down the Bay—Satchel Paige and Willie McCovey sure did—but there was no better place to play ball than Toulminville," maintained Aaron. "There were open spaces in Toulminville, and before long, enough kids had moved in that we could generally get up a game."

Aaron's mention of Paige brings to light the fact that he was not the only native Alabamian to view sports as a means of escaping the racial injustice and economic hardship of his home state. Joe Louis, the world heavyweight boxing champion for most of Aaron's childhood, was born in the Yellowhammer State in 1914. Louis grew up in Lafayette with his widowed mother and six siblings. He began picking cotton at age 4, two years before he learned to speak. The youngster waited three more years before someone taught him to read. When his mother remarried she moved the entire family to Detroit, where Louis played hooky from his violin lessons and learned how to box. Although Detroit liked to claim the "Brown Bomber" as its own, the people of Alabama never forgot about their native son. "When Louis would fight, everyone would get together and crowd around the radio," Aaron recalled in *I Had a Hammer*.

Jessie Owens also brought honor to Alabama on the world stage. The youngest of ten children, he was born in Oakville a year before Louis. His family also headed north in search of opportunity during the early 1920s, settling in Cleveland. Owens parlayed his athletic prowess into a scholarship at Ohio State University, where he broke several world records. At the 1936 Olympics, he single-handedly shattered Adolf Hitler's myth of Aryan supremacy. Owens's father, himself the son of slaves, once told his son that "it don't do a colored man no good to get himself too high" because "it's a helluva drop back to the bottom." This warning proved prophetic, for in an age when black consumers did not possess the buying power to warrant paying black athletes huge endorsement fees, Owens was quickly reduced to racing against dogs and motorcycles—and eventually became a playground instructor.

The story of Willie Mays, born in Fairfield three years before Aaron, had a much happier ending. Though he too traveled an arduous road to stardom, the "Say Hey Kid" had the benefit of good timing and good bloodlines. During his career, he achieved what is now called "crossover" appeal and thus was able to augment his baseball income with commercial endorsements and appearance fees. Mays also attained superstardom in an era when black Americans wielded considerably more economic might than they had in decades past, so he also benefited financially from his fame in this sector of the market. Mays's mother had once been a track star, and his paternal grandfather and father were both talented baseball players, thus success in sports came quite naturally to him. Cat Mays, his father, was well known around the highly competitive industrial baseball leagues of Birmingham, and was an occasional fill-in player with the Black Barons of the Negro American League.

As a teenager, Mays gained recognition for his exploits on the baseball diamond and the gridiron. He was greatly influenced by Jackie Robinson, as was Aaron, and a year after the Dodger star reached the big leagues Mays decided to focus solely on baseball. A shortstop with the Fairfield Stars in sandlot ball, he had just started to play semipro ball with the Chattanooga Choo Choos when he signed his first professional contract with the Birmingham Black Barons in 1948 at the age of 17. Mays starred in the Negro League World Series that fall, and under the tutelage of manager Piper Davis he developed his immense skills quite rapidly. When he signed with the New York Giants organization in 1950, every kid in Alabama heard about it. When Mays spurred the Giants to a pennant the following summer, the state suddenly had a record number of Giant fans.

In Aaron's hometown, fans also followed the St. Louis Browns. That was because the Browns, the southernmost team on the major league map, had under contract Satchel Paige, Mobile's most famous baseball export. Nicknamed "Satchel" as a child when he held a baggage-handling job at a train station, the ageless hurler was born in the vicinity of Mobile Bay in 1906. Legend had it that Paige already possessed his trademark pinpoint accuracy as a child, and could quite effortlessly bring down a chicken with a rock.

Paige sharpened his accuracy during a stretch in reform school, and upon his release pitched for a number of semipro teams around Mobile, including the Tigers—the top local team during the 1920s. In 1926, he signed a professional contract and within a few seasons came to be regarded as one of the world's best pitchers, white or black. By the time Paige reached the majors with the Cleveland Indians in 1948, he had amassed an estimated 2,000 victories, including 300 shutouts and 55 no-hitters. During his rookie season with the Tribe, Paige, then in his forties, recorded six victories and a 2.47 ERA, helping Cleveland capture the American League pennant. When baseball writers discussed him as a candidate for Rookie of the Year, Paige joked, "Which year?" Interestingly, Paige was nearly a teammate of Aaron's two decades later, when the Atlanta Braves put him in uniform for a publicity stunt, although he never played in an official game.

Paige was among the players Aaron watched at Hartwell Field, the home of the Southern League's Mobile Bears, which transferred from Knoxville in July of 1944. A minor-league affiliate of the Brooklyn Dodgers, the Bears boasted a number of future big leaguers, including George "Shotgun" Shuba, Cal Abrams, and Chuck Connors, who went on to fame in TV's *The Rifleman*. Because of its large working-class population and proximity to several spring training sites, Mobile was a regular stop for major league teams heading north to start the season.

According to *The Hank Aaron Story*, written by Milton L. Shapiro in 1961, Aaron made his first visit to Hartwell Field in the spring of 1945. Using money he earned from mowing lawns and working on an ice truck, the 11-year-old bought a ticket for a game between the Boston Red Sox and Brooklyn Dodgers.

"Henry was seeing a diluted version of big league baseball," wrote Shapiro. "The Brooklyn Dodgers and the Boston Red Sox, as did all other teams in organized baseball, fielded patchwork clubs while the stars were serving in the Armed Forces." Henry was nonetheless impressed by the sight of men in major league uniforms. He might not have recognized the faces, but the names of players such as Eddie Stanky, Dixie Walker, Augie Galan, Luis Olmo, Curt Davis, Eddie Lake, "Indian Bob" Johnson, and Boston manager Joe Cronin, a future Hall of Famer, would have been familiar.

The player who captured Aaron's imagination more than any other was Jackie Robinson, who signed with the Dodgers after the 1945 season. Aaron got his first glimpse of Robinson in person in the spring of 1947. Brooklyn was in town on a preseason swing as the club made its way back to New York. By this time, Robinson, who was about to begin his rookie season, had become a hero to African Americans across the country. During his stay in Mobile, he appeared at a local church and gave a speech about the challenges before him and the struggles of minorities. "When I finally put my eyes on him, he seemed bigger than life," Aaron remembered in *Chasing the Dream*. "He truly changed the world for me."

Though Aaron had talked before about playing in the big leagues, he embraced the idea more passionately than ever after Robinson joined the Dodgers. Kahn referred to this catharsis in his article in *Sport*, observing that Aaron's behavior "changed radically" after watching professional baseball for the first time—most notably a black man playing professional baseball.

Aaron addressed the point directly in Summerall's book. "Jackie Robinson was my hero," he said. "He was the man who inspired me to be where I am today."

Hopelessly hooked on the national pastime, Aaron completely immersed himself in baseball. "If he wasn't playing the game, he was reading about it," Estella Aaron told Kahn. "He was reading every newspaper and magazine about baseball he could find. All the time he was around the house he was reading."

Aaron's childhood friend Corneil Jiles has similar memories. "We talked baseball, ate baseball, and slept baseball twenty-four hours a day," he recalled in *Chasing the Dream*.

Even when he had no one to play with, Aaron invented games to feed his love of the sport. He would fashion a crude baseball out of old dress rags, roll it toward the top of the roof, then sprint to the other side and grab it before it fell to the ground.

When Aaron teamed up with Jiles, he was even more imaginative. Their two favorite games were "cockball" and "fireball"—both designed to be contested by two people. The equipment required for cockball was a broom handle and soda bottle caps. Hits and outs were recorded based on where and how far the batter smacked a cap. Aaron usually dominated his friend, slugging offerings from Jiles as far as a block and a half away. He has since said that cockball was a key to his success as a hitter in the major leagues, especially in the way it helped develop his quick wrists.

Fireball was played with a rag ball soaked in kerosene, which Aaron and Jiles lit on fire and tossed back and forth. The two played the game deep into the night during camping trips in the country. These evenings gave Aaron plenty of opportunity to dream about his future as a baseball player.

On other occasions, Aaron joined the neighborhood kids who gathered most days to play sandlot games. The first pitch was usually delayed because Aaron, whose parents allowed him to play only after he finished his chores, often showed up late. He was by far the best player around, and thus the choosing of sides could not proceed until the automatic first pick had arrived.

By his 14th birthday, Aaron was so convinced of his destiny that he decided to attend a tryout held by the Dodgers in Mobile. This was 1949 and the Dodgers had become a powerhouse club thanks to their black talent, with former Negro leaguers Robinson, Roy Campanella, and Don Newcombe playing starring roles. Brooklyn hoped to stock its farm system with more black players, and the organization knew from its affiliation with the Bears that southern Alabama was a hotbed of baseball talent, both black and white. Aaron felt this was a perfect opportunity to showcase his talents. Not surprisingly, the Brooklyn scouts disagreed, barely giving the short, skinny kid a second look. Or for that matter, even a first look. "It broke my heart to be turned away," Aaron said in *Chasing the Dream*.

To help soften the blow, Aaron went fishing, which was one of his few pastimes aside from the national one. Others included camping (Aaron was a member of the Boy Scouts) and reading Dick Tracy comic books. "Other than playing ball and eating," he admitted in *I Had a Hammer*, "we didn't do a whole lot."

This included school, where Aaron was rarely excited or challenged in class. He conceded in later years that he "made a mess" out of his academic career at Central High School, a public school in Mobile. Put bluntly, he believed getting an education was a waste of his time. Once Robinson had broken the color barrier, Aaron felt certain he had the ability to play in the big leagues. And attending class would not help him get there.

"I knew I was going to be a ballplayer," he stated in *I Had a Hammer*. "There was no doubt in my mind. So school didn't matter to me. School couldn't teach me how to play second base like Jackie Robinson."

Needless to say, this attitude troubled Aaron's mother. So did the coddling her son received from teachers who seemed to have a different set of rules for the school's reigning sports star. "He was quite an athlete, so all of us teachers knew who he was," said Virginia Hunt of her former student in Kahn's article. "We never had any trouble with Hank. He was polite, alert and outstanding in baseball."

He was also hardly ever in class. By the time Aaron turned 17, in fact, he had more or less dropped out. He was so sure of his future in the majors he saw no reason to bother staying in school for more than a few minutes a day. He would show his face in the morning, then quickly disappear. Not even the school's sports teams could hold his interest. Central had a softball program, but no baseball program. Aaron participated for a couple of seasons (catching and playing third base), but softball seemed kind of pointless when he knew there were pickup hardball games being played all over town.

Aaron and Jiles began spending their mornings at a local pool hall. "I would go to school in the morning, walk in the front door, walk out the back, and then go to Davis Avenue and shoot pool until the Dodger game came on or the movie house opened up," Aaron recalled.

They kept this schedule for several weeks until Herbert Aaron learned of his son's truancy. The elder Aaron was furious. But instead of angrily confronting his son and demanding that he return to school, Herbert relied on logic. He reminded his son of the sacrifice he made every day for his family, explaining that he left lunch money of 50 cents for each of his children, while *he* took only 25 cents. The least Henry could do in exchange was finish his high school education.

Aaron agreed and soon transferred to the Josephine Allen Institute, a private school where he could learn a trade. Unfortunately, Allen didn't field a baseball team either.

Aaron's memory of his confrontation with his father remains vivid to this day, but not because of its life-affirming effect on him. That very same fall day in 1951 also marked Bobby Thomson's "Shot Heard 'Round the World," the three-run homer that lifted the New York Giants over Aaron's beloved Dodgers for the National League pennant and capped one of the most thrilling races in baseball history. Though Thomson's blast ended the season for the Dodgers, Aaron was swept away by the emotion of the moment. The drama only reinforced his desire to play in the majors.

By this time, Aaron was becoming a little more realistic about what it would take to sign with a major league club. The odds of simply "being discovered" were not good. White scouts were still looking primarily for white ballplayers. "If I had waited in Mobile for a white baseball scout to find me, I don't know if I'd ever have been discovered for the big leagues or not," Aaron offered in *Aaron, r.f.*, a collaboration between him and Furman Bisher, published in 1968.

Though baseball had been integrated for several years, teams were not exactly rushing their talent evaluators into the Deep South in search of the next Jackie Robinson. Aaron correctly surmised that the smartest road to the major leagues would be through the Negro Leagues. In the 1920s, '30s, and '40s, black baseball boasted incredible talent. In the early 1950s, major league clubs believed that the smartest way to integrate was to allow the Negro League teams to continue plucking talent out of the small towns and sandlots, then skim off the best players. Owners of these teams knew that in the long run this would destroy their little slice of pro ball (and indeed it did), but they could get rich by selling off their best young stars for big-league money.

Aaron began to showcase his talent for the Mobile Black Bears, the local all-black semipro club. Estella would not let her son travel with the club, which barnstormed around the South during the week, but agreed to let him play on Sundays when the team hosted games at Mitchell Field in nearby Prichard. The team's youngest starter, Aaron played shortstop and was the Black Bears' best hitter. He received $20 per game, while the rest of his teammates got $10. Lela Tucker, the wife of team owner Ed Tucker, paid him the difference on Mondays so the other players wouldn't find out.

Playing for the Black Bears was a terrific opportunity for Aaron. It enabled him to compete against men for the first time, as the majority of players in the league were much older and more seasoned than he. It also got the grapevine going, and soon enough there were scouts in the stands from several well-known teams. The team that eventually signed Aaron was the Indianapolis Clowns of the Negro American League. Ed Scott, the player-manager of the Black Bears, happened to double as a bird dog for the Clowns, so he did not have to go very far to find the best young hitter in south Alabama.

Getting Aaron to sign, however, was a bit more trying. The teenager feared his mother would frown upon his joining the team, and he avoided Scott like the plague. Try as he might to deliver his sales pitch, Scott never could corner his young shortstop; Aaron always managed to see him coming and slip away. Scott would not be denied. From his first at bat with the Bears, Aaron had impressed Scott as one of those once-in-a-lifetime-type players. "He was green as he could be," said Scott in *I Had a Hammer*. "He stood up there at the plate upright, no crouch at all, and the other team figured he wasn't ready. The pitcher tried to get a fastball by him, and he hit a line drive that banged against the old tin fence they had around the outfield there—nearly put the ball through the fence. They walked him the rest of the time."

What most impressed Scott was Aaron's phenomenal bat speed. "This guy got some wrists," he told Bunny Downs, the traveling secretary for the Clowns. Downs knew Scott well from his days as a player with Indianapolis, and the two remained friends. When Scott continued to rave about Aaron, Downs arranged a game between the Black Bears and the Clowns. Unaware of the informal tryout, Aaron went about his business as usual and stung the ball all day long. Afterward, Downs introduced himself and informed the youngster that Indianapolis had decided to offer him a contract. The offer, he promised, would come the following spring.

Good as his word, Downs sent a contract, worth $200 a month, after the first of the year in 1952. Aaron quickly realized that he no longer had reason to worry about his mother's misgivings about baseball. Indeed, as soon as Estella saw the contract, she changed her attitude.

"$200 A MONTH TO PLAY BASEBALL," Aaron wrote in *Aaron, r.f.*, "You can't imagine how big that looked to a little Negro boy in Mobile, Alabama. It even looked big to my mother, who had not been inclined to be impressed by baseball before."

As soon as he signed, Aaron was given a train ticket to join the Clowns in Winston-Salem, North Carolina, for spring training. He left immediately, even though he had not completed his final year of high school. Leaving school was not a problem; leaving his family was a different matter. In *Chasing the Dream*, Aaron admitted that he found it very difficult to go. "I was excited and terrified at the same time," he recalled. His mother was beside herself. It broke her heart to see one of her sons leave the fold. To help ease the pain, Aaron agreed to return and pursue a college degree if he failed.

The Indianapolis Clowns proved a perfect setting for Aaron to mature and flourish as a ballplayer. According to Aaron, however, the veterans on the club initially treated him harshly. Since a rookie in camp usually meant an older player was going to lose his job, most of the Clowns had little incentive to extend a warm welcome to their newest teammate. Many of the players on the Indianapolis roster were also jealous of Aaron. He was one of the new boys, one of the up-and-coming players who had a real shot at the major leagues. Most of the Clowns had been around a long time and their skills were eroding. They knew their chances of playing in the majors were zero. To see someone as young and talented as Aaron, whose nonplussed, nonchalant nature made him seem oblivious to the opportunity before him, was more than some could take.

Aaron acknowledged this in *I Had a Hammer*. "Looking back on it, I can understand how the Clowns must have felt about somebody like me," he said. "To start with, being as quiet as I was and knowing as little about the world, I was an easy target . . . For the guys on the Clowns, though, it was more than that . . . They knew they were going nowhere . . . They could see that a guy like me would get the chance they never had."

Indianapolis had joined the Negro American League in 1946, the same year Jackie Robinson began playing in the minors for the Dodgers. Over the next few years, as the NAL's top stars were siphoned off by the majors, attendance began to droop and the quality of play began to deteriorate. The Clowns were one of the more successful clubs of this era, in part because they blended entertainment with talent. Trick pitching, hitting, and fielding were staples for the Clowns, and several times during a game they would halt the action and go right into one of their comedy routines—all of which would be considered politically incorrect by today's standards. The team's batboy, a dwarf, was immensely popular with fans. A year after Aaron left the team, the Clowns hired a woman named Toni Stone to play second base.

Aaron was an infrequent and highly reluctant participant in these high jinks. Years later he characterized the Clowns as a baseball version of the Harlem Globetrotters, which was not far off the mark. Like the Globetrotters, the Clowns were usually far superior to their opponents and quite capable of playing good baseball when they had to. For his part, Aaron took every at bat seriously. You never knew when a scout for the Yankees or the Dodgers might be in the stands, even in some of the small towns the Clowns visited on their barnstorming adventures.

Team owner Syd Pollock was a good man to be in control of Aaron's destiny. He encouraged the teenager to keep working hard on his game and did not pressure him to mug for the crowd. Pollock was also highly respected and trusted by organized baseball, having won several awards from the National Baseball Congress for helping to build the game's popularity. And he knew a prospect when he saw him—if Syd said a kid had a future, people listened.

Aaron's initial concern was that his manager with the Clowns, Buster Haywood, would be unwilling to showcase his talents. Haywood had played in the Negro leagues from 1940 to 1950. Though small and possessing only marginal skills as a hitter, Haywood molded himself into a top-notch catcher. His managers had liked him because he always hustled, and pitchers loved him because he knew the game inside out. Haywood joined the Miami Ethiopian Clowns in 1941, and stayed with the team during its move north where it laid claim to two cities (Cincinnati and Indianapolis) during the war years before making Indianapolis its permanent home. An All-Star in 1944 and 1946, he toured with Jackie

Robinson's All-Stars in 1947. Pollock hired Haywood to manage the Clowns in 1948, a job he kept until 1954. He was named skipper of the East for the Negro League All-Star Game in 1952 and 1953.

At first, Haywood resisted using Aaron, who was young and seemingly unenthusiastic. Aaron was not comfortable performing the comedy routines the older players had down pat. But when a rash of injuries beset Indianapolis, Haywood had no choice but to play his rookie shortstop. Aaron responded by scorching opposing pitching, smashing singles through the infield, lining doubles in the gaps, and launching home runs to all fields.

"As frightened as I was about everything else, it never occurred to me that I might not hit," Aaron said in *I Had a Hammer*.

The offensive outburst helped ingratiate Aaron to his teammates. They soon took to calling him "Little Brother," a nickname conceived by second baseman Ray Neil, the Clowns' leader on and off the field. With the veterans in his corner, Aaron began feeling more and more comfortable. The nonstop travel, which even the most energetic players found grinding, did not bother him, though he seldom knew where the team was or where it was going next. "I never paid any attention to geography," he admitted in *Aaron, r.f.* "I just put on my uniform and played and dressed and got on that bus and rode all night and put on my uniform again and played again."

He also grew accustomed to a subsistence-caliber diet. The days of steaks and chops were still years away. "We were only getting two dollars a day meal money," he recalled in Summerall's book. "We used to take our two dollars and put them together. We would buy a loaf of bread and some peanut butter, and I would insist upon having some jelly."

One thing on the road that did disturb Aaron was the shabby treatment he and his teammates received from fans, especially when they traveled north. "They let us play ball in their towns," he said in *Chasing the Dream*, "just not sleep there."

The most notable incident occurred in a diner in the nation's capitol, where establishments were compelled to serve black customers. After the table was cleared, Aaron and his teammates heard their dishes being smashed in the kitchen. No one in the group reacted to the insult, but no one forgot the episode either.

Aaron believed that the racial problems he encountered in the North stemmed from the ambiguity of the region. "The South can be kinda easier than the North," he told Kahn. "There you know where you can go and where you can't. In the North sometimes you find out you can't go where you thought you could."

Aaron reasoned that the best way to make a difference was "to keep hitting that ball." And that is exactly what he did. Several weeks into the season, he was leading the Clowns with a .467 average—this despite batting with his unorthodox cross-handed grip. Word about Aaron had now begun to filter up to major league teams. Scouts watched the youngster more and more, and they were in awe. Many believed he was the best prospect to come out of black baseball since Willie Mays. In no time, the race to sign the next great black ballplayer was on.

The story of how Aaron eventually joined the Braves has been told over and over, always with a different wrinkle or two. Common threads, however, run through all accounts. Though several teams, including the Philadelphia Phillies, were interested in Aaron, the bidding came down to the Boston Braves and the New York Giants. The asking price of $10,000 was unusually high, and Syd Pollock, who stood to collect this fee, held firm on his terms. He dictated that the team securing the rights to Aaron would have to pay $2,500 up front and $7,500 after Aaron proved himself in the minors. Pollock also imposed a deadline that gave the Braves the first right of refusal.

"The Day the Braves Almost Gave Up on Hank Aaron," a story penned by Maury Allen for *Sports Today*, claimed that Boston came dangerously close to giving the young slugger away to the Giants. "If we had waited five more minutes, the Giants would have him," said Donald Davidson, then the team's publicity director. "They would have had Willie Mays and Hank Aaron in the same outfield. Can you imagine that?"

Such a development would have been particularly galling to Boston, because the team had already passed up a chance to sign Mays. In 1949, a scout for the Braves reported that Mays was not worth signing because he "would never hit" in the majors.

In his article, Allen reported that Boston general manager John Quinn found out about Aaron after receiving a glowing letter from Pollock. Since Quinn had dealt with Pollock before, he knew the Clowns' owner would not steer him in the wrong direction about a prospect. Boston sent one of its top scouts, Dewey Griggs, to take a look at Aaron. Griggs came back raving about the youngster's potential. He was so impressed, in fact, he told Quinn he would make the $2,500 down payment himself. That was all that Quinn needed to hear. He immediately called Pollock to offer a deal to Aaron, only to learn that the Giants had already done so. "I had a contract with the Giants in my hands just before I signed with the Braves," Aaron confided in Allen.

Boston's deal promised him $50 a week more than New York's, a sum that seemed princely to the young slugger. Though the Braves would start him with their Class-C affiliate in Eau Claire, Wisconsin, Aaron liked the fact that the team valued him enough to pay him like a Class-B player.

Allen's story is supported by Aaron's version in *I Had a Hammer*, though some of the details differ slightly. For example, Aaron said that Pollock had written to Braves' owner John Mullen and that these two had struck a verbal agreement in mid- to late April. The deal stated that Boston had thirty days to offer Aaron a contract. Once this deadline passed, Pollock would contact the Giants.

According to Aaron, Boston eventually dispatched Griggs to scout him, but he did not catch up with the Clowns until May 25, when the team stopped in Buffalo, New York. There, on a wet, blustery day, Aaron put on a show, launching a home run in his first at bat and beating out a bunt in his next trip to the plate. Griggs fired off a letter to Mullen, telling him that, while he questioned Aaron's defensive ability in the infield, there was no doubt he was a *bona fide* hitting prospect. "This boy could be the answer," Griggs concluded in his letter.

By the time Mullen received this evaluation, however, Pollock's deadline had expired. He hurriedly called the Clowns' owner, who was attending a league meeting in Chicago. Pollock informed Mullen that he was close to a deal with the Giants, exactly the news Boston did not want to hear. After some haggling, Mullen convinced Pollock to allow the Braves at least to make an offer to Aaron.

On May 29, Pollock received Boston's proposal via telegram, which, according to Aaron, paid him $100 more than New York's offer. He chose the Braves for this reason, as well as for a typo in the Giants' contract, which he took as a slight. "I thought my chances to make the Braves were better and that they were being fairer to me, paying me more money to play in a lower classification," Aaron said. "Besides, the Giants spelled my name "Arron" on their telegram."

The account in *Aaron, r.f.* varies from both of these in several ways. In his collaboration with Bisher, Aaron references an article from the *Saturday Evening Post* for many details. The most telling difference, however, is the emphasis he placed on Pollock's self-serving role in the drama. "If I had been one of these smart kids, I'd have said that I'd go with the club that made me the biggest offer," Aaron remarked. "I didn't have to go with the one that made Syd Pollock the biggest offer."

Aaron also talked about a cardboard suitcase that Pollock gave to him as a bonus. "After I signed, Syd Pollock gave it to me for a going-away gift and in undying appreciation of the $10,000 I was putting in his pocket," Aaron said with a measured amount of sarcasm. "But, as I said, I didn't know any better then, and it really didn't make any difference to me, and I don't know why I let it bother me now. Oh, I do know, too: I just hate to look back on something and realize that somebody took advantage of me because I was a kid who didn't know any better."

The suitcase, by the way, disintegrated in a rainstorm the first day Aaron used it.

Kahn's article in *Sport* focused a great deal of attention on the urgency of Boston's decision. In the story, the writer has Griggs calling Quinn at 6:57, three minutes before a 7:00 deadline imposed by Pollock. The scout tells the GM in impassioned tones that Aaron is worth the money "just for his swing." Two minutes later, "give or take a few seconds," the Braves supposedly contacted Pollock and signed Aaron.

Regardless of how the events actually unfolded, there is no doubt that Griggs was a key player. His evaluation of Aaron convinced the Braves to sign the budding star. As Allen wrote, "Two careers were on the line, Hank Aaron's and Dewey Griggs's. A scout who recommends an expensive purchase that fails often loses his job. A scout who declines a recommendation on a player who becomes a star, as the Boston scout did on Mays, also disappears. Griggs never hesitated."

The final contribution made by Griggs to Aaron's future came in the form of some advice. He told the rookie to start holding the bat like everyone else. Aaron said he would think about it.

It did not take long for Aaron to make an impression on the Class-C Northern League. Just 18 days after arriving in Wisconsin, he was selected to play in the All-Star Game. Several months later he was named Rookie of the Year. In 87 games as a shortstop, Aaron batted .336 with nine home runs and 61 RBIs.

That was all the more impressive considering that, despite the tip from Griggs, Aaron continued to bat in his unorthodox style. Though he actually felt more comfortable with his right hand positioned correctly on the bat above his left, the old habit was hard to break. "I hit cross-hand until two strikes were on me," he admitted to *Baseball Digest* in 1966. "Then I'd switch, because I had more confidence in myself that way." (Interestingly, Aaron said in his 1999 book, *Home Run: My Life in Pictures*, that he also experimented as a switch-hitter, but gave up batting from the left side after he lost control of the stick one day in practice and it struck a teammate.)

One of the reasons for Aaron's rapid development at Eau Claire was his manager, Marion "Bill" Adair, who was also the team's second baseman. Adair seemed to know just how to handle the young phenom, serving as a double-play partner, an authority figure, and a supportive friend. "A guy couldn't have asked to break in under a better manager than Bill Adair," Aaron said in *Aaron, r.f.* "He had been a lot more than a manager to me."

Adair's insight and compassion surprised the rookie shortstop. Like Aaron, he had grown up in Mobile. Given the racist sentiments prevalent throughout Alabama, Aaron expected his white skipper to be unsympathetic and unforgiving. "I knew how white people from Mobile thought about black people from Mobile, and I wondered if I could ever be the equal of a white player in his eyes," Aaron said in *I Had a Hammer*. "As it turned out, Adair was a fair and good manager—he was virtually a legend in Eau Claire—and he gave me every chance to prove myself."

Aaron needed all the support he could find. There were few places in the world that were whiter than Eau Claire in 1952, and there were times when he must have felt like an alien walking on a strange planet. During his summer there, he met just one black resident. It is not that Aaron believed Eau Claire was "a hateful place," but making the transition to life in a small, reserved, Midwest town was not easy. Of course, he had been warned of the difficulties he might encounter by veterans on the Indianapolis club. "Best keep your mouth shut and mind your own business," he remembered one telling him in *The Hank Aaron Story*. "You'll find a lot of white folks expect a kid like you, coming from the South especially, to act like the end man in a minstrel show."

Aaron was friendly with few people in town and close to only two players on the team, Wes Covington and Julie Bowers, both of whom were a few years older and both of whom were black. Bowers had been a backup catcher for the New York Black Yankees in the late 1940s in the final days of the Negro National League, and stayed with the club when it became a barnstorming outfit after the league's demise. His prospects of making the majors were not good, but he was playing baseball, cashing a check, and passing on his wisdom to the young pitchers who went through Eau Claire on their way up the system. Covington, like Aaron, oozed with unrefined talent. A murderous left-handed hitter, he feasted on right-handed fastballs, of which there were plenty in the Northern League. As an outfielder, Covington sometimes took a gladiatorial approach to fly balls, but his immense physical gifts enabled him to recover quickly from his occasional errors in judgment. He was from North Carolina, and also in his first year of organized baseball. He came out of spring training with the club and thus played the entire season, finishing with 24 homers, 99 RBIs and a .330 average.

There was only so much support this trio could offer one another. For the most part, Aaron kept to himself. During his frequent bouts with loneliness, he wondered whether he should quit and head back to Toulminville. A defensive play during a game against Fargo-Moorhead, an affiliate of the Cleveland Indians, almost pushed him over the edge. While turning a double play, Aaron's relay throw to first struck the incoming runner in the head. He was taken off the field on a stretcher and rushed to the hospital. His career ended soon after. "That thing shook me up for two or three weeks," Aaron admitted in *Aaron, r.f.* "I'd have bad dreams some nights, and just about every time I had one, somewhere in it this guy would come sliding into second base, and every time he slid I'd wake up shivering and sweating."

One night, Aaron called home in tears. His mother handed the phone to his older brother, Herbert Jr. He told his younger brother to keep his head up and play ball. There was nothing worth coming home to in Alabama.

Mullen and Quinn certainly would not have been happy to hear such talk from the hottest prospect in their system. Boston had invested a lot of money in Aaron, and the team was determined to see its investment pay off. Therefore, Mullen and Quinn sent Billy Southworth, who had managed the Braves for six years beginning in 1946, to evaluate the young infielder. Southworth had started his career with the St. Louis Cardinals in 1926. A disciplinarian with a reputation for getting the best out of young players, he guided the Redbirds to three straight pennants from 1942 to 1944. After the 1945 season, the Braves offered him the unheard-of sum of $50,000 to manage in Boston. Southworth remained the club's skipper for six years, and in 1948 brought the National League pennant back to the city for the first time since 1914. His career-winning percentage of .593 ranks among the top 10 of all time. After watching Aaron for several games, Southworth filed the following report:

Dear Mr. Quinn,

Will send along player report on Henry Aaron shortstop at Eau Claire club.

Aaron has all the qualifications of a major

league shortstop. He runs better than average so I would have to call him fast but not very fast.

On the latest official Northern League batting averages Aaron is hitting .345 he is a line drive hitter altho he has hit a couple of balls out of the park for home runs. He has good hands, also quick hands, gets ball away fast accurately. He gets good jump on ball and can range far to right or left. I saw him go deep in the hole to his right and field a slow hit ball, he came up throwing and virtually shot his man out going to first. This was a big league play in my book because I did not think he had a chance to retire the man at first. He has a strong arm.

Aaron started two double plays and completed one from the pivot position in his first game he accepted six chances without an error.

Aaron throws a lot like Maranville not overhand but more side arm, his arm is strong and he does not have to straighten up to throw.

Aaron told me that he turned eighteen years of age last Feb. consequently I like his chances of becoming a major league player far more than I do Gene Baker, shortstop Los Angeles or James Pendleton of Montreal, first because of the difference in ages, then too, I think he has better hands than either Baker or Pendleton. He has proven his ability in the short time he has been here.

Baker and Pendleton are faster men but this boy will outplay them in all departments of the game when he has had more experience.

2nd Game—On Aaron's first trip to plate he hit long home run over left centerfield fence. He collected three hits for the evening and had three RBI's. He had four chances with one error. Oh yes, he also had one stolen base.

For a baby face kid of 18 years his playing ability is outstanding.

I will see the remaining game tonight but will send this report now, cause regardless of what happens tonight, it will not change my mind in the least about this boy's ability.

Please don't get the impression from what I have said above, that Aaron isn't a good runner cause he is fast and his running will continue to improve for the next couple years.

Also sending along individual player report and clippings.

The very next year, 1953, proved to be a turning point for Aaron. As Kahn wrote, "he won the attention of all of baseball." The season almost ended that spring for Aaron before it began, however, when he found himself looking down the business end of a rifle. The Braves' Jacksonville club was training in Waycross, Georgia, where the team had rented the grounds of an old World War II air base. Both the barracks and playing facilities were within the chain-link fence that surrounded the base, which was still manned and guarded by gun-wielding soldiers. One day Aaron took the team bus downtown to get a haircut. By the time he returned to the bus, it had already left, so he walked back to the base. Night had fallen and the gate was locked. The only way in was up and over the fence. Aaron put a toe in the fence and boosted himself up. Suddenly, shots rang out. "The camp guard spotted me, and all he saw was a strange Negro, and he started shooting," Aaron explained to Mike Capuzzo in a *Sports Illustrated* article.

Ironically, Aaron had specifically requested an assignment to Waycross to escape the clutches of Tommy Holmes, who managed the organization's top farm team, the Class-AAA Milwaukee Brewers. Originally, the Braves assigned Aaron to spring training with the Brewers in Kissimmee, Florida, as a reward for his fine performance with Eau Claire. But Aaron soon sensed that he would not make the team. The 36-year-old Holmes, who had been fired as Boston's player-manager the previous year, was back after playing out the season as a pinch hitter with Brooklyn. He was just coming to grips with the fact that his playing career was over, and seemed jealous of Aaron's eye-popping skills. After seeing the young slugger lash a home run over the right field fence, the Milwaukee skipper informed Quinn that Aaron would never succeed in the big leagues because he was unable to pull the ball. When Aaron learned of the comments, he asked for the reassignment. He certainly had read about Holmes as a boy, and knew that he had set a National League record with a 37-game hitting streak. Aaron might even have recalled that Holmes was the only player in history to lead the league in home runs and fewest strikeouts in the same season. If so, he had every right to be outraged. If anyone could appreciate the benefits of going with a pitch and driving the ball the other way, it should have been Holmes. Aaron exacted a small amount of revenge later in the preseason when he launched a long home run to dead center in an exhibition game against the Brewers.

Aaron played the entire 1953 season with the Braves' Class-A team in Jacksonville, Florida. The experience would have a long-lasting impact on him. No black had ever played there before. Several years earlier, in fact, a padlock had been placed on the stadium entrance to prevent Jackie Robinson from going in. The Braves sent Aaron and two other dark-skinned players—Felix Mantilla and Horace Garner—to break the color line. Mantilla, a

Puerto Rican, was a sure-handed infielder with a little pop in his bat. It was his second season in the organization. He had spent his first with Evansville of the Three-I (Illinois, Indiana, and Iowa) League, where he batted .323 with 11 home runs and 28 steals. Mantilla was a real prospect and a better shortstop than Aaron, who was shifted to second base.

Garner was a strapping 28-year-old outfielder who stood six foot three and rarely encountered a pitch he did not like. Aaron knew of him from his days in Indianapolis and Eau Claire. Two years before Aaron's stint with the Clowns, Garner had been one of their top players. He was signed by the Braves in 1950 and spent 1951 in Eau Claire, where he tore up the league with a .359 average and 44 stolen bases. In 1952 he was a teammate of Mantilla's in Evansville, where he slugged 23 homers and knocked in 107 runs. Despite his numbers, Garner was not regarded as a can't-miss prospect because scouts thought him too old and undisciplined to become a quality major leaguer. Opponents knew he would hack at anything close to a strike, so they fed him a steady diet of pitches high, low, and off the plate. At Evansville, he walked 111 times in 112 games, and probably could have walked 200 times had he shown any patience.

Aaron, Mantilla, and Garner were not sure what they would encounter in Jacksonville. According to their white teammates, however, it was a wonderful place to play. The scene before games (the majority were played in the evening) was like a Hollywood premiere. A World War II searchlight swept across the sky proclaiming each night's contest. A dwarf named Meyer "Shorty" Segal sold box-seat tickets from a wooden stand outside the stadium. Despite afternoon showers, rain almost never postponed a game. When it did, business manager Spec Richardson waited until the very last second to make the announcement. The delay provided him extra time to sell hot dogs. The Jacksonville fans did not mind.

They loved the team, they loved the ballpark, and most of all they loved baseball.

Despite all of this, they still were not quite ready for Aaron, Mantilla, and Garner. They boycotted games, picketing the stadium with signs that called the trio "niggers" and "jigaboos." Those who ventured inside the stadium were appalled to see hundreds of black faces in the stands, crammed into the remote blacks-only section in left field. "It was still segregated then," wrote Hubert Mizell in the *Sporting News* in 1974. "White spectators had the entire grandstand plus the first base bleachers. There was a 'Colored Only' sign over the gate to the third base bleachers."

In addition to the bigotry of the fans, Aaron also faced taunts from teammates and opposing players. In his *Sports Illustrated* profile, Capuzzo wrote how one teammate remarked that "a nigger's gonna croak every time" after Aaron ended a close game with a pop-up to the infield. Beanballs and high spikes were commonplace. The chin music did not bother Aaron and Garner, but Aaron had to take throws at second with his back to the base runners, which could get scary at times. Mantilla, mindful of his teammate's vulnerability, got him the ball as quickly as he could. One wonders whether an intolerant white shortstop might not have hesitated a half beat in the same situation.

Mantilla, who had played in the Caribbean his entire life and had never set foot in the Deep South, was appalled at the treatment he received at the hands of white players and fans. "Maybe it was easier for Henry because he came from Alabama and had seen it before," Mantilla said in the November 1982 issue of *Baseball Digest*. "He didn't like it, but he could adjust. He helped me and I probably helped him, too. That made him like a brother to me."

Road trips were especially harrowing. Heat, alcohol, and racism made for a volatile mix, and sometimes a riot seemed just a play away. In Macon, for instance, Mantilla charged the mound after being hit by a pitch. The police were summoned to the field to restore order. They remained there the rest of the game, ready to draw their weapons at the slightest provocation.

Aaron responded to the insults and abuse the same way he always had. He hit. In Jacksonville's first exhibition game, a home contest against the major league Boston Red Sox, he slammed a home run. In *Chasing the Dream*, announcer Dick Stratton remembered his call of the historic blast. "Jacksonville baseball has just been integrated," he told his listening audience.

"There's only one way to break the color line," Aaron said in *Aaron, r.f.* "Be good. I mean, play good. Play so good that they can't remember what color you were before the season started."

Aaron was true to his word. He tore up the league during the first month of the campaign. By midseason, Jacksonville was being hailed as perhaps the greatest Class-A team ever. They were playing at better than a .700 clip, staying a few games ahead of the Sally League's other powerhouse team in Columbia, South Carolina, and Aaron's name was starting to appear in the *Sporting News* almost every week. The entry of July 15, 1953, gives a flavor of how things were going. It said that Jacksonville, "paced by their three Negro players, who reached base 13 out of 14 times . . . trounced Augusta 13–5." Later in the story mention is made that Garner played left field instead of his customary right field, because on the Braves' previous visit to Augusta, fans in the right field bleachers had thrown rocks at him during the game.

Five members of the Braves were selected to play in the Sally League's 50th Anniversary All-Star contest. Aaron was joined by white teammates Joe Andrews, Len Morrison, Joe Casey, and Larry Lasalle. Mantilla and Garner were left off the squad, no doubt to their great relief. Aaron garnered All-Star honors despite playing a new position. The change had come as no great surprise to Aaron. He knew all along that it was his bat, not his glove, that had the front office most excited about his future. Still, second base is considered by many to be the hardest position to master in a short period of time, and Aaron did a decent enough job.

The All-Star game was scheduled for Savannah, where Georgia Governor Herman Talmadge planned to throw out the first ball. The media seized on the irony of the situation. Here was Talmadge, a staunch supporter of segregation, appearing at the first Sally League All-Star Game in which blacks were included. Fate quickly diffused the political powder keg, however. The night before the game, Aaron was sidelined when he was spiked in a rundown. The injury prevented him from walking without pain, much less digging in at the plate to face the league's best hurlers. Deciding not to further aggravate the wound, Aaron chose to sit out. The timing and location of the injury seemed all too convenient to those who believed Aaron was scared to play, and they let anyone who would listen know it. Aaron has always bristled at this thought. "I think some of those silly people thought I didn't show up because I was afraid," Aaron said in *Aaron, r.f.*

This was one of many stories that began circulating that questioned Aaron's commitment, his intelligence, or both—stories that followed him right to the majors. All cast him in an unfavorable light, sort of a cross between a court jester and a country bumpkin. Often, these stories ignored the fact that Aaron possessed a sharp but very subtle wit. In Kahn's article, for instance, there was a story about Jacksonville manager Ben Geraghty changing his signs midway through the season. In his first at bat after the change, Aaron stepped to the plate and was given the "take" sign. He swung away and belted a home run. When the manager informed Aaron that he had mistakenly reacted to the old sign, he reportedly responded, "Damn, I only got around to learning it yesterday."

A few years later, another tale picked up by the media detailed how Aaron received personal hitting instruction from Stan Musial. Again, this misunderstanding came about as a result of Aaron's dry sense of humor. After a couple of nights without a hit, Aaron was asked by a teammate how he planned to end his "slump." With perfect deadpan timing, he responded that he had already consulted Musial, who advised him to keep swinging. No one in the locker room, including a local reporter, got the joke. An article in the paper the next day detailed the budding relationship between Aaron and Musial! Such stories contributed to Aaron's reputation as being either arrogant or clueless, an analysis both unfair and inaccurate. "The quick conclusion—that Aaron was either an absurdly cocky rookie or a naive country boy—was too quick," Kahn cautioned in his *Sport* article.

Indeed, in Jacksonville, Aaron remained aloof from his manager and teammates, not out of choice but as a reaction to his trying circumstances. Imagine shouldering the responsibility of integrating a league at the age of 19—enduring endless streams of racial slurs, eating and sleeping apart from your teammates, and being excluded from the clubhouse banter. Imagine, too, being instructed how to speak, act, dress, and eat, as if you had been doing it incorrectly your entire life. Quiet by nature, Aaron grew even more detached. On bus rides he almost always slept, his ability to nap ultimately becoming a running joke among his teammates. Identical behavior years later helped brand him as lackadaisical.

"The most relaxed kid I ever saw," said Geraghty in the August 12, 1957, issue of *Sports Illustrated*. "From the time he got on the bus until we got to the next town, Hank was asleep. Nothing ever bothered him."

Geraghty's observations are of particular note because of the tremendous respect Aaron had for his manager. He called him the best skipper he ever had in Mizell's 1974 article in the *Sporting*

News. In *Aaron, r.f.* he said Geraghty did more for him than any manager before or since. "I guess he was one reason I didn't realize I was 'crusading' because he crowded out a lot of the stuff and never let it get close to me," Aaron added.

He echoed those sentiments in *Get That Nigger Off the Field*, written by Art Rust Jr. in 1992. "Who had the greatest influence on my baseball career?" Aaron pondered. "I think the one manager that I can remember was . . . Ben Geraghty of the Jacksonville team. I was literally going through hell down there. Ben used . . . to give me the inspiration and the things I needed to carry on and be a professional baseball player."

Aaron thought so much of Geraghty partially because he simply let Aaron play. For instance, instead of trying to convince Aaron to pull the ball to take advantage of his lightning-quick wrists, Geraghty encouraged him to wait an instant longer, recognize the pitch, and then just hit it hard. Aaron produced only 22 home runs in 1953—a respectable total for a teenager—however many of the 186 singles, doubles, and triples he hit that year sounded like rifle shots when they came off his bat.

Geraghty, who was 41, knew what it was like to be on the fringe. He played short and second in the Brooklyn organization during the 1930s, but never hit well enough to stick in the majors. During the war, he caught on as a utility man with the Braves, then retired after the players began returning from military service. Perhaps for these reasons, he had some notion of the struggle that outsiders like Aaron, Mantilla, and Garner faced. Geraghty always made a point of visiting with the trio on the road, just to have a beer and talk baseball. The effort meant the world to Aaron, helping ease the pressure he felt.

Geraghty did not coddle Aaron, however. On the contrary, he was quick to pounce on his young star when Aaron made a mistake. In one game, Aaron got picked off second three consecutive times. Though he was livid, Geraghty sensed the appropriate moment to launch into Aaron. "Ben did something I appreciated—something I've always admired in a manager," Aaron said in *I Had a Hammer*. "Instead of screaming at me in front of the whole team—Lord knows, I was embarrassed enough already—he waited until he could get me alone after the game. Then he told me how stupid I had been, and I couldn't disagree. I was a better base-runner from there on in."

Geraghty also helped Aaron become the Sally League MVP. The second baseman finished the year with a .362 batting average and 125 RBIs. Aaron was among the league leaders in just about every statistical category, including errors: he committed thirty-six in all. "If I was a bad shortstop at Eau Claire, I was a worse second baseman in Jacksonville," he said in *I Had a Hammer*.

Yet for every miscue in the field, Aaron more than compensated at the plate. His hot hitting carried Jacksonville to the Sally League playoffs. The team struggled through its best-of-five semi-final series against Savannah, taking the last two games to win 3–2. Against Columbia in the final, however, Aaron and his mates faltered. Though disappointed by the defeat, Aaron did not lose sight of his larger victory.

"We had played a season of great baseball in the Deep South, under circumstances that nobody had experienced before and—because of us—never would again," he said years later. "I'm not sure I've ever done anything more important."

The other significant event in Aaron's summer was his engagement to Barbara Lucas, whom he married on October 6, 1953. He had first seen her earlier in the season as she passed him on the street. Instantly smitten, he introduced himself and found out as much as he could about her. His pet name for her was "Half Breed" because neither he nor anyone in his family had ever seen a black person with green eyes.

"She lived right down the street across from the ballpark," he recalled in *Aaron, r.f.* "She was living at home and going to business college. She had been going to Florida A&M, but it came time for one of her brothers to go to college, so she had dropped out to give him a chance. The cost was a lot less for her, living at home and going to school there in Jacksonville. I learned all this while walking down the street with her."

Lucas's father, a Pullman porter, had settled his family in a government-funded project apartment in a section of Jacksonville known as "Durkeeville." It was commonplace to see Aaron leave the building and walk across the street to the stadium each day to prepare for a game. Part of the reason he enjoyed spending time there was the feeling of security provided by the Lucases. "I got to talk to older folks who sort of filled in for my own family while I was away from home," he said.

Aaron proposed to Barbara on the day he was awarded the Sally League MVP. Jacksonville fans, white and black, took up a collection of "going home" money and presented it to him at the ballpark. Before Aaron spent one dime on his fiancée, though, he bought a television set for his parents. When he returned to Toulminville with it, the Aaron home quickly became the most popular house on the block. But Estella and Herbert had an even better reason to feel proud. The following spring their son would have a chance to make the Braves.

CHAPTER TWO:

THE QUIET MAN

IN PROFILES WRITTEN SOME FIFTEEN YEARS APART, Roy Terrell and George Vecsey seized on the irony of Henry Aaron's early major league career. In a 1957 issue of *Sports Illustrated*, Terrell wrote, "Perhaps the most unusual part of the Aaron story is the fact that no one gets very excited about it." Vecsey concurred more than a decade later in *The Sports Immortals*, observing that "pitchers talked about him more than the sportswriters wrote about him."

Vecsey's assessment was particularly insightful, as Aaron often left National League hurlers muttering to themselves, totally frustrated in their inability to pitch to him. Indeed, during his first dozen years in the big leagues, Aaron drummed pitchers to the tune of 398 home runs and 1,305 RBIs while maintaining a .320 batting average. The bulk of those numbers came after his first two seasons with the Braves, in which he established himself as a dependable everyday player. Four years later, by the time he turned twenty-six, Aaron had joined the ranks of baseball's elite, winning the NL batting crown twice, capturing the only MVP award of his career, and leading the team to a World Series title.

Still, accolades were difficult to come by. Though many inside baseball acknowledged Aaron as the game's greatest talent, fans and the media paid more attention to the things they felt he did *not* do. Writers liked to describe his appearance in the batter's box as "sleepy" and his loping strides in the outfield as "casual." Instead of exploring the amazing odds he overcame to reach the big leagues, stories about Aaron usually portrayed him as a simpleton who could not grasp the enormity of his accomplishments. His first manager with the Braves, Charlie Grimm, called him "Stepin Fetchit," explaining that his prized rookie just kept "shuffling along."

Such aspersions seemed to matter little to Aaron. In fact, he helped perpetuate myths, playing the role of country rube like an Oscar-winning actor. Appearing unconcerned with headlines, regardless of whether they praised or criticized him, the shy and reserved star hesitated to reveal himself to the public. He was content to play baseball. Endearing himself to fans and chatting up reporters were chores best left to others more comfortable in the spotlight. "Certain players are cut out for being recognized," Aaron told Vecsey in 1972. "There would be more recognition if I played in New York or Los Angeles, but I have no regrets."

As he matured, however, Aaron learned that recognition provided certain advantages, including the ability to effect change. By the mid-1960s, no longer content to remain overshadowed by the likes of Willie Mays, Mickey Mantle, and Frank Robinson, he grew more outspoken, becoming an increasingly controversial figure unafraid to take an unpopular stand. Embracing Jackie Robinson as your hero, Aaron realized, came with certain responsibilities. Aaron understood these better as he got older.

If fans and reporters were slow to acknowledge Aaron's immense talent, the Braves were not. His breakthrough year in Jacksonville convinced the team that he was a special player. Only two questions remained in the minds of owner John Mullen and GM John Quinn: What position should Aaron play and when would he be ready for the majors? Both were answered before Opening Day of the 1954 campaign.

The more the Braves' brain trust saw of Aaron, the more it suspected that he was best suited for the outfield. Though the strength and accuracy of his arm were unproven, he was athletic and ran well. The Braves also loved Aaron's attitude. No one in the organization was easier to coach. The youngster picked up the subtleties of the game quickly and instinctively. With the proper tutoring, believed Mullen and Quinn, Aaron could become an accomplished outfielder.

As soon as the Sally League season ended, Quinn contacted Aaron about playing winter ball in Puerto Rico. Felix Mantilla was set to join a team in Caguas and the Braves encouraged Aaron to accompany him. The youngster did not hesitate. Every year the Puerto Rican league attracted a bevy of big-league pitchers, from veterans looking to make extra money to rookies eager for a regular spot in a starting rotation. Aaron viewed the opportunity as a way "to find out how ready I really was as a hitter."

He and the Braves also felt Puerto Rico was the perfect place for him to learn the basics of outfield play. Without the pressure from the hostile crowds he encountered in southern towns, Aaron would be free to make mistakes and learn from them. They did not want him dodging stones the way Horace Garner had.

One thing Aaron would not bother with was the Spanish language. Running down a ball in the gap and throwing to the correct base seemed to be as much as he wanted to think about. "I could have stayed there for twenty years and I wouldn't have known what they were talking about," he joked in *Aaron, r.f.* "Besides, I didn't have my mind on Spanish lessons."

Aside from his obvious career goals, there were other reasons Aaron looked forward to a trip to a scenic island destination. It served as his and Barbara's honeymoon, though the new Mrs.

Aaron would have to take it easy. She was pregnant, having recently entered her third trimester. The newlyweds expected their first child before the first of the year. In *Aaron, r.f.*, Aaron claimed that wedlock changed him on and off the field. "I know it may sound artificial, like I'm trying to score a few points at home, but marriage was the best thing that ever happened to me," he said. "If my career had a turning point, it was standing up there that day before the preacher. I'd been getting a little wild, I won't deny that . . . Getting married developed some sense of responsibility for me."

Winter ball also delayed Aaron's possible entry into the army. With war raging in Korea, the U.S. draft board indicated that Aaron would soon be called for duty. Upon learning this news, the Braves stepped in on Aaron's behalf. Fearing it would lose its budding superstar, the club intimated that the youngster would be assigned to the Atlanta Crackers when the 1954 season began. This gave the draft board a great deal to consider. Atlanta competed in the Southern League, which had yet to be integrated. As the Braves hoped, this put Aaron's future into an entirely different perspective. The army had a powerful dilemma on its hands. Did it really want to stand in the way of history? Feeling that Aaron could do more good for his country at home than in a frozen foxhole half a world away, the draft board ultimately answered *No* and chose to drop the matter.

In *I Had a Hammer*, Aaron admitted his relief at having sidestepped military duty. The thought of breaking a color line for a second time, however, was only slightly less appealing. "It makes me shudder now to think about integrating another league in the South," he said. "But I did plenty of things back then that I can't imagine doing now—that I wouldn't do now."

The high point of Aaron's experience in winter ball was the opportunity to play for Mickey Owen. Aaron had lucked out once again, being paired with a manager who knew how to squeeze the most out of his prodigy's immense talent. Cerebral and authoritative, Owen possessed the type of baseball mind that major league teams usually looked for in a manager. His thoughtful approach to the game complemented Aaron's raw skills perfectly.

"If anyone deserves help for teaching me it must be Mickey Owen, who managed me in Puerto Rico winter ball in 1953," said Aaron in the August 1966 issue of *Baseball Digest*. "Owen was working for the Braves then. He'd get me out to the ballpark a couple of hours before the game and make me hit for one hour to right and one hour to left."

In addition to Owen's desire to see Aaron improve as a batter, what made the two a good fit was that, in his own way, the skipper had also been a victim of discrimination. A highly regarded defensive catcher for the Brooklyn Dodgers in the 1930s and '40s, Owen was nonetheless known far and wide for his infamous "dropped third strike." The play occurred in the ninth inning of Game Four in the 1941 World Series. With the Dodgers clinging to a two-run lead and two men out, Owen called for a curve from reliever Hugh Casey. Instead he got a spitball, which darted low and inside, fooling both Owen and the batter, Tommy Henrich, who flailed helplessly for strike three. Owen stabbed at the pitch but it bounced off his glove and Henrich made it to first base. The Yankees went on to win the game and the series, and Owen spent the rest of his playing days, quite unfairly, as a symbol of Dodger ineptitude.

After the game, second baseman Billy Herman suggested to reporters that Owen may have been nonchalant. Regarded as an observant player, Herman was taken at his word. When this version of the story reached the Yankee clubhouse, the New York players did nothing to quell it. Owen had barreled into their diminutive shortstop, Phil Rizzuto, trying to break up a double play, and this seemed as good a way as any to get back at him. Little did anyone at the time realize that Owen's miscue would remain one of the most vivid gaffes in sports history. A dozen years later the play was as fresh as Bill Buckner's 1986 error is to today's baseball fans.

Owen was in Puerto Rico trying to lay the groundwork for a managing career. He had caught what he assumed was his final major league game in 1951 for the Cubs (he actually came out of retirement in 1954 and played in 30 games for the Red Sox at age 38) and knew he would have to build a résumé that would convince someone that the good he would do might outweigh the public relations nightmare that would likely accompany his hiring. He had actually begun this process several years earlier, when he accepted an offer to be a player-manager in the renegade Mexican League for the 1946 season. The league was run by the Pasquel brothers, a pair of war profiteers who hoped to lure enough returning players to form a third major league. Commissioner Happy Chandler threatened to ban anyone who played in the league, so Owen simply stayed on the bench and managed his players. When the league disbanded and he tried to rejoin the majors, he found that he was among the group of blacklisted players anyway. Owen and the others were reinstated after missing two seasons, and he toiled from 1949 to 1951 as Chicago's backup catcher.

By the time he and Aaron connected, Owen had not moved much off square one—his reputation had been forever sullied by a blunder that may not have been his fault, and a desire to expand his baseball horizons abroad. He was glad for the opportunity to mold a player of Aaron's caliber. In *I Had a Hammer*, Owen fondly remembered the first time he worked with Aaron on his outfield skills. "I sent him out there and hit him some fly balls," he recalled. "He just turned and ran and caught them. I thought, well, he can catch the ball, but can he throw it? I'd never seen him throw any way but underhanded. So I hit him some ground balls and told him to charge and throw them to second base. He threw the ball overhand, right to second base. Then I told him to cut loose and throw one to third. So he cut loose and that ball came across the infield as good as you ever saw. That was it. He was an outfielder."

Aaron initially struggled at the plate in Puerto Rico. A few weeks into the season, his average had dipped far below .200. There was talk of sending him back home, but as Aaron became more comfortable in the outfield, his average began to climb. He was selected to play in the All-Star Game, where he dazzled fans with his speed and power. Before the game, Aaron won the 60-yard dash competition. During the game itself, he slammed two long home runs, both sailing over the bleachers and disappearing into the night. Only one other ball left the stadium the entire season.

Aaron continued his torrid hitting during the second half of the year and finished third in the league with a .322 average. He also tied for the lead in homers with nine, which kept him fully stocked in Chesterfield cigarettes. Like many athletes of his time, Aaron smoked. In Puerto Rico, he received cigarettes for every home run he hit. But a free pack of Chesterfields in Caguas was no bargain. In Puerto Rico, the cigarettes are significantly stronger than in the United States, and Aaron found them hard to handle.

Although the Aarons enjoyed their time in Puerto Rico, they were eager to return to the States. Spring training was only a few weeks away, and Aaron needed time to rest. He also wanted to introduce Gaile, the newest addition to the Aaron family and the first of Henry and Barbara's four children, to her grandparents, uncles, and aunts in Mobile.

The Braves invited Aaron to spring training with the big club as a reward for his outstanding season the year before. No one, not even Aaron, expected him to make the majors. The organization had actually elevated him above the Southern League and placed him on the roster of its Class-AAA Toledo club in the American Association. Even so, Owen had to cheer up the youngster before he left Puerto Rico. The manager reminded him that the American

Association was a "man's league" and that his promotion to Toledo represented a major leap for someone so inexperienced. Don't be impatient, Owen advised, you'll be in the majors soon enough.

On the first day of spring training, Aaron pulled on a Braves uniform and donned a cap emblazoned with a big, white *M*. The Braves belonged to Milwaukee now; Boston was just a distant memory. Aaron had heard about the move while in Waycross the previous spring, when the team announced what was the first franchise shift in the majors since 1903. What he did not realize was how warmly the Braves had been received in their new home. Attendance in 1953 soared to 1.8 million from the 281,000 that had paid to see the Braves in Boston during all of 1952—a figure the Braves equaled after just 13 home dates at Milwaukee's County Stadium. The players responded by surging from seventh place in '52 to second in '53.

The people of Milwaukee treated the Braves like gods. Pitcher Lew Burdette once said he only paid for two things in Milwaukee, fruit and soap. Everything else was handed to him for free. "The team nobody wanted to see in Boston the year before, everybody wanted to see now in Milwaukee," wrote Milton Shapiro in *The Hank Aaron Story*. "Nothing could keep the fans away."

"Andy Pafko, voted the fans' most popular player, received a Cadillac and thousands of dollars in other gifts," Shapiro added. "Warren Spahn got a tractor for his farm. Sid Gordon got a $1,000 bond and dozens of other valuable gifts. Rookie Bill Bruton [an African American] was given three rooms of furniture and a down payment on a house."

A team that improves so dramatically generally does so on the strength of its pitching. This was true of the Braves, whose starting staff was led by Spahn and Burdette. To keep the momentum going, the team had to make trades to shore up vulnerabilities in its pitching, hitting, and defense. This meant acquiring veterans either to play leading roles or fill in if and when needed. There was little room in this picture for a 20-year-old with one year of Class-A ball under his belt.

And that is just how the Milwaukee veterans treated Aaron when he arrived in camp. They did not think of him as a piece of a winning puzzle. "Some of the fellows were skeptical when the Braves' front office told us this young kid, Henry Aaron, would be in spring training with us," confirmed Bobby Thomson in "Where Does 'Bad Henry' Rate?" an article Dan Schlossberg wrote a few years after Aaron retired. "Everybody had said he was bound to be a great one, but nobody gave him much thought. He'd hit well in the minors, sure, but we figured he'd be like so many other rookies before him—come to camp with a reputation, really see the curveball for the first time and bomb out."

Thomson, a versatile slugger who had become the Giants' top hitter in 1953 while Willie Mays was in the army, was Milwaukee's key acquisition heading into spring. The Braves gave up left-hander Johnny Antonelli—a former bonus baby who at 23 was finally becoming the pitcher everyone thought he could be—and Don Liddle, a diminutive spot starter who specialized in retiring left-handed hitters. Thomson was to take over in left field for Sid Gordon, who had been dealt to the Pirates for infielder Danny O'Connell. These moves solved a couple of problems for the Braves. In Thomson, they had a 30-year-old player who was typically good for 25 homers and around 100 RBIs. Gordon had been the same type of hitter, but at 35 he had begun to slip. The addition of O'Connell gave Milwaukee a solid hitter and fielder at second base to replace Jack Dittmer. After coming to the Braves with much fanfare from the University of Iowa, Dittmer had produced three stellar minor-league seasons in which he hit .373, .334, and .356. At the big-league level, however, his defense proved erratic and he struggled to stay above .250. He would be more valuable off the bench, a role he would play for the Braves through the 1956 season.

With the trade of Liddle, the Braves were without a reliable lefty in the bullpen, their only major concern as spring training began. The outfield was considered to be one of the team's strengths. In addition to Thomson, right fielder Andy Pafko was an excellent all-around player, and center fielder Bill Bruton was the best base stealer in the league. The fourth outfielder, converted shortstop Jim Pendleton, had hit .299 in limited duty the year before with seven homers, including three in one game.

Alas, the baseball gods did not smile on the Milwaukee outfield that spring. Or at least, that is how it looked to manager Charlie Grimm. First, Pendleton was a no-show. A star in the Negro Leagues, at Class-AAA, and in the Venezuelan and Cuban winter leagues, he was unhappy with his salary and role on the team, and decided to hold out. Apparently, Pendleton hoped to eat his way to stardom, for when he finally reported to camp he was grossly overweight (Aaron described him as a "blimp"). This would not have been a great concern were it not for an injury suffered by Thomson. During a March 13 game against the Yankees in St. Petersburg, he tried to stretch a single into a double and snapped his ankle going into second base.

"It was getting late in the game," Aaron remembered in *Aaron, r.f.* "I had already been in as a pinch hitter, and was showered and dressed and standing in a little alleyway between the third-base stands and the bleachers at Al Lang Field.

"I was . . . drinking a Coke when Thomson got hold of a pitch and hit a line drive to left field. He tore around first and went into second with a big slide. Then he didn't get up. I could see his leg doubled underneath his body and he was just lying there on the ground like he'd been shot."

To fill Thomson's spot, Grimm used Aaron and Pendleton. But Pendleton just was not ready, so as the weeks passed Aaron got more and more playing time. Picking up a hit or two every game, he was making believers out of everyone who saw him. Aaron's first taste of big-league competition had come a few games earlier against none other than the Dodgers and his idol, Jackie Robinson, in the Braves' first exhibition series of the spring. Before the opening game, Robinson approached the nervous rookie and wished him luck. Aaron, slated to hit third in the lineup, could barely contain himself. In his first appearance at the plate, he lined a double off Carl Erskine. The Dodgers quickly sensed they were watching a superstar emerge. "The boy's gonna be murder on us in a couple years," Roy Campanella said afterward. "He's a natural swinger, and I don't think a pitcher's gonna be able to find a weak spot on him once he gets a little more experience."

By the time Thomson got hurt, Aaron was hitting right around .400. He had passed every spring-training test a 20-year-old could, and finally Grimm had no choice but to cancel his ticket to Toledo and hand him the starting left field job. Aaron laid claim to a permanent roster spot with the Braves after slamming a long home run against the Red Sox. The blast even got the attention of Ted Williams. "Who the hell is that?" Williams demanded of some nearby sportswriters after hearing the crack of the ball off Aaron's bat. When told it was a newcomer named Aaron, he responded, "Write it down and remember it. You'll be hearing that name often."

Despite Aaron's Grapefruit League heroics, the news that he had secured not just a spot on the roster, but the role of starting left fielder, was still met with skepticism by some of the veterans on Milwaukee. Having a 20-year-old kid patrolling the outfield and hitting fifth in the order was a scary prospect, unless it was just a stopgap measure until a veteran could be acquired.

"We expected to have a good outfield with Bobby Thomson out there, and the veterans were concerned about how good we would be with a rookie as his replacement," recalled Lew Burdette in the November 1982 issue of *Baseball Digest*. "After all, Aaron was just a young kid who had to prove himself. We all wondered if he could do it. But it didn't take us long to discover how good he was. He was better than anything I'd ever seen."

Aaron went hitless on Opening Day in four at bats as Milwaukee lost, 9–8, to the Cincinnati Reds. The young outfielder, in fact, spent most of the afternoon chasing line drives off the bat of fellow rookie Jim Greengrass, who set a big-league record with four Opening Day doubles. Aaron's debut had gotten off to a rocky start long before the game's first pitch was ever thrown. First, as he walked through the locker room, several teammates mistook him for the clubhouse boy. When he arrived at his locker, he found his name misspelled. He then learned the Braves had assigned him uniform number 5, though he preferred a double digit. Team executives, however, felt he was "too skinny" to wear anything but a single number.

Regardless of the adversity that met him on and off the field, the rookie still felt encouraged by his first exposure to the big leagues. "You read about the other guys and you play against them in spring training," Aaron remembered in an article in *Baseball Digest* from December of 1974. "But this was getting down to the nitty-gritty. Then, you find out everything's the same as in spring training."

Aaron's confidence and relief were tempered somewhat by the fact that he did not become an instant star. "I don't remember Henry as an instant success," *New Yorker* writer Herbert Warren Wind once observed. "When I first saw him, I didn't have that feeling of impending greatness. It takes time to appreciate Henry Aaron. He does everything so smoothly that it makes you wonder if he's loafing or not."

Wind was right. During his rookie year in Milwaukee, Aaron practically went unnoticed. He acknowledged as much in *I Had a Hammer*. "I wasn't the one the fans came to watch," he said.

"[Eddie] Mathews . . . was such a hot young star that in August he appeared on the cover of the first *Sports Illustrated* ever published. Spahn was already a superstar by the time the team arrived in Milwaukee, and in 1954 he won twenty-one games, which was about his average. Bruton led the league in stolen bases. Those were the guys the fans wanted to see."

Aaron, however, did establish himself as an important part of the Braves, batting in the heart of the lineup all season long. When Pafko was forced to the bench because of a hernia, Aaron moved to right field. There he performed consistently, remaining the starter even after the return of Pafko, who was relegated to pinch-hitting duty.

Despite the surprisingly cool play of Aaron, Milwaukee had dropped to dead last in the NL by the end of April. Prognosticators who felt the loss of Thomson was too much for the Braves to overcome seemed like psychics. The usually affable Grimm, known best for his undying sense of humor, had seen enough. He ripped his club in a private meeting, promising to shake up the lineup.

One of his changes was to shift Aaron to the third slot in order. The move energized the rookie, who immediately collected five hits in a game against the Cardinals. He stayed hot throughout May, helping the Braves climb steadily up the standings. As the month drew to a close, Milwaukee had pulled even with the Dodgers in first place. Then, with his team set to square off against the Cubs in a doubleheader at County Stadium, Grimm made a curious move. Tinkering with the lineup again, he flip-flopped Aaron and power-hitting first baseman Joe Adcock in the 3–4 spots in the order. Conventional wisdom said that the pressure of batting cleanup would be too much for the young outfielder, but Aaron made his manager look like a genius. He roped a two-run triple in the eighth inning of the first game to key Milwaukee's 7–6 victory, and belted a game-tying home run in the second game before scoring the winning run with two out in the ninth. The sweep propelled the Braves into sole possession of first place.

Milwaukee's stay atop the standings was short-lived. As quickly as their bats heated up, the Braves' hitters cooled down—including Aaron, who started to press in the four hole. Grimm re-adjusted the lineup, switching Aaron and Adcock once again. But his moves could do little to halt his slumping team's slide. Injuries did not help matters either. Adcock missed time because of a sore hand, and Mathews split a finger. Milwaukee received encouraging news in July when Thomson returned to the lineup. But even his presence failed to wake up the Braves. They fell to third place, behind the Giants (who were getting great pitching from Antonelli) and Dodgers, in early September. Then misfortune struck again. This time it was Aaron who experienced the setback.

In Cincinnati for a doubleheader, the Braves, five and one-half games back of New York, felt very much alive in the pennant race. The team's outlook changed in the ninth inning of the second game. Legging out a triple in a 9–2 Milwaukee rout, Aaron slid hard into third and fractured an ankle. Ironically, the runner sent in to replace him was Thomson.

The break was not all gloom and doom for Aaron, who at the age of 20 needed permission from his parents before doctors could operate on him. By this time the army had seen through the organization's integration charade, but the injury now eliminated any chance of Aaron serving in the Korean War. "My number had come up," he observed in *Aaron, r.f.* "I was due to report in October. I wouldn't break my ankle to keep from going, but since it happened that way, and my draft board had to reclassify me, and it kept me from losing some good baseball years, I'm not going to turn liar and say that I'm mighty sorry I didn't get a chance to be a soldier."

Aaron's injury did hurt his chances of winning NL Rookie of the Year. His final stats—a .280 average, 27 doubles, 13 home runs, and 69 RBIs in only 122 games—impressed many. But Wally Moon of the Cardinals, who batted .304 and scored 106 runs over the course of a full season, claimed the award.

Moon was not the only young star to overshadow Aaron in 1954. Willie Mays, the 23-year-old wunderkind of the Giants, emerged from two years of military service and put up astounding numbers. Along with his .345 average, he slammed 41 homers, 13 triples, and 33 doubles. Mays also drove home 110 runs while scoring 119. His extraordinary play enabled New York to overtake both the Braves and the Dodgers for the NL pennant. Then, with the eyes of the nation on him in Game One of the World Series, he stole a victory from the powerhouse Cleveland Indians with a stunning over-the-shoulder catch. Robbed of their momentum, the Indians fell in four straight.

As the preeminent young black outfielder in baseball, Mays was the yardstick by which all other young black outfielders would now be measured. Mays never had another season like he did in 1954, and no player has ever made a bigger catch. No one was more a man of the people—all the people—than Mays, either. Still, Aaron would soon find himself trying to meet these impossible standards. "Mays was at the top of the game when I broke into baseball, and from the beginning he was the guy I was measured against," he said in *I Had a Hammer*. "It went on for as long as we played in the same league—twenty years—and then some. There were Willie Mays comic books, Say Hey baseball caps, and a dozen songs about Willie. It wasn't New York that made Mays what he was though, and it wasn't Leo Durocher. It was his amazing ability. And it wasn't just me who suffered from comparisons to Willie. That year, he became the standard for all other players.

"Meanwhile, I was just a guy filling in for Bobby Thomson. To give you an idea of how important I was in 1954, on the Braves' highlight film from that year, it showed me hitting a foul ball. That was it."

As the years passed, there developed a small but vocal group that believed Aaron was every bit as good as Mays. Braves' announcer Ernie Johnson Sr. liked to say, "Hank Aaron does everything Willie Mays does, but his hat doesn't fall off."

With his leg in a cast, Aaron spent the off-season at home with his family in Mobile. Meanwhile, other top black players of the day joined Jackie Robinson's All-Stars, a troupe that had been barnstorming since 1947. Aaron would have gladly made the tour had he not been injured, but then, had he not been injured, he most certainly would have been sweating through basic training somewhere. He accepted the trade-off, using the time to play with his daughter and reflect on his good fortune.

For one thing, Aaron realized how lucky he was to play in a city where the fans treated him so well. Having endured a season in Jacksonville, Milwaukee seemed like paradise. "I suppose I'll always have a warm spot in my heart for Milwaukee, because I grew up there," Aaron once told writer Samuel A. Andrews. "I made a lot of mistakes when I first came up, and those people lived with me through those mistakes. I wasn't scarred or booed, or anything like that. They let me develop, without considerable pressure."

He reiterated those sentiments in *Chasing the Dream*. "Milwaukee seemed like a million miles from the Jim Crow South where I grew up," he said. "Sometimes I had to pinch myself. Here I was 20 years old, and already my dream had come true."

Aaron also began to consider deeper questions, those exploring race and the role he could play in the plight of African Americans in the United States. By 1954, 14 of 16 major-league teams had been integrated (the Yankees and Red Sox were the lone holdouts). Aaron and his fellow black players saw this as a positive step. The Supreme Court's ruling in *Brown v. Board of Education* in 1954 was also reason for hope. There was a much greater sense of optimism in the black community. It seemed the climate was right for change. Aaron came to the understanding that he could be a player in a much larger and more important drama, and this realization shaped him for years to come.

To many of his teammates (and Milwaukee's front office) Aaron seemed like a different player after his rookie season. More confident in his ability to handle big-league pitching—and more secure in his role with the Braves—he quickly became a team leader, though not the type likely to deliver an impassioned clubhouse speech. Aaron, rather, led by delivering key hits in clutch situations, taking an extra base late in games, and deflating opponents with sparkling defensive plays.

A prime example of Aaron's newfound confidence was his request to change his number. Before the 1955 campaign began, the second-year outfielder went to Donald Davidson, who counted traveling secretary among his duties for the Braves, and again asked for a double digit. Davidson responded incredulously. How could a skinny kid like Aaron fill out a jersey with two numbers? Didn't he realize that all of the game's biggest stars, from Ruth to Musial, had carried single digits?

Aaron did not budge. He told the diminutive Davidson, who stood four foot something and received unending ribbing for it, that he would look great in a double number. When Aaron arrived for spring training, he found uniform number 44 hanging in his locker. Ironically, he totaled forty-four home runs four times in his career. Years later, Davidson joked that he should have assigned number sixty-six to Aaron instead.

Though Davidson seemed to delight in ripping into Aaron, the two enjoyed a strong relationship. "The fact is, Donald was one of my best friends in baseball," said Aaron in *I Had a Hammer*. "I think because of the prejudices we both faced, we understood each other. Once, he and I sat down for breakfast at our hotel in Pittsburgh and the waitress wouldn't wait on me. Donald never scheduled us in that hotel again."

Opposing pitchers often felt Aaron's wrath for such slights. In 1955, for instance, he batted over .300 for the first time, more than doubled his home run total to 27 and led the NL in two-base hits. He also scored 105 runs, starting a streak of 13 consecutive seasons in which he topped the century mark. In addition, Aaron made his maiden voyage to Cooperstown, New York, traveling with the Braves for a preseason game against Boston. The second-year outfielder saw no significance in his initial visit to the Hall of Fame, a place that had yet to enshrine a black player.

"Why should I be excited about my first trip to Cooperstown?" Aaron asked writer Dave Hirshey in 1974. "I was young then. I didn't really think about ending up there. All I remember is that I was there to play an exhibition game against the Red Sox and it was raining and we spent the whole day at the hotel swimming pool."

Much like their young right fielder, the Braves used the 1955 season to establish themselves as a force to be reckoned with in the National League. They did so by playing winning baseball despite injuries and off years of several key players. Spahn won just three more games than he lost, Adcock and pitcher Gene Conley suffered season-ending injuries, and O'Connell's average plummeted more than 50 points to .225. The Braves fell ten games behind the Dodgers in the spring and never made the games up. In the end, huge years from Roy Campanella, Don Newcombe, and Duke Snider were the difference. Had the Braves gotten the years they expected from their top players, the race would have been much, much closer. As it was, they finished in second place, 15 games over .500 with 85 victories.

The team Milwaukee put on the field the following year was a superb one. Catcher Del Crandall was just entering his prime, yet had been the everyday backstop since completing his military commitment in 1953. Crandall, who first caught for the Braves in Boston when he was 19, had become the defensive equal of Campanella. Though Crandall was not on the same level as a run-producer, he did have 20-homer power. First base belonged to Adcock, who murdered left-handed pitching. O'Connell, the second baseman, was no threat at the plate, but he hustled all the time and never made mental errors. Shortstop Johnny Logan, who had made the All-Star team in 1955, was a scrappy fan favorite who loved to pick fights with bigger players. A star for the minor-league Milwaukee Brewers in the early 1950s, he was welcomed as a returning hero when the Braves moved from Boston. At third, Eddie Mathews entered the 1956 campaign as the undisputed star of the Braves (despite the fact that Aaron was named team MVP in '55) and one of the most exciting young power hitters of all time. Just 24 years old, he had already amassed 153 home runs in four seasons. Mathews was a patient and selective hitter, and a fine fielder. Many sportswriters were already penciling him in as a future Hall of Famer.

The Milwaukee outfield in 1956 was a strong one. Center fielder Bill Bruton was still one of the fastest men in the league, and had developed a little power to go with his speed. In left, Bobby Thomson, then 32, was beginning to fade. But he was backed up ably by veteran Andy Pafko and Aaron's old friend from Jacksonville, Wes Covington. After spending 1954 in the army, Covington returned to Jacksonville where he led the Sally League in hitting. A good spring won him a permanent spot on the roster.

Milwaukee's pitching was anchored, as always, by Spahn and Burdette. Spahn, 35, no longer had the popping fastball he needed to blow away right-handed hitters, so he compensated by adding a devastating screwball and changing speeds and locations. Burdette, 29, made hitters crazy with his fidgeting and mumbling on the mound, and frustrated them with his sinker and slider.

When he had these deliveries working, it was almost impossible to put runs on the board against him. The third starter, Bob Buhl, seemed ready to become a big winner. A paratrooper in Korea, he feared no one. Buhl's herky-jerky motion and mixed bag of pitches made him unpleasant to face. By 1956, he had learned everything he needed to know about NL hitters. The end of the staff was held up by towering Gene Conley—who had played pro basketball for the Boston Celtics during the 1952–53 season—and Ray Crone, a control artist who had won 19 for Jacksonville the year Aaron played there.

And then there was Henry Aaron. When a 21-year-old hits .300, scores and drives in 100 runs, and raps out 73 extra-base hits as Aaron had in 1955, it is hard to know what he will do at 22. In the preseason publications, however, none of the experts had any doubt about his abilities. They expected bigger and better things from Aaron, and the Braves, in 1956.

Aaron did not disappoint. He hit well in 1956 from the first weekend to the last. And the Braves improved to 92 wins. But when the final out was recorded, Milwaukee fans had little to cheer about. The Braves went into the season's final series (against the Cardinals) with a one-game lead over the ancient Dodgers who seemed to be falling apart. Brooklyn did what it had to do, however, beating the Pirates in three straight. The Braves choked against St. Louis, losing two out of three. By this time, Fred Haney had replaced Grimm, who was sacked in June when the team was languishing below .500. The conservative Haney just let his players play, and Milwaukee surged into first. But he could do little more than watch in frustration as those same players faltered down the stretch.

For his part, Aaron had a terrific year. He led the league in hits (200), doubles (34), total bases (340), and batting (.328), and finished third in runs and slugging. His 14 triples ranked him second behind teammate Bruton, who hit 15. In the Most Valuable Player voting, Newcombe and Sal Maglie finished 1–2, with Aaron garnering more votes than any hitter in the league.

The Braves were definitely trending upward as the 1957 season began. Haney looked at the team he had in finishing 1956 and believed it was good enough to win the pennant with just a few adjustments. Feeling his players might have tired down the stretch, he aimed to give more playing time to a group of youngsters who had performed well in limited action. Frank Torre, a left-handed first baseman, would spell Adcock more frequently. Covington, also a lefty, would get more playing time in left field, as would Pafko, the veteran righty. Catchers Del Rice and Carl Sawatski would give Crandall more days off. And Felix Mantilla would get an occasional start at second or short. Haney's main area of concern was second base, where O'Connell was no longer getting the job done. The Milwaukee front office could not make a trade over the winter, but kept an eye out for a top second sacker as the season began.

As expected, the Braves started well, while the Cardinals and Phillies hung with them. Neither opponent had the pitching the Braves did, but they were good enough to move into first if Milwaukee faltered. By June, the only thing clear about the 1957 pennant race was that the Giants would not be a part of it. Outside of Mays, who was tearing up the league, no one could get a clutch hit. New York's second baseman, Red Schoendienst, had been a perennial All-Star since the 1940s. The Giants had picked him up from the Cardinals a year earlier for Al Dark and Whitey Lockman, and he finished as he had in four of the previous five seasons, with a .300 average. But with the Giants floundering and attendance drooping, he had become a luxury they could not afford.

The Braves traded the Giants O'Connell, Thomson, and Crone for the 34-year-old Schoendienst, who collected 122 hits in his 93 games in a Milwaukee uniform to end up as the league leader with an even 200. Thomson's spot was split between Covington and Pafko until Bruton was lost to a knee injury. Aaron then moved to center, Pafko replaced him in right, and Covington became the everyday left fielder. To shore up the outfield, Haney dipped into the farm system and pulled 26-year-old Bob Hazle out of Wichita. A .275 hitter in the minors, he caught fire during the last couple of months and became part of baseball folklore. "Hurricane Hazle" hit Milwaukee, and everything else for that matter, finishing the year with a .403 average in 41 games. "He was unbelievable," remembered Aaron. "I was hitting about .330, and he made me feel like I was in a slump. I thought I was having a pretty good season, and he made me feel downright embarrassed."

Haney also had Wichita to thank for relief ace Don McMahon, a converted starter who used a live fastball and overhand curve to tame enemy batters an inning or two at a time. He was called up prior to the All-Star break and saved nine games with a 1.53 ERA in 32 appearances. Haney's final bit of good fortune came in the person of Torre, who was thrust into the everyday first base job when Adcock broke his leg. The slick-fielding Brooklyn native came through with a .272 average and saved countless runs with his glovework.

A six-game winning streak in September lifted the Braves into first place, but the second-place Cardinals hung close. Aaron, who was having a spectacular season, was in contention for the league lead in hits, runs, homers, and RBIs.

The undercurrent beginning to circulate around baseball whispered of Aaron ascending to the title of "best in the game," a sentiment confirmed by Bill White in *Chasing the Dream*. "Hank could flat out hit," recalled the first baseman, who was regarded as one of the National League's most observant players. Warren Spahn echoed White's remarks when discussing Aaron's developing power stroke. "When Hank hit 'em," he said, "they were like tee shots."

On September 23, with Milwaukee up by two games, the Cardinals invaded County Stadium for the final series of the regular season. One win would clinch the pennant for the Braves. In the opening game, Aaron singled and scored his first time up to give the Braves a 1–0 advantage. Milwaukee maintained its lead until the sixth, when a base hit by Dark plated two for St. Louis. The Braves responded in the bottom of the inning as Mathews drove home Schoendienst to tie the score. Over the next four innings, neither team could break the deadlock. In the top of the 11th, Haney replaced Burdette with Conley, who set the Redbirds down in order.

Logan led off the home half of the 11th with a single off Billy Muffett. Two outs later, at 11:34 p.m., Aaron stepped to the plate. He described the ensuing drama in *My Greatest Day in Baseball*.

"In that situation as a hitter, you don't think about winning the pennant . . . all you think about is getting a good pitch to hit," he explained. "Muffett's first pitch was a curveball, and I knew I hit it well, very high to straightaway center. On the way to first I saw Wally Moon go back to the wire fence and jump for it. I didn't know it was in there until I saw people scrambling for the ball on the other side of the fence."

The blast set off a raucous celebration. Aaron's teammates met him at home plate and carried him off the field on their shoulders. The Braves celebrated long into the night, as did their fans. Aaron remembers feasting on a spread of ribs, chicken, and shrimp in the clubhouse, telling the reporters assembled around him that "for the first time I felt like I could let my guard down and really act excited." He later called the moment his "shiningest hour."

Vecsey tried to pinpoint Aaron's jubilation in *The Sports Immortals*. "For several seconds of Milwaukee's finest hour, Henry Aaron wasn't there," he wrote. "Running between second and third base, he was back on Edwards Avenue in Mobile. . . . The day was October 3, 1951, and Henry had just heard on somebody's radio that

Bobby Thomson had homered to win the pennant. . . . The Negro sandlotter from Toulminville was Bobby Thomson that day until he rounded third base, saw the reception committee and knew it was at least as much fun to be Henry Aaron."

A picture of Aaron on his teammates' shoulders appeared on the front page of the *Wisconsin CIO News* the next day. Next to it was a story about the riots that had erupted in Arkansas after the Supreme Court's ruling to integrate Central High School in Little Rock. The National Guard was called in to restore order. The irony was thick, which Aaron noted in *I Had a Hammer*.

"Milwaukee's dusty Hank Aaron blasted the Braves into the World Series only a few hours after an insane mob of white supremacists took the Stars and Stripes in Little Rock and tramped it on the ground in front of Central High School," he quoted from the *CIO News*. "The cheers that are lifted to Negro ballplayers only dramatize the stupidity of the jeers that are directed at those few Negro kids trying to get a good education for themselves in Little Rock."

Aaron had to block all these distractions from his mind. Game One of the 1957 World Series was less than a week away, and the fearsome Yankees were lying in wait. The media billed the Fall Classic as a showdown between Aaron and Mickey Mantle.

The Milwaukee outfielder did not mind the comparisons to Mantle, except that once again he found himself on the losing side of the argument. Mantle had enjoyed one of the greatest seasons in baseball history a year earlier, winning the major-league Triple Crown with a .353 average, 52 home runs, and 130 RBIs. In 1957, Mantle raised his average and walked more than once a game as American League pitchers wanted nothing to do with him.

But was Mantle's year better than Aaron's? It was hard to say. In 1957, Aaron himself claimed two legs of the major-league Triple Crown, with 44 home runs and 132 RBIs. His .322 batting average was second to Stan Musial's in the NL. But next to Mantle and his throng of adoring fans, Aaron seemed almost ordinary. "Just my luck," he said, "I finally got out of Mays' shadow, and there was Mickey Mantle."

The Yankees were given the edge over the Braves on the basis of experience and home-field advantage. The series, everyone agreed, would come down to pitching. Milwaukee had Spahn and Burdette in top form, but Buhl was coming back from a broken finger. Casey Stengel put together a patchwork staff that featured three starters returning from injuries: Whitey Ford, Bobby Shantz, and Bob Turley. Whichever team could squeeze the most out of its mound corps would prevail.

In the opener, Aaron accounted for one of just five hits the Braves got off Ford. Milwaukee scored only one run, when Schoendienst singled home Covington in the seventh, while the Yankees reached Spahn for three. The game ended with New York treating 69,000 fans in Yankee Stadium to a 3–1 victory.

Burdette took the mound the following afternoon and pitched masterfully, going the distance while allowing two runs on seven hits. The Braves drew first blood when Aaron led off the second inning with a triple off Shantz to dead center field, right over Mantle's head. The next batter, Adcock, flicked an outside pitch to right center and Aaron scored. Shantz then wriggled out of trouble thanks to a leaping grab of Covington's liner by Milwaukee native Tony Kubek. Burdette allowed the Yanks to tie the score when Jerry Coleman drove in Enos Slaughter by beating out a slow roller to Mathews with two down, but the Braves bounced back in the third to take the lead on a homer by Logan. Not to be denied, the Yankees knotted the score when Hank Bauer drilled a ball into the left field seats. But the Braves took control in the fourth when Covington blooped a single over shortstop Gil McDougald's head to score Adcock, and Slaughter's throw trying to nail Pafko at third skipped through the legs of

Kubek, the relay man. Burdette gave up just four more hits to close out a 4–2 win.

The victory swung the home-field advantage to the Braves, who flew straight to Milwaukee. The Yankees, however, chose a different route. They first flew to Chicago and then boarded a train north for the final leg of their journey. On the train, reporters pressed Stengel for a remark that they could use to lead off their stories. He obliged when he echoed the jeers of Yankee fans who had taken to calling Milwaukee "Bushville."

The behavior of the fans at County Stadium in Game Three did nothing to change this image. In batting practice, they cheered for every line drive. As each player was announced, they rocked the stadium. And once the game started, every time the Braves recorded an out they received loud and enthusiastic applause. When the Braves were overwhelmed 12–3, however, they started cheering for the hometown boy, Kubek, who slugged two home runs and drove in four. Still, the day's biggest ovation was reserved for Aaron, who made a spectacular catch and rocketed a two-run homer over the screen in right field to make the score 7–3. Aaron's four-bagger might have been the hardest ball he ever hit, but it went to waste. Don Larsen, the hero of the 1956 World Series, pitched seven and one-third innings in relief of Turley for the win.

Game Four was a must-win game for the Braves and they played it that way. Spahn cruised into the ninth with a 4–1 lead on a three-run homer by Aaron. Before the homer, Stengel was on the mound discussing the situation with starter Tom Sturdivant. The manager assured his hurler that he had nothing to fear with the wind blowing in, adding that not even Babe Ruth could hit one out in this gale.

In the top of the ninth, Spahn ran into trouble after retiring the first two batters. Yogi Berra and McDougald singled, then Elston Howard (the Yankees' first black player) pulled a three-run homer to left to tie the score. In the top of the 10th inning, Spahn again got the first two batters, but Kubek reached first when he beat out a grounder to Schoendienst. Bauer then shocked the crowd with a triple off the left field fence to give the Yankees a 5–4 lead. Spahn got Mantle to fly out and end the inning, but the damage was done. The Braves were dead if they did not find a way to score.

The Milwaukee 10th began when pinch hitter Nippy Jones was awarded first base after being grazed on the foot by reliever Tommy Byrne. At first, umpire Augie Donatelli called the pitch a ball, but when shown a smudge of shoe polish on the ball he changed his decision and motioned Jones to first. Right-hander Bob Grim, the Yankees' top reliever, came into the game and Schoendienst dropped a bunt down the first base line. First baseman Joe Collins pounced on the ball and threw Schoendienst out, while Mantilla (who was running for Jones) took second. Logan came up and laced a double into the corner, scoring Mantilla to tie the game. Now Stengel had to make a decision. Should Grim, a right-hander, face left-handed Eddie Mathews? Or should Mathews be walked to face the right-handed Aaron? National League managers had faced this decision many times during the season. Those who walked Mathews contributed to Aaron's league-leading RBI total. But those who pitched to Mathews did not fare much better. Stengel let Grim go after Mathews, and according to Aaron, this was the turning point of the series. County Stadium exploded moments later as Mathews crushed the ball over the right field fence for a game-winning homer.

"There's a strange little point of interest in the case of Nippy Jones," said Aaron some 10 years later. "The day that pitch hit his toe and he argued his way to first base was his last appearance in the Major Leagues. He never came to bat again for the Braves."

Haney handed the ball to Burdette in Game Five and the righty twirled a shutout. One Yankee he did not have to face was

Mantle, who had injured his shoulder and was on the bench. It was a good thing, because Milwaukee did not get much off of Ford who allowed just one run. The winning hit for the Braves was supplied by Adcock, who followed singles by Mathews and Aaron with a single of his own.

Down three games to two, New York was not dead, however. The series returned to Yankee Stadium where Bob Turley gave the pinstripers a terrific effort, holding the Braves to just two runs and striking out eight. Trailing 2–1 in the seventh, the Braves tied the score when Aaron homered into the left field bullpen. But Bauer connected for a round-tripper in the bottom of the inning and the game went to the Yankees 3–2.

Now it was Haney who faced the big pitching decision. Spahn had thrown 10 exhausting innings four days earlier, while Burdette had pitched far more economically a day later. The Milwaukee skipper tabbed Burdette who went out and pitched splendidly in Game Seven. Every time a Yankee reached base, the next man pounded one of Burdette's sinkers into the dirt or lifted a fastball harmlessly into the air. "The way he was going, I think Burdette could have pitched if he'd been up all night working in one of those coal mines back in West Virginia," Aaron said in *I Had a Hammer*.

Meanwhile, the Braves knocked the well-rested Larsen out of the box in the third inning when Mathews doubled home Hazle and Logan. Shantz came in to pitch to Aaron, who smoked a ball past the slick-fielding pitcher and into center field to score Mathews. Aaron scored the inning's fourth run on a force-out. Del Crandall finished the Milwaukee scoring in the eighth with a solo homer off Byrne. The Yankees mounted threats in the sixth and again in the ninth, but Burdette worked out of trouble each time. The series ended when Moose Skowron pulled a ball down the line with the bases loaded. Mathews lunged to his right, gloved the ball, and calmly stepped on third.

Needless to say, Burdette was named World Series MVP. But the Braves could not have done it without Aaron, who hit in all seven games and was the only Braves starter to bat over .300. His .393 average, three home runs, and seven RBIs were the highest of any player in the series.

The celebration that awaited the Braves in Milwaukee was stupendous. For a night, at least, Milwaukee changed from "Bushville" to the "City That Never Sleeps." "I suppose that if you've seen one World Series celebration you've seen them all, but I kind of doubt that, when I stop to think again of Milwaukee on the night of October 10, 1957," said Aaron. "Those people were out of their minds. We got involved in the damnedest parade you ever saw . . . anything I might say about the victory celebration after we got back to Milwaukee would be strictly hearsay. Some say I had a great time. I hope I did. I know I had a great time winning the World Series."

Baseball writers recognized Aaron's accomplishments a week later by voting him National League MVP. The balloting surprised Aaron, who assumed that one of his chief competitors for the award—Schoendienst or Stan Musial—would walk away with it. Both were well-liked veterans who had the sentimental support of voters. Each was also near the end of his career and might never again be in position to win the MVP. The baseball writers, however, could not overlook Aaron, who was unquestionably the best player on the league's best team. He finished first with 239 points, Musial was second with 230, and Schoendienst was a close third with 221. Only once before (1931) had three NL MVP candidates been separated by fewer points. The award provided the perfect ending to the 1957 campaign, which Aaron later called the "best year of my baseball life."

Aaron had more reason to count his blessings in 1957 when Henry Jr. was born. Less than a year later, however, Barbara gave birth prematurely to twin boys, Gary and Lary. Gary died before leaving the hospital but Lary survived. Though doctors saw little hope for the infant, the Aarons brought him home to Mobile. Estella cared for the baby around the clock, keeping him well fed and warm. Although he later developed epilepsy, Lary grew up happy and otherwise healthy.

The eight years following 1957 marked the steady maturation of Henry Aaron. Season after season, he recorded dazzling numbers, batting higher than .300 and scoring at least 100 runs in every year. Three times he belted 40 or more homers. Five times he topped the century mark in RBIs.

The Braves entered 1958 as the odds-on favorite to take the pennant, and they obliged the experts by finishing eight games in front. At no time during the season did a serious challenge materialize, although there were several crises to be dealt with. Buhl's funky delivery finally caught up with him and he hit the DL with a sore shoulder, while Conley hurt his arm and failed to win a single game. Once again Haney dipped into the farm system for pitching.

This time he came up with Juan Pizarro, Carlton Willey, and Joey Jay. Pizarro, a 20-year-old Puerto Rican with an overpowering fastball, struck out 84 batters in 97 innings and won 6 of 10 decisions. Willey, called up from Wichita at the end of June, shut out the Giants in his first start and was the top rookie hurler in the National League, finishing with a 9–7 mark. Jay, a bonus baby who languished on the bench as a teenager in the early 1950s, made the team out of spring training and filled in nicely with seven wins and a 2.13 ERA. Haney also used veteran Bob Rush in the rotation. An above-average pitcher who toiled in near anonymity for the lackluster Chicago Cub teams after World War II, he was best known for his high leg kick. Rush won 10 games for the Braves in 1958, and behind Spahn and Burdette—who won 22 and 20 games, respectively—was Milwaukee's most reliable starter.

Haney had less luck filling the hole left by Schoendienst, who contracted tuberculosis and missed two months. Mantilla, Mel

Roach, and Casey Wise played in his place, and together made Milwaukee fans long for Danny O'Connell. Also lost for a couple of months was Bruton, who once again injured his knee. Aaron shifted to center as he had the year before, keeping the position warm until Bruton returned for the stretch run.

The rest of the Braves' offense picked up the slack. Crandall raised his average into the .270s. Torre and Adcock split first base and combined to hit over .290. Mathews led the team with 31 home runs, Covington hit 24, and Logan chipped in 11. Aaron led the Braves in extra-base hits, amassing 34 doubles, four triples, and 30 home runs, and also had a team-high 109 runs and 95 RBIs. There was no "Hurricane Hazle" this year (in fact, Hazle was traded to the Tigers a couple of months into the season), but the Braves had enough to finish well ahead of the surprising second-place Pirates—a team Haney had a significant hand in building before he came to the Braves.

Milwaukee's opponent in the 1958 World Series was the Yankees again. Like the Braves, New York had swept to a pennant rather easily, and the team was healthy and well rested. This time the Braves had experience and home-field advantage on their side, but skeptics pointed to the emergence of Bob Turley as a big-time starter and questioned whether Burdette and Aaron would produce as they had in 1957. The slightest edge was given to the Braves.

Spahn and Ford hooked up in the opener, which started with three scoreless innings. Moose Skowron opened the top of the fourth with a bases-empty homer, but the Braves came right back to take a 2–1 lead when Aaron singled and scored and Spahn later singled in another run. The Yankees regained the lead immediately on a two-run shot by Hank Bauer. Up a run in the eighth, Ford walked Mathews and then gave up a long opposite-field double to Aaron. Covington tied the game with a sacrifice fly off reliever Ryne Duren, and when neither team scored in the ninth, the game went into extra innings. In the bottom of the 10th, Bruton, who had come into the game as a defensive replacement for Pafko, delivered the winning hit with a single that drove home Adcock.

Game Two was a blowout as Turley, a 21-game winner, was shelled in the first inning. From there, it only got uglier for the Yankees. The Braves—who scored seven times (including a three-run homer by Burdette) before the Yankees recorded three outs—added six more runs over the next seven innings to win 13–5.

The shell-shocked Yankees returned to the Bronx determined to win Game Three at all costs. Don Larsen took the mound against Rush and had a whale of an outing, combining with Ryne Duren to shut out Milwaukee 4–0 on six hits. Expecting to tie the series the next day, the New Yorkers ran into Spahn, who had all his pitches working. The 37-year-old southpaw embarrassed the Yankees, allowing just four runners to reach base and no one to score. Once again, Ford pitched well. But this time he was undone by left fielder Norm Siebern, who lost two fly balls in Yankee Stadium's notorious afternoon sun.

Up three games to one, with the final two games scheduled for County Stadium, the Braves were feeling very upbeat about their chances. Only one other team in postseason play had come back from such a deficit, which meant Milwaukee had history on its side. The Yankees were the team in the other dugout, however, and they were not in the habit of giving up. In Game Five, New York turned the tables, bombing Burdette for six runs and getting a shutout from Turley.

Two days later, in Milwaukee, Haney pushed the panic button. Rather than throwing Rush or one of the kids in Game Six so Spahn would be rested for Game Seven, the manager trotted Spahn back out, hoping he might repeat Burdette's three-win miracle. To Spahn's credit, he nearly pulled it off. Aaron and Spahn delivered run-scoring singles in the first and second innings to give the Braves a 2–1 lead. In the sixth, Haney sent Bruton into center field for defensive purposes, but the move backfired when the outfielder fumbled an Elston Howard single, allowing the potential tying run in the person of Mickey Mantle to go from first to third. Berra then made it 2–2 with a sacrifice fly, which is how it remained for the next three innings. In the New York 10th, Gil McDougald touched Spahn for a leadoff homer. Five batters later, Don McMahon gave up another run-scoring hit to make it 4–2. In the bottom of the 10th, Logan reached second and Aaron singled him home. Adcock singled up the middle, with Aaron advancing to third, but that is where he stayed. Torre hit a shot, but right to second baseman McDougald who snagged it to end the game.

Burdette and Larsen tangled again in Game Seven, and for seven innings it was as tense a contest as any fan could want. Milwaukee scratched out a 1–0 lead on a bases-loaded groundout in the first inning, but the Yankees manufactured two runs in the second. Crandall tied the game in the sixth with a home run off Turley, who had taken over for Larsen, and the Braves were suddenly looking like champions again. Burdette retired the Yankees easily in the seventh and got the first two batters in the eighth. But then Berra pulled a double into the left field corner and Howard drilled a single to center, giving New York a 3–2 lead. Burdette, clearly laboring, could not get the last out. Andy Carey hit a hard grounder to Mathews, who could not make the play. Skowron then came up and blasted a three-run homer to left center field. The Braves went quietly in the eighth and ninth and the Yankees swarmed Turley in front of 46,000 crestfallen Milwaukee fans.

Once again, Aaron had an excellent World Series. He reached base 13 times in seven games and hit .333. He took no consolation from his stats, of course. The Braves had blown it, and he was as responsible as anyone. Aaron and his teammates vowed that, when they made it back to the World Series, they would never let up until they had the final out.

As bad as they felt, it was probably inconceivable to the Milwaukee Braves and their fans that they would never reach the World Series again. They certainly did not expect to find themselves in a life-and-death struggle with the Dodgers and Giants in 1959. Both clubs had moved west in 1958 and finished a combined 33 games behind the Braves. Yet as the final weeks of September rolled around, San Francisco was in first place and Los Angeles and Milwaukee were in a virtual tie for second.

The Braves just were not the team they had been in the past. Schoendienst, sick again, missed the entire season. Covington, who should have been entering his prime, injured his knee and hit just seven home runs. With the exception of rookie Lee Maye, the bench was awful. And although Spahn, Burdette, Buhl, and McMahon pitched well, none of the other hurlers was able to reproduce his 1958 performance. Aaron and Mathews, however, were awesome. The big third baseman clubbed a league-high 46 homers, while Aaron led the majors with 223 hits, a .355 batting average, and a .636 slugging percentage. Aaron's 400 total bases were 48 more than the runner-up, Mathews, and 99 more than the American League leader, Rocky Colavito.

Aaron had clearly reached a new level as a hitter. Though not a classically trained batter, he succeeded "on the strength of his natural skill," as Roger Kahn put it—much of which depended on the unnaturally quick snap of his wrists. Indeed, despite hitting off his front foot (a cardinal sin for most batters) Aaron was able to make solid contact by keeping his hands back and whipping his bat through the hitting zone at the very last moment. "With those wrists," observed Rogers Hornsby, the preeminent right-handed hitter of the 1920s, "he can be fooled a little and still hit the hell out of the ball."

Aaron proved this point in the 1959 campaign. Two months into the season, his average stood at .468. Even more amazing, through those 40 games he had walked only 13 times. Even if opposing teams wanted to pitch around him, Aaron made it virtually impossible by swinging at anything remotely close to the strike zone. As long as he was hitting, no one had much to say about his form. "A manager would have to be crazy to bother a hitter like that," laughed Haney. "You look at his average and you leave him alone. I've seen him hit like that for stretches before, only not that early in the season. He does it early and everyone's amazed. He's done it in July or in August lots of times since I've been here and nobody was much surprised."

Sal Maglie, known during his playing days as the "Barber" for the number of close shaves he gave to opposing hitters, had his own theory on Aaron's hot streak. Baseball had legislated a new rule into the game, imposing a $50 fine for knockdown pitches. Maglie felt that without the threat of the beanball, hitters throughout baseball, including Aaron, were free to extend their arms and dive out over the plate.

"The only way I could handle Aaron was to get his face in the dirt," said the 42-year-old Maglie, who was finishing his career in the minors. "Then he'd be edgy and I could work on him. Not always, but sometimes. It was the only way I could pitch to him."

As long as his average hovered around .400, Aaron had to answer endless questions about what it would take to stay at that magical figure throughout the season. At one point, when asked about his goal for the season, Aaron answered that he hoped to get at least two more hits. "Then I'll only be 2,000 behind Musial," he deadpanned.

When asked years later about the best statistical season of his career, Aaron pointed to 1959, explaining that his 400 total bases represented a plateau that contemporaries Mantle and Mays never reached. "You can't excel in total bases unless you are an all-around hitter, and the best all-around hitter will produce the most total bases," he said.

The '59 season would once again bring postseason disappointment for Aaron and the Braves. Just as they were about to concede the pennant to San Francisco, the Giants imploded, losing seven of their final eight games. The Braves and Dodgers surpassed them, each winning on the season's final day to end up with 86 victories apiece. The ensuing best-of-three playoff still leaves a bad taste in the mouths of old-time Milwaukee fans. The Braves had leads in each of the first two contests only to lose both.

In Game One, Willey relinquished a 2–1 advantage when he gave up three singles in the third inning, then lost the game when Los Angeles catcher Johnny Roseboro led off the sixth with a home run. Reliever Larry Sherry (who would star in the World Series later that week) shut down the Braves over the final seven innings to preserve the Dodgers' 3–2 win. In Game Two, Burdette went into the ninth with a 5–2 lead, but gave up three hits and had to yield to McMahon. The National League saves leader did not add to his total, allowing a run-scoring single to make it 5–4. Haney called Spahn into the game and he gave up the tying run on a sacrifice fly, and then a hit to Maury Wills. Jay finally got the last out, but not without help from Aaron, who made an excellent running catch. Stan Williams came on for the Dodgers and pitched three hitless innings, although the Braves loaded the bases on walks in the 11th. The Dodgers won the game in the 12th when Mantilla fielded Carl Furillo's grounder with two out and two on and threw it into the dugout.

For the second time in four years, the Braves had let the pennant slip from their grasp. This time it cost Fred Haney his job. It also caused people in and out of Milwaukee to look a lot less favorably on the Braves' key players. Incredibly, the seemingly unassailable Aaron was a favorite target.

By 1959, Henry Aaron was producing astounding numbers so consistently that they had almost become commonplace. (He has since admitted that his success on the television show *Home Run Derby* convinced him that putting up big power numbers was the quickest way to riches in the big leagues.) Fans and the media alike expected Aaron to perform at such a high level that they raised a collective eyebrow when he did not. Somehow, his rare 0-for-4s did not have the pizzazz that Mays's and Mantle's did. Consequently, Aaron was often accused of being aloof and lazy.

Bill Furlong addressed Aaron's supposed lackadaisical attitude in *Baseball Stars of 1959*. "There are many who suspect that Henry's apparent indolence is his own quiet little joke on the world," wrote Furlong. An anonymous source in Milwaukee's minor-league system admitted that "we couldn't make up our minds whether he was the most naive player we ever had or whether he was dumb like a fox."

Aaron, at times, seemed to enjoy this reputation. "A long time he ago," he once said, "my daddy told me, 'Henry, never hurry unless you have to.' I've remembered that ever since and here I am playin' in the majors."

His "theories" on hitting served to reinforce his public persona. "I just grab a bat and go up lookin' for one thing—and that's the baseball," he told Furlong. "If it's near the plate, I'm gonna swing at it."

There were other times, however, when Aaron tired of being characterized as a lethargic nitwit. He confided as much to Roger Kahn. "Listen, if you hear a lot of silly things, ask me about 'em before you write," he pleaded with the writer in 1959 in a story for *Sport*. "I know what happened and what didn't. I mean a guy once wrote something about me and it wasn't much. There was a lot of, uh, dumb stuff. Like every time I said 'I,' he spelled it 'Ah.' I don't like those Uncle Tom stories. They're all wrong and they never happened."

Obviously, in five short years as a major leaguer, Aaron had grown wary of the media. At this point in his career, for instance, he only spoke to reporters whom he trusted would not "hurt" him in the press. Years later, Aaron still talked as if he were suspicious of the media. "Just because I don't jump and holler and run to and from the outfield doesn't mean that I don't go all out," he said to Vecsey. "Maybe I don't look like I'm hustling but that's just my way. It's the only way I know. I couldn't change if I wanted to. If I did, I'd probably foul myself up."

Managers and players close to Aaron had no problem with his playing style. On the contrary, they appreciated his effort and praised his attitude. "Aaron's loping style is deceptive," admitted Haney. "You'd almost get the impression he wasn't hustling at times. But he's about the last player you'd accuse of that. He just runs as fast as he has to and he always seems to get the fly ball or to a base in time when there's any chance of making it."

"The funny thing about Henry Aaron is you're not going to be impressed with him at first sight," offered Bill Bruton in "What It's Like to Be a Neglected Superstar," an article written for *Sport* by Jim O'Brien in 1968. "He just isn't very colorful."

Indeed, Aaron suffered his reputation partly because he made the game look so easy. He was neither flashy nor presumptuous, always willing to contribute in whatever way a manager asked. From 1954 to 1967, for example, though he had developed into an accomplished outfielder, Aaron played second base 43 times, third base 7 times, and first base once.

Playing in a city like Milwaukee, hardly a major market, did not help matters. "For a long time," said Eddie Mathews in 1982, "he didn't get any publicity because we were in areas that didn't get much publicity."

While reporters or baseball fans did not always show Aaron proper respect, opposing players saw the brilliance in the slugger's game. Sandy Koufax, for instance, referred to Aaron as the toughest batter he ever faced. Koufax and his teammate Don Drysdale, in fact, are credited with giving Aaron the nickname he likes most, "Bad Henry." "That's just how I felt about him," Koufax said in *Chasing the Dream*.

Regardless of how simple Aaron was portrayed in the media, the young star was gaining a clearer understanding of the world around him. An incident that occurred on his way to spring training in 1958 crystallized his feelings. Heading to Florida in a brand new Chevy purchased with prize money he won on *Home Run Derby*, Aaron was run off the road in the Deep South by a white driver. For the first time in his career, he sought out the press and told the story. "Something inside was changing," he recalled in *Chasing the Dream*.

Among those changes was the dominance minority players were asserting in the National League. More than a decade after Jackie Robinson had broken the color line, teams had grudgingly accepted the fact that developing talent from the overwhelming pool of blacks and Hispanics was essential to success on the field.

This was particularly the case in the National League, where the style of play favored players like Aaron, who combined speed and power. With the exception of the White Sox, American League teams tended to move from station to station. They preferred sluggers who launched high, majestic drives over gap hitters whose line-drive homers barely cleared the fence. The lily-white Yankees were the perfect example. Mickey Mantle filled seats by swinging from the heels, and like the Babe, his prodigious clouts were the stuff of legend. The Bronx Bombers constantly searched for similar hitters. They assumed they would not find them in the black and Hispanic communities because these players, who sometimes grew up using broom handles as bats and rolled-up socks as balls, learned different skills as youngsters. It is hardly a coincidence that Elston Howard and Hector Lopez—their first dark-skinned regulars—were slow-footed sluggers. Ultimately, this stereotype would help hasten the fall of the once mighty Yankees.

Also contributing to the imbalance of minority stars between the two leagues was that Bill Veeck, the owner of the Chicago White Sox, was the top recruiter of blacks and Hispanics in the AL. During the 1940s, he had schemed to break the color barrier several years before Branch Rickey. As president of the Browns and Indians in the postwar years, Veeck brought Negro League stars Larry Doby, Luke Easter, Satchel Paige, and Minnie Minoso to the majors. Veeck was perhaps the most colorful promoter the game has ever seen, and for this (and his open-mindedness on the color issue) he was disliked quite intensely by his fellow owners, who felt his wild stunts inflicted more harm than good on baseball. Thus, when he began stocking his farm system with black and Hispanic players, other American League owners instinctively shied away from the practice, suspecting that Veeck was again more interested in making headlines than in winning pennants.

AL clubs needed to look no farther than their rivals on the junior circuit to see that Veeck and the White Sox were on the right track. Mays and Aaron were no longer alone in their battle for best in the league. Ernie Banks of the Cubs claimed back-to-back MVP awards in 1958 and 1959, and Frank Robinson of the Reds was becoming a terrific all-around player. On the horizon was a group of exciting young stars, including Roberto Clemente, Bob Gibson, Juan Marichal, Bill White, Orlando Cepeda, Maury Wills, Vada Pinson, and Curt Flood.

"The early to mid sixties were probably the peak years of the black ballplayers," Aaron said in *I Had a Hammer*. "We were the Jackie Robinson generation. By 1963, black players were leading the National League in so many things you wonder what the quality of baseball was like before Jackie joined it—and what the quality of Negro League baseball was like before Jackie left it."

As minority players expanded their influence in the early '60s, they also realized the importance of unity. As in the Civil Rights Movement, presenting a unified front was the key to fighting the discrimination that still existed in baseball. Aaron learned this lesson after his good friend Bill Bruton was traded to Detroit after the 1960 season. Thoughtful and soft-spoken, Bruton had long been the mouthpiece for his black teammates on the Braves. With the center fielder gone, Aaron assumed the mantle. At the time, one of the most significant issues among minority players was the segregation at hotels in Florida during spring training. Since he had broken into the majors, Aaron had spent every spring at a boarding house run by a matronly black woman named Mrs. Gibson. Along with players from several other teams, including Bill White of the Cardinals, he hoped to curtail this practice.

White, as it turned out, had the most powerful arsenal in the fight. After he spoke to a St. Louis newspaper about the bigotry he encountered every spring in Florida, fans protested the unfair treatment. When mention of a beer boycott surfaced, Cardinals owner Augie Busch took action. "The result was that the Cardinals were the first team to rectify the situation of segregated hotels," said White. "Their solution was to segregate everybody, not just the black players. They leased a motel in St. Petersburg and just took the whole thing over."

Once the first domino fell, it was not long until others followed. After a meeting with Braves management, Aaron convinced the team to find alternative lodging. For the white players on the Braves who had grown accustomed to the frills of the luxurious Manatee River Hotel, the team's new digs in the Twilight Motel paled in comparison. For Aaron, however, the move was imperative, though he too made a sacrifice. Leaving Mrs. Gibson's meant passing up her "first-rate chicken and biscuits."

The integration of Milwaukee's spring training facilities had little impact on the team's performance on the field, which disappointed Aaron. He believed that team unity would help the Braves return to the top of the NL. But complacency proved to be Milwaukee's greatest enemy. After losing to the Dodgers in 1959, general manager John McHale failed to address the club's weak spots and decided he already had the horses to make a run at the pennant in 1960. The core players performed as expected—Aaron and Mathews were 1–2 in the NL RBI race and Spahn, Burdette, and Buhl accounted for 56 wins—but the Braves were getting long in the tooth and a little tattered around the edges. The new manager, Chuck Dressen, brought more enthusiasm to the clubhouse than Haney, but not enough to overtake the Pirates, who built a modest lead in the spring and held off Milwaukee all summer long.

The inevitable tumble began in 1961, when the Braves found themselves in fourth place at season's end. The Dodgers and Giants oozed with young talent, while the Reds slapped together an unimpressive squad and managed to win the pennant with two things the Braves lacked: timely hitting and deep pitching. Adcock, Mathews, and Aaron were all that was left from the great offensive teams of the 1950s and Spahn and Burdette had no one to follow them in the rotation or bullpen. Dressen was fired and replaced with Birdie Tebbetts in September, but the Braves only got worse.

Milwaukee finished fifth in 1962 and sixth in 1963 as the team continued to disintegrate. Whereas the Braves had once been able to restock through their farm system, now they were forced to pluck talent before it had ripened sufficiently. Called up too soon were pitchers Tony Cloninger and Wade Blasingame, infielders Denis Menke and Woody Woodward, and catcher Joe Torre, who was Milwaukee's everyday receiver at the ridiculous age of 20. By the end of 1963 only three players from the championship years—Spahn (who won 23 times at age 42), Mathews, and Aaron—remained key contributors.

Aaron, now entering his prime years, was truly a fearsome hitter. In 1962, he batted .323 with 45 home runs, 127 runs, and 128 RBIs. In 1963 he led the league in runs, homers, and slugging average. Yet with Milwaukee now situated closer to the expansion Mets and Colt .45s than to the National League front-runners, Aaron was hard pressed to gain the accolades he deserved. Despite his gaudy numbers and growing maturity as a hitter, he got no respect from baseball writers. Despite consistently excellent seasons from 1960 to 1963, he finished 11th, 8th, 6th, and 3rd in the MVP voting and failed to win a Gold Glove award after 1960, as if something had "gone wrong" with his fielding.

The problem was not with Aaron's performance, although it may have been partly Aaron's fault. Despite everything he had done for his team, his city, and his sport, he was still viewed with a skeptical eye.

Take the way he was portrayed in the annual Baseball Stars series. These paperback books, the publication of which more or less coincided with the entire span of Aaron's career, profiled the top players of the day in each league. Read by a wide audience—including millions of young and impressionable school-age fans—the Aaron features almost always seemed to place him in a questionable light. Al Silverman called him the "Relaxin' Slugger" in the 1960 issue. The moniker used the next year by Ray Robinson was the "Sleepy Slugger." Two years later, the same scribe tabbed Aaron as the "Casual Clouter." Granted, each feature acknowledged Aaron as one of baseball's preeminent talents, but they tended to lay on the superlatives with a backhanded stroke. For example, Aaron was not an intelligent hitter; rather, he was "dumb like an atomic physicist." Compliments were peppered with adjectives such as "catnapping," "dozing," "insouciant," "careless," and "comatose."

Though he initially courted such characterizations, by the 1960s Aaron was growing increasingly tired of them. And in his own quiet way, he had started to change his image. There was his new role on the Braves as spokesman for black players, the role he assumed after Bruton was dealt away. He also became more politically active. In 1960, for instance, Aaron worked on John Kennedy's presidential campaign. Four years later, he shook hands with Lyndon Johnson after the president signed the Civil Rights Act into law.

Then, in 1965, Aaron took his most significant off-field gamble. In a controversial interview with Jerome Holtzman, he stated emphatically that blacks had the ability to manage a major-league team. This piece of baseball heresy appeared in *Sport*, which asked its readers, "Are You Ready for a Negro Manager?" Aaron certainly was, saying "I could do the job." He went on to name contemporaries whom he felt were promising managerial candidates, including Willie Mays, Jackie Robinson, Bill White, Bill Bruton, Junior Gilliam, and Ernie Banks. "You don't have to cut this list off," he added. "It can go on and on."

Agreeing to the interview was a daring move for many reasons. First, Aaron risked alienating fans, especially with the Braves set to move their franchise to Atlanta. Major League Baseball had yet to establish a presence in the Deep South, where explosive racial issues continued to fester. Aaron's personal safety, not to mention less his reputation, was at stake.

Another potential problem was the reaction of team management. Would the Braves' front office look kindly on Aaron's comments? And if not, how long would they hold them against Aaron? For a player admittedly considering a career in baseball after his playing days ended, rebuffing management seemed an odd choice. He also took the chance of scaring off endorsement deals. Commercial sponsors wanted black athletes who ingratiated themselves to—not provoked—white America. But Aaron ignored the consequences.

He believed in the message he delivered. Besides, could his image really be damaged? Public recognition still eluded him. Consider the limited fanfare from baseball or the media that greeted Aaron and Mathews in 1965 when they passed Duke Snider and Gil Hodges in the record books for most home runs by teammates in the National League. Mathews clouted the tying homer, number 745, in the first game of an early-season doubleheader with the Phillies. Aaron made it 746 with a blast off Bo Belinsky in the second game. But, as Aaron lamented in *I Had a Hammer*, "Nobody seemed to care."

Bob Wolf of the Milwaukee Journal was one of the few members of the media who did. While checking on the most prestigious long-ball tandem in baseball history, Babe Ruth and Lou Gehrig, he found that they had actually slammed only 793 homers during their years together on the Yankee, 77 less than originally calculated. That meant that by the end of 1965 Aaron and Mathews would likely become the most powerful duo the big leagues had ever seen. Today an event would be built around this milestone. Back then it was treated as an unimportant footnote. Indeed, when Mathews hit his 28th home run of the year on August 20th to boost their total as teammates to 794 and surpass Ruth and Gehrig for the all-time mark, the story received scant attention in the press.

Actually, Aaron should have set the record two days earlier against the Cardinals, when he lunged after an outside pitch by Curt Simmons and drove it over the right field fence. But catcher Bob Uecker, a former teammate, argued successfully that Aaron had stepped out of the batter's box when he swung. Umpire Chris Pelekoudas called Aaron out, nullifying the home run. This incident, forgotten by all but Aaron and Uecker, came to light many years later, when Aaron finished the 1973 season one home run short of 714. "I believe that was a home run," Aaron once joked. "I blame the whole thing on that damn Uecker."

The lack of excitement generated by his home run record with Mathews showed that Aaron was still several years from winning widespread fan gratitude and media appreciation. Ironically, it would not come until after the Braves left Milwaukee, the town he loved for the way it had opened its heart to him. Still, Aaron's final two years in Milwaukee were encouraging ones. The team seemed to be righting itself, replacing old players with new ones and finding the puzzle pieces necessary to contend for the pennant.

In 1964, the Braves brought up the rear in a wild five-team race that was up for grabs until the final week of the season, finishing just five games off the pace. Lemaster and Cloninger had replaced Spahn and Burdette as the team's top starters, Torre matured into a clutch-hitting catcher, Maye batted .303 as a regular, and Menke clubbed 54 extra-base hits from the shortstop position. New talent was also on the rise, in the persons of hurlers Clay Carroll and Phil Niekro and left fielder Rico Carty, who tore up the league with a .330 average in his first full season. Another important contributor was sweet-swinging Felipe Alou, whom the Braves had stolen from the Giants in a multiplayer deal. Had Alou not injured his knee, and had Mathews not suffered through the worst year of his career, the Braves might well have finished atop the standings.

In 1965 the Braves ended up fifth again, but were not part of the mix as the season headed down the home stretch. Not that anyone in Milwaukee cared. The Braves had already announced their move to Atlanta, thus acrimony was high and attendance low. On the field, injuries stalled the progress of several up-and-coming players, but Lemaster matured into a top starter and Mathews regained his old form. It was hard to tell what the Braves had and what they still needed, but the nucleus of an excellent team seemed to be present.

On the final day of the '65 campaign, Aaron received a standing ovation as he stepped to the plate with one out and a runner on in the bottom of the ninth. It was the afternoon's lone positive note. When Aaron lined into a double play to end the season, it was the last swing ever taken by a Milwaukee Brave. Baseball would return to the city five years later, and Aaron would follow five years after that. But both would be changed by the time of their reunion.

CHAPTER THREE:

PLAYING CATCH-UP

THOUGH NEVER CONSIDERED A "SLUGGER" IN THE conventional sense, Henry Aaron was hot on the trail of baseball's top home run hitters heading into the 1966 campaign. His 398 round-trippers put him 6 behind Ernie Banks, 75 behind Mickey Mantle, 79 behind teammate Eddie Mathews, and 107 behind Willie Mays. Of this group, Mantle and Mathews were done as power hitters, and Banks was beginning to show his age. Only Mays, the MVP in 1965, seemed to have the staying power that would be required to mount an assault on Babe Ruth's all-time home run record of 714. Few outside baseball realized at the time how good a "dark horse" Aaron was.

Aaron had clouted nearly 400 homers despite playing half of his games in Milwaukee's County Stadium. The ballpark was not considered friendly to home run hitters, despite the fact that the Braves always seemed to have a power-laden lineup. Milwaukee's often frigid early spring temperatures and the ballpark's uninviting dimensions robbed Aaron of at least a couple of round-trippers each year. Still, he managed an average of 33 home runs a season, while maintaining a lifetime batting average well over .300. As statistician Bill James illustrated in his *Historical Baseball Abstract*, however, Aaron did a good part of this damage away from home. Indeed, from 1954 through 1965, 213 of his home runs came on the road. "At his peak," James maintains, "Aaron would have hit 50 home runs, and probably more than once, had he been playing in an average home run park."

With the Braves set to move to Atlanta in 1966—where the climate was warmer and the ballpark cozier (and also 1,000 feet above sea level)—it stood to reason that Aaron's home run totals might actually increase as he got older, rather than decrease. No one gave any serious thought to this interesting set of circumstances, least of all Aaron himself, who was busy pondering the ways in which his life would change as he led Major League Baseball's first foray into the Deep South. He knew that, despite the impressive gains of the Civil Rights movement during the 1960s, things and people had changed little in this part of the world. Aaron had changed, however. This time around he was not willing to keep quiet about issues that affected him personally. He could only imagine what lay ahead.

Aaron had grown more than just comfortable in Milwaukee. He and his family had adopted the city as their home. "To this day, whenever I'm in Milwaukee, which is often, I'm reminded that the people there still haven't gotten over the Braves leaving," Aaron said in *I Had a Hammer*. "If it helps, they should know the players haven't either."

When rumors began to surface in 1964 that the Braves might be headed south, Aaron was naturally concerned, as were thousands of fans across the Midwest, including politicians who were already at work to stop the team from moving. As Huston Horn wrote in *Sports Illustrated*, "The squeal of the wheels was highly reminiscent of the noise in Boston 12 years ago when the Braves pulled out for Milwaukee."

The plot to move the Braves to Atlanta had actually been hatched in the summer of 1963, soon after Ivan Allen was elected the city's mayor. One of Allen's primary objectives was to bring big-league baseball to Atlanta. It was a goal shared by the Georgia legislature, which in 1960 had created a stadium authority to oversee the construction of a new baseball/football complex. The state's movers and shakers felt professional sports teams were essential to Atlanta's plan to develop into one of the country's foremost urban centers.

"Once Scarlett O'Hara and David O. Selznick had passed through town, things never really got back to being the same in Atlanta," wrote Horn in *SI* in November of 1964. "Having thus nibbled on greatness, the city has been yearning ever since for one more bite. Atlanta takes quiet satisfaction in the fact that its jet airport is the busiest in the whole U.S. between 11 in the morning and—imagine—2 in the afternoon, that four million of its citizens went bowling last year, that 383 of Fortune's 500 top businesses have branch offices in the vicinity."

No longer a source of pride, however, were the Atlanta Crackers, the Class-AAA affiliate of the Braves. The team had suffered through a miserable season in 1964, finishing dead last in the International League, despite the presence of future National League stars Jim Merritt and Randy Hundley and IL batting champ Sandy Valdespino. With the Crackers crumbling, Mayor Allen began to search for a big-league replacement as soon as he took office.

His first suitor was Charles O. Finley, the owner of the Kansas City Athletics. In the spring of 1963, Allen and Arthur Montgomery, president of the Coca-Cola Bottling Company and chairman of Atlanta's stadium authority, hosted Finley on a tour of their fair city. Fully impressed with Atlanta's accommodations—not to mention the potential seven-state television package that included Coke and Gulf Oil as advertisers—the fast-talking Finley told Allen and Montgomery that "if they provided a stadium, he would provide a team." After a few phone calls, the two soon realized that Finley's word was worth less than a nosebleed seat at a Crackers game. The search continued.

Shortly after Finley's visit, Montgomery heard from his friend Delbert Coleman, a director of the Milwaukee Braves and part of an ownership group that had recently purchased the team. He discussed his concerns about Milwaukee with Montgomery, citing among other things the franchise's dwindling attendance figures and the soaring costs of operating out of County Stadium. He went on to mention that the new owners were actively investigating other homes for the team, especially if it would help them recoup their investment quickly. Montgomery, who later admitted he was amazed by Coleman's revelations, could barely contain himself. He immediately set up a meeting with representatives from the Braves. The two sides formed the foundation of an agreement during the weekend of the All-Star Game in Cleveland. Less than a year later, Montgomery and Coleman sealed the deal with a handshake in Chicago.

The next challenge for the folks in Atlanta was erecting a stadium by the start of the 1966 baseball campaign. As Allen admitted years later, this was no easy task. In *Chasing the Dream*, in fact, he conceded that the city built its new ballpark on "land we didn't own, with money we didn't have." Using the best features from stadiums around the country—as Horn noted in *SI*, these included "the sun's course across Candlestick Park, the color of the concession stands in Washington, D.C., the compass direction Mets' pitchers face when serving up home run balls to Ken Boyer (N39°E)"—architects designed a then-state-of-the-art complex that would seat 50,000 for baseball games and an additional 7,500 for football games (the NFL-expansion Falcons would also begin play in 1966). Work on the $18-million project began in March of 1964.

Allen, Montgomery, and the Braves' ownership initially took great pains to keep their scheme a secret. They knew that once word spread, the backlash from Milwaukee fans would be severe. A sudden surge of support for the team would not help them slip painlessly out of town. In fact, the hope among the principals was that Milwaukee would continue to play mediocre baseball and fans would continue to stay away from the ballpark.

During the early 1960s, the Braves were usually out of the pennant race by August. The fan response was predictable, as gate receipts fell steadily. In 1964, for instance, the Braves' paid attendance was only 910,911. While not the lowest figure in baseball, it was a far cry from the more than two million that flooded County Stadium each year in the late 1950s. Aaron, ever loyal to his hometown supporters, blamed himself and his teammates for the small crowds. "Sure, it used to be that every year almost we were one, two, three in the league, and the people always expected us to win and when we didn't win they were saddened," he said. "It was only natural that attendance started to fall off. We went from two pennants in a row to losing a playoff for the pennant to second place to fourth and then fifth."

News of the Braves' move could be kept quiet for only so long, however. In October of 1964, when the team's directors approved the relocation to Atlanta, the cat was officially out of the bag. Fearing summers without their beloved Braves—not to mention the annual loss of an estimated $3.5 million in local revenue—fans, lawyers, and businessmen reacted angrily, refusing to believe that the change was a *fait accompli*. In November, as National League representatives gathered in New York's Commodore Hotel to vote on the move, judges in Milwaukee issued one restraining order after another to block the meeting. Eugene Grobschmidt, chairman of the Milwaukee County Board of Supervisors, delivered a scathing speech laced with such phrases as "breach of contract" and "antitrust litigation"—ideas meant to put any right-thinking baseball executive on the defensive.

Of all the injunctions passed by Milwaukee courts, the most troublesome to the Braves' owners was the one that forbade them from even approaching the league for permission to move the team. When they asked the federal court to rule on the issue, the city of Milwaukee responded like a scorned lover. "The very minute they vote to approve the transfer, we'll slap an injunction on everybody," said George E. Rice, a county attorney. "We'll chase all these fellows down . . . and we'll slap them all in jail, players and all. You're not going to have big-league baseball in Atlanta next year—at least not with our Milwaukee Braves."

Meanwhile, Braves' GM John McHale was performing a song and dance that would earn him the eternal hatred of Milwaukee faithful. "The Braves will be in Milwaukee today, tomorrow, next year and as long as we are welcome," he said at one point. Several days later he added that the team was "positively not moving . . . whether you're talking about 1964, '65 or 1975."

By Opening Day in 1965, McHale's performance proved to be a charade. It was common knowledge that the Braves were playing their last season in Milwaukee. Fans composed songs denouncing McHale and created the Atlanta Braves "Boo-ster" Bag, which contained, among other things, a Confederate flag. The collection of sarcastic novelty items sold like 10-cent pitchers of beer.

Unfortunately for Aaron and his teammates, they were caught in the middle of the fracas, a dilemma detailed by William Leggett in *Sports Illustrated*. "During a 10-day period ending last Saturday evening in Milwaukee's County Stadium, the 27 men who play for the Braves went through an almost unbelievable odyssey," he wrote. "They went through it with flair, dignity and spirit which baseball the game can be proud even though baseball the business should hang its head in shame for forcing them to go through it all."

The "odyssey" Leggett described began on Thursday, April 8, 1965, when the Braves traveled to Jacksonville, Florida, for an exhibition against the Yankees. The game was noteworthy for two reasons. Not only was the contest the first of 19 games that future

Braves fans up in Georgia would be able to see on TV, it also marked the debut of Mel Allen as the voice of the Atlanta Braves. For the previous 25 years, Allen had been in the booth for virtually every pitch of every Yankee game. He delighted listeners with his calls of "Ballantine Blasts" and "White Owl Wallops" and his trademarks, "Going, going, gone!" and "How 'bout that!" But the Bronx Bombers canned him after the 1964 season. Atlanta, hoping to attract more fans, quickly signed the man whose peers called him "The Voice." Always the professional, Allen sounded genuinely happy to be part of his new team for its maiden telecast. "Evenin' everybody, and welcome to this historic telecast back to Atlanta of your 1965 Braves," he drawled. Allen then suggested "that all you fine people give them a real southern welcome."

According to an informal survey conducted by *Sports Illustrated*, it seemed that not too many heard Allen's advice. Of 10 bars in downtown Atlanta, the magazine noted, seven had tuned in to *Perry Mason*. If those patrons were seeking drama and ultimate victory, they were watching the right channel. The Braves went down without much of a struggle, 6–1.

All was forgotten the next day as 40,000 lined the streets of Atlanta for a parade to welcome the Braves. Swaying to the soothing beat of "Georgia on My Mind" played by a full marching band, fans cheered as Aaron and his fellow Braves rumbled through the streets of the city in open convertibles. That evening the Braves christened Atlanta Stadium with an exhibition game against the Detroit Tigers. Atlanta won by a score of 6–3, then took the next two over the weekend for a tidy sweep. Attendance was excellent for all three games—an achievement that pleased the team's owners, especially since they were competing against the Masters golf tournament and NASCAR's Atlanta 500 on the same weekend.

The following Monday the (still Milwaukee) Braves took the field in Cincinnati for the regular-season opener. Though wearied by their hectic schedule, the Braves beat the Reds, 4–2. After losing the next day, Aaron and his teammates boarded a plane and flew home to face the music. When they landed, a mock debate ensued about who should exit first. Someone suggested Aaron, joking that the new suitcase he purchased in Cincinnati might protect him from the gunfire of unhappy fans. But as Leggett revealed in *SI*, "Aaron had nothing to worry about. In the old days the Braves used to draw 5,000 people when they came back from lunch. Now there was no one to meet them."

Aaron hoped there was a simple solution to the fans' distress. "When I heard we were moving, I was just another fan—I grew kind of sad," he said at the time. "But I think if we win this year the people will come to see us."

Aaron must have been encouraged to see a crowd of 33,874 show up for the home opener. But later it was learned that this was largely the doing of Team, Inc., a group of local citizens formed to keep Milwaukee's image as a big-league city intact. Not only did Team, Inc., buy out the entire ballpark, it brought back most of the starting nine for the first game ever played by the Braves at County Stadium.

"Johnny Logan trotted out to shortstop, and then the only Brave from 1953 still with the club, Eddie Mathews, sprinted to third," wrote Leggett. "The public-address announcer got as far as the first "r" in Warren Spahn when the people jumped to their feet, applauding." Spahn, who had been sold to the Mets in November of 1964, acknowledged the appreciative crowd, covering the tears welling up in his eyes. Aaron also received a warm reception from fans who recognized him both for his fine performance in Milwaukee and his loyalty to the city.

The Braves delighted their hometown fans by beating the Chicago Cubs, though not many outside the stadium knew it. While TV stations in Atlanta had secured rights to 19 games, not a single contest in 1965 was broadcast in Milwaukee.

After the home opener, it was as if the team were playing on a desert island. Only 3,362 showed up to watch the second game of the series on a cold, windy Saturday afternoon. When manager Bobby Bragan strolled to the mound in the fifth, he was booed roundly. "You have to expect it under the circumstances," said the philosophical skipper.

The response must have disappointed Aaron. He really thought the fans would support a good team, and the Braves featured a quality lineup. Milwaukee stayed within striking distance of the leaders for most of the season, with solid pitching and timely hitting. No fewer than seven Braves reached double figures in home runs, including Aaron and Mathews, who swatted 32 apiece. But the fans never came in significant numbers. Those who did show sometimes seemed like mourners at a wake.

The Braves faded from the race and ended their final year in Milwaukee 86–76. An average of slightly less than 7,000 fans came to watch their games, and their final appearance at County Stadium drew a few thousand more. It was hardly a fitting send-off for a team that had electrified the city for so many years. But the fans were bitter. Baseball in Milwaukee was officially dead.

After a winter that was not without trepidation, Aaron reported to spring training and renewed acquaintances with his teammates. He saw essentially the same cast of characters that had populated the clubhouse the previous fall, with the only obvious scenery change being the script *A* replacing the block letter *M* on the team's hats. The rest of the home uniform remained unchanged; a script *Atlanta* now graced the road jersey.

As the team took shape in March and early April, it appeared that Atlanta might be getting a better team than it had bargained for. Middle infielders Woody Woodward and Denis Menke had matured into confident young veterans, while outfielder Rico Carty had his act together again after a disastrous sophomore season.

The middle of the lineup looked set with Aaron, Mathews, Mack Jones, Felipe Alou, and Joe Torre. The pitching staff was led by Tony Cloninger, now one of the league's best young hurlers, and veteran Ken Johnson, who had won 13 games after being picked up from the Astros during the 1965 campaign in a trade for Lee Maye. Talented young arms filled out the rest of the rotation, with Denny Lemaster, Wade Blasingame, Dick Kelley, Pat Jarvis, and Hank Fischer all vying for starting jobs. The bullpen held promise, too. Young gun Clay Carroll, knuckleballer Phil Niekro, and old-timer Chi Chi Olivo gave the Braves three interesting righties to complement southpaw Billy O'Dell, who was coming off an 18-save season. Still percolating in the minors were prospects Bill Robinson, Felix Millan, Mike Lum, Cecil Upshaw, and six-foot-seven-inch Ron Reed, who had finally given up on his NBA career and devoted himself full-time to baseball. When the team broke camp it seemed as if the pieces were there for a competitive season.

Not long after the season started several things became clear, and not all of them were good. Mathews could no longer handle a big-league fastball. Cloninger had lost the magic he had found the year before. And the Braves' bench would be no help at all. If the starting eight did not get the job done, the job would not get done. The early-season positives included the blossoming of Carroll into a lights-out reliever, the continued development of Torre as a middle-of-the-lineup hitter, and the complete recovery of Menke from knee problems in 1965.

What was especially clear was that Atlanta Stadium (aka Fulton County Stadium) would be a very different ballpark than what the Braves had grown accustomed to in Milwaukee. When you hit a ball in Atlanta, it carried. Aaron, ever conscious of his hitting environment, immediately recrafted his swing to suit his new environs. Anything from the middle of the plate in he now tried to pull to left field, where the thin air and pleasant climate transformed warning-track flies into home runs. It took a while to get the timing down, but with a little extra snap of those marvelous wrists, balls began disappearing into the Georgia night at a league-leading pace. The "Launching Pad" was born. Aaron's countdown to 714 had unofficially begun.

The new ballpark was a revelation of sorts for Aaron, who had devoted much thought over the winter to his change of address. Blacks were still treated as second-class citizens in the South, and Aaron was determined to make a difference. He knew that the first (and perhaps greatest) contribution he could make to the cause was to win over the white fans. The new homer-friendly stadium provided him with a means to do this. He would lead the league in home runs his first two years in Atlanta, and in the process show the white world that combining the qualities of power, consistency, and courage had nothing to do with the color of a man's skin.

This he did before a large and enthusiastic audience. On Opening Night, 50,000 people jammed into Atlanta Stadium. The scoreboard read in big letters: April 12, 1861: First Shots Fired on Fort Sumter . . . April 12, 1966: The South Rises Again. For one of the few times in his career, Aaron felt pressure to deliver.

"I don't know if I had ever wanted to hit a home run as badly as I did that night," he admitted in *I Had a Hammer*. "As much as I'd loved Milwaukee, and as warm as the fans of Milwaukee had been to me, I wanted things to be a little different in the new city. This time, I was a charter member of the local team, and I saw the opportunity to secure an important place in the community. I also knew that, as a black player, I would be on trial in Atlanta, and I needed a decisive way to win over the white people before they thought of a reason to hate me. And I believed that the way was with home runs."

Aaron came up empty in his first game in his new home, however, and so did the Braves. Despite a heroic effort by Cloninger, who labored through 13 innings, Atlanta fell to the Pirates 3–2 on Willie Stargell's two-run homer. Torre had the honor of belting the first official home run in Atlanta Stadium, and then slammed a solo shot in the Braves' final at bat. For his part, Aaron became the answer to at least one trivia question: he stole the first base in the new stadium.

By the All-Star break, Aaron had 26 home runs, which put him on pace to approach Hack Wilson's NL mark of 56 round-trippers. "The reason I'm hitting the long ball this season is that I'm feeling stronger at the plate," he told Charles Dexter in *Baseball Digest*. "Last year I had bone chips in my ankle and took only three days of spring training before I went to Milwaukee for an operation. In the latter part of the season I had a second operation for the removal of hemorrhoids. This year I feel great."

Aaron also acknowledged that he had adjusted his batting style to fit his new surroundings. Indeed, he took advantage of the favorable conditions in '66 by leading the league in home runs with 44 and in RBIs with 127. But the increase in his power numbers did not come without a price. For only the second time since his rookie year, Aaron's average fell below .300. "I'm not as good a hitter as I was in my early years when I hit to all fields," he added in his interview with Dexter. "I've become a pull hitter. . . . I used to hit as many home runs to right as to left, although I have more power now."

Aaron reiterated this point in *Aaron, r.f.* "I started the season not hitting well at all," he confided to Furman Bisher. "I don't have to look at the averages to tell when I'm hitting the ball the way I like to. I look at my right shoe. It's worn from dragging when I move into the ball the way I should."

If anything was worn out during the Braves' first season in Atlanta, it was the nerves of some of the team's minority players. The city's political machine had done a wonderful job of selling the image of the "New South" as a place where people of all races and religions were welcome. The unsettling reality was that the New South had a way to go. The crowds at Atlanta Stadium, for example, while enthusiastic and supportive, were predominantly white. "As much as I wanted the city on my side, I just couldn't bring myself to be buddy-buddy with a crowd of white Southerners—especially after what I'd seen in our first few months in Atlanta," said Aaron.

His wife, Barbara, often experienced the type of abuse Aaron referred to. Away from her husband, she was just another black woman in the South, which exposed her to constant racial slurs and taunts. Even in a box seat at a Braves game, she was not immune. On one occasion a white man seated behind her became so loud and obnoxious with his insults that she had to leave and collect herself under the stands. She returned to her seat with a hamburger practically swimming in ketchup and mustard. She calmly waited for the bigoted fan to start again. As soon as he did, she whirled around and threw the burger at him.

Aaron, feeling increasingly frustrated by such incidents, finally had enough. In an interview with Roscoe Harrison of *Jet* magazine, he tore into Major League Baseball, blasting the league for its history of racism. At first, he felt vindicated, as his comments seemed to bring about immediate change. Soon after the interview was published, for example, Monte Irvin was appointed to a newly created position in the commissioner's office.

But progress remained slow, and the discrimination faced by Aaron and his teammates had a profound effect on the Braves on the field. There were four black players in the everyday lineup who also happened to be respected team leaders, and they were not enjoying the summer at all. As a result, Atlanta never really got it going during the first 100 games—winning a few, losing a few, and hovering around the .500 mark. The Braves' front office, perplexed by the malaise, ultimately blamed the manager, Bobby Bragan. He was fired in early August and replaced by coach Billy Hitchcock, who had joined the organization as a scout the year before. Hitchcock, a longtime coach with the Tigers and manager of the Baltimore Orioles for two seasons, coaxed 33 wins from the Braves in the season's final 51 games, which was enough to slip past the retooling Cardinals into fifth place and avoid a second-division finish.

Although the team's play picked up over the final two months, the firing of Bragan bothered Aaron, partly because he and the manager had long enjoyed a friendly relationship. Almost a decade earlier, in fact, when Bragan was managing the sad-sack Pirates, he called Aaron a "million-dollar" player, saying the slugger was "not only a good hitter, he's a great hitter."

When Bragan took over the Braves in 1963, he quickly ingratiated himself to Aaron by treating him with respect and honesty. "He made me feel I was important," Aaron recalled. "I don't mean that he put me on a pedestal and posed me and painted 'Our Hero' on a sign and hung it around my neck. He made me feel my value to the ball club, that's what I mean. In fact, I give Bragan credit for making me a complete ballplayer."

Among other things, the Milwaukee skipper encouraged Aaron to be more daring on the base paths and gave him the green light to steal a base whenever the opportunity presented itself. In his first year under Bragan, in fact, Aaron nabbed a career-high 31 bases. He also batted .319 and topped the league in homers and RBIs.

Years later, in *Home Run: My Life in Pictures*, Bragan revealed that his relationship with Aaron benefited greatly from his days with the Dodgers as a teammate of Jackie Robinson's. Ironically, the native of Birmingham, Alabama initially told Branch Rickey that he would rather be traded than step on the field with an African American. He even signed a petition saying as much. But Rickey called the bluff of his white players, and Bragan learned a valuable lesson. "Had I not had that experience with Jackie, I might not have been able to identify with Aaron," he said. "I became friends with him."

For his part, Aaron felt fortunate to survive the tumultuous 1966 campaign. There were even times when he was able to forget the troubles that surrounded him. The high point of the year came on April 20 in Philadelphia, when Aaron launched the 400th home run of his career. A rocket shot off pitcher Bo Belinsky, the homer easily cleared Connie Mack Stadium's short left field porch, continued to soar, and after landing finally rolled to a stop in a parking lot across the street. "[The ball] was found by some kid under an automobile on the far side of the lot," he remembered. "Gene Oliver stepped it off himself, and came back saying the ball had traveled 725 feet."

Such highlights were few and far between. At about the same time the Braves turned to Hitchcock, the team also hired Paul Richards as general manager. Richards's first act as GM was to rankle everyone in the clubhouse, including Aaron, by announcing that no one was too valuable to be traded. They knew he meant it. Considered a baseball genius during his managing days, Richards was not averse to swapping big-name players for spare parts if he thought it would help his team. He made good on his threat when he dealt Mathews to the Houston Astros on New Year's Eve. "He was devastated, and so was I," said Aaron of his longtime teammate in his autobiography. "This was a guy who had played more games at third base than anybody in the history of baseball and who shared a record for most home runs with one team. He was the only Brave to play in Boston, Milwaukee, and Atlanta. As far as I'm concerned, he was Mr. Brave. I'm not a man who forgives easily, and I haven't forgiven Paul Richards for trading Eddie Mathews the way he did."

To loyal Braves fans, the Mathews trade bordered on heresy. In return, Atlanta agreed to take Dave Nicholson—at the time, the easiest batter in major-league history to strike out—and pitcher Bob Bruce, whose best years were three seasons behind him. The two Astros contributed nothing to the Braves. Even worse, Richards made speedster Sandy Alomar a throw-in on the deal. Alomar, who ended up on the Angels, would be an All-Star by 1970. The happy part of the story is that Mathews ultimately finished 1967 in the thick of a pennant race with the Tigers, and got a second World Series ring when Detroit won it all in 1968.

Looking back on his first season in Atlanta, Aaron had little to smile about. He did, however, come to appreciate the positive effect the Braves had on the region. As he admitted in *Chasing the Dream*, he never imagined "how much major league baseball meant to people of the South." President Jimmy Carter agreed. "It was sports—integrated sports teams—that brought about the changes that saved the South," said the former Georgia governor also in *Chasing the Dream*, adding that he would never have been considered seriously as a presidential candidate had the Braves not moved to Atlanta.

The next two years brought more disappointment and disillusion for Aaron. The Braves had never gone through a rebuilding period during Aaron's career, but that would probably be the best way to characterize the team's approach to the 1967 and 1968 seasons. Also, most of the people Aaron had grown up with in the game were either retired or headed that way.

Then there were new pressures in the outside world. The Civil Rights Movement had found success in part through its many high-profile supporters, both black and white. Aaron felt pressure to join the cause, but agonized about when and how—and what effect it might have on the bridges he was attempting to build in Atlanta. Vietnam was also bursting into the national consciousness. From an obscure anti-Communist military adventure on the other side of the world, it had become a real war almost overnight, and tens of thousands of young men—a great many of them poor and black—were being shipped overseas.

After the 1966 season, Aaron signed on to do a morale-building tour of Southeast Asia with several other players, including Stan

Musial, Harmon Killebrew, and Brooks Robinson. The experience opened Aaron's eyes to the brutality of war. One of his most vivid memories was watching an American helicopter obliterate two suspected Vietcong sampans.

"But not all of my memories of that trip are violent," he recalled years later. "It was rewarding to do something for the servicemen, and I was also able to develop a greater friendship with my roommate, Stan Musial."

Unquestionably, Aaron came back a changed man. Upon his return, he signed a new contract with the Braves calling for an annual salary of $100,000—in 1967 the single, indisputable measure of sports superstardom. Now more squarely in the spotlight than ever before, Aaron began to enjoy the trappings of celebrity. "I wasn't content anymore to let other guys have all the fortune and fame," he admitted.

Aaron's fresh take on life affected him in many ways. Unfortunately, this included his relationship with his wife, Barbara. He began spending more time with teammates, including Joe Torre and Bob Uecker, who rejoined the Braves during the 1967 season. Known as the "Playboys of Peachtree," the two catchers partook with considerable enthusiasm of the city's nightlife. They drank hard and stayed out late. It was a lifestyle Aaron was unaccustomed to, but as he said, he was "in search of new perspectives."

One perspective that never sat right with Aaron was seeing Mathews in an Astro uniform. The first time the Braves faced their old teammate in 1967, Mathews beat them with a triple late in the game. The loss reinforced Aaron's feelings about the trade, and amplified his misgivings about the direction the team was headed in. Richards and Hitchcock seemed satisfied to let the pitching staff (which was essentially unchanged from 1966) work through its assorted problems. Richards had plugged the hole left by Mathews with Clete Boyer, but it had cost him Bill Robinson, the team's top hitting prospect. Luckily, Boyer responded with a solid year at the plate and in the field. However, the offense was ill-equipped to deal with baseball's shifting currents and management was paralyzed to do anything about it.

With the exception of Aaron, Atlanta's hitters were one-dimensional. They swung for the fences and were incapable of manufacturing runs. Since the mound was raised and the strike zone adjusted in the mid-1960s, pitchers had gained a huge advantage over hitters—particularly the kind of hitters the Braves put on the field. Situational hitting and team speed had become very critical to scoring runs, and Atlanta was sorely lacking in these areas. Aaron was particularly frustrated with the play of Rico Carty who had the tools to be a productive team player but chose to follow his own path. Aaron characterized the Dominican native as extremely selfish in *I Had a Hammer*. Indeed, the two never saw eye to eye, and even once came to blows on a flight to Los Angeles.

By September, the Braves were hopelessly mired in the second division. Woodward and Menke, so promising the year before, had taken steps backward instead of forward. Clay Carroll, seemingly on the verge of a breakthrough, was hammered by enemy batters all year long. The lone high points for the Braves in 1967 were the emergence of Pat Jarvis as a quality starter, and the astonishing transformation of Phil Niekro into an effective starter. Long considered a middle-relief novelty act, the knuckleball specialist gained full command of his dancing delivery and led the National League with a microscopic 1.87 ERA.

Still, for the first time in his career, Aaron was ashamed to be a member of the Braves. "I had never been on a ball club, one that played 150 games or more, that finished under .500," he said to Joe Heiling of *Baseball Digest* early in 1968. "It wasn't just embarrassing to me, but the management, too. We had guys who just weren't trying. I'm not mentioning names, but they know who I'm talking about."

Aaron could feel proud, however, about several of his accomplishments during the 1967 campaign. He collected the 2,500th hit of his career, making him one of only 41 major leaguers to do so. In addition, he surpassed several other milestones, including 1,600 singles, 1,500 runs, 4,500 total bases, and 1,500 RBIs. Aaron led the league in home runs again with 39 and in runs scored with 113. He also raised his average to .307 and knocked in two fewer runs than league leader Orlando Cepeda who finished with 111. Only one other player in baseball—AL Triple Crown winner Carl Yastrzemski—topped 100 runs, 100 RBIs, and 30 homers with a .300 average.

Aside from the losing, the weirdest thing about 1967 for Aaron was a bizarre feud that started with announcer Milo Hamilton, for which Aaron later accepted responsibility. It all began when Hamilton introduced Roberto Clemente at a luncheon in downtown Atlanta as "the man who beat out Hank Aaron as the National League's All-Star right fielder." Aaron bristled at the remark. He had actually received the most votes among NL outfielders. But when manager Walter Alston asked Aaron to play left, he agreed without complaint. Now he felt that Hamilton, his hometown announcer, was belittling him on his own turf.

The next day against Pittsburgh, still seething from Hamilton's comments, Aaron went 4 for 4 including two two-run homers. He also threw out Clemente when he tried to take an extra base on a single to right. In the locker room after the game, Aaron responded to questions about his sterling performance with a wry smile, "When you're second best, you have to try harder."

The quarrel between Aaron and Hamilton would not die, mainly because Aaron would not let it. "The whole thing went on for a couple of years, and at one point *Newsweek* even wrote about it," said Aaron in *I Had a Hammer*. "Eventually, it blew over, because Milo and I had to do a lot of appearances together during the Ruth chase. I regret the whole episode, and I realize now that I should have let it ride from the beginning."

The 1967 season also marked the first time Aaron faced Tom Seaver. Ironically, the two had almost become teammates the year before. Atlanta, in dire need of pitching since the heydays of Spahn and Burdette, had tempted the right-hander off the USC campus with a $40,000 offer. This skirted the rules of the just-instituted amateur draft, exposing a loophole Commissioner Billy Eckert immediately moved to close. Eckert, whose experience as an Air Force general left him ill-prepared to deal with the connivances of major-league owners, decided the fairest way to handle the Seaver situation was to allow any team willing to match Atlanta's offer to participate in an informal lottery. Slips with the names of the Braves, Indians, Phillies, and Mets were placed in a hat, and New York got Seaver. Several years later, in 1969, Eckert, whose contract ran through 1972, was given his walking papers by the owners.

Although the casual fan could not have known it in 1967, the Mets and Braves were only two seasons away from a series that would decide the pennant. When Seaver and Aaron first dueled, they were toiling for sub-.500 clubs in meaningless games. Of course, for these two, no game was meaningless. No at bat was meaningless. No pitch was meaningless.

In his book, *How I Would Pitch to Babe Ruth*, Seaver admitted that he had idolized Aaron as a boy and recalled their first encounter in the big leagues. "I have faced Henry Aaron many times over the course of seven seasons in the majors, and I'm still not sure if I've gotten over my childhood hero-worship of him," he wrote. "I used to play that I was Henry Aaron in my backyard when I was 12 years old, imitating his swing and his mannerisms.

"I got him to hit into a double play with an inside fastball," Seaver said of their first encounter. "The next time he came up, I threw him another inside fastball. He hit it for a home run and I learned that hitters can remember pitchers, too."

The sequence against Seaver illustrated Aaron's brilliance as a hitter. "Pitchers don't set Henry up," teammate Gene Oliver once said. "He sets *them* up. I honestly believe he intentionally looks bad on a certain pitch just so he'll get it again."

Los Angeles closer Ron Perranoski, who was all too familiar with Aaron's cat-and-mouse games, agreed with Oliver's assessment. At one point in Perranoski's career, in fact, Aaron had gone 13 for 16 against him. "He not only knows what the pitch will be, but where it will be," he said to Jack Mann of *Sports Illustrated* in 1966. "He hit one home run off me, and he went after that pitch as if he'd called for it."

Indeed, a good deal of Aaron's success later in his career can be linked to reaching this new plateau as a hitter. In baseball's long history, only a handful of stars have become so proficient in their approach that they could actually "set up" pitchers. As an older hitter's skills begin to fade, he can significantly prolong his effectiveness by focusing on the one thing he can still do well and then using his head to "guide" situations to that one remaining strength. One such player was Pete Rose, who piled up five 200-hit seasons after the age of 30 and eventually broke Ty Cobb's all-time record for hits. Rose prided himself on his ability to get a pitcher to throw the precise ball he was waiting for, thinking that it was the ideal pitch with which to get Rose out.

In Aaron's case, he knew he would always have quick, strong wrists—perfect for powering inside pitches down the left field line. His job was to coax enemy hurlers into throwing the ball he wanted, when he wanted it. The pitchers knew this was Aaron's plan, so he had to "convince" them (often through an elaborate yet subtle series of body signals) that he was preparing himself for something very different. Only then would they dare put a fastball in his wheelhouse.

"He changed himself into a home run hitter, because of the changed circumstances," Leonard Koppet of the *New York Times* once observed. "He was in a different ballpark, being pitched to differently, and he reacted by becoming a more dangerous hitter."

Coming off the frustration of the 1967 season, Aaron expected a big year for the Braves in 1968. His optimism was well founded. For one thing, the team had cut bait on Menke and Woodward and injected some speed into its lineup. Woodward was benched and later packaged with Carroll and Cloninger for Cincinnati starter Milt Pappas. Menke was sent along with Lemaster to the Astros for shortstop Sonny Jackson. One of the fastest men in baseball, Jackson, like Menke, had slogged through his worst season in 1967. The Braves' new second baseman was Felix Millan, a solid defender who had matured into a capable top-of-the-lineup hitter at the age of 24. Finally, Atlanta had a couple of table setters. "If I have any kind of year," Aaron told a reporter before the season, "I ought to drive in 100 runs."

Another new addition was first baseman Deron Johnson, acquired from the Reds in exchange for Mack Jones. A former Yankee farmhand, Johnson had blossomed after coming to the NL in 1964. The right-handed slugger had a lethal swing, but his numbers had dropped sharply since leading the league with 130 RBIs in 1965. The emergence of Lee May in Cincinnati had rendered him expendable, and Jones—who could supply left-handed power off the bench—was a good fit for the Reds.

The pitching staff looked okay. Niekro, Jarvis, Pappas, and Ron Reed figured to hold their own in the starting rotation, with help from the likes of Ken Johnson and Dick Kelley. The bullpen was solid with Cecil Upshaw, Jim Britton, and Frenchie Raymond, who was reacquired from Houston in 1967 for sore-armed Wade Blasingame.

The Braves' only obvious weak spot was in the outfield, where a vacancy was created when Carty was diagnosed with tuberculosis. Among the candidates for this position were young Mike Lum, Sandy Valdespino, veteran Tito Francona, and Tommie Aaron, who had been toiling for two years with the Braves' new Class-AAA team in Richmond, Virginia. Also in camp that spring were a couple of impressive prospects named Ralph Garr and Dusty Baker, but they did not figure to contribute for a few more years.

Right from the end of spring training, however, things began going wrong. Perhaps because of all the promise this season held, it went down as Aaron's most disappointing. The most bitter pill he had to swallow came in early April when Martin Luther King, whom Aaron greatly admired, was gunned down in Memphis. When he heard of King's death, he reacted with anger, fear, and grief. Now living separately from Barbara, Aaron called her in the middle of the night to clear his head and make sense of the tragedy. King's funeral was held the day before the season opened. The Braves considered postponing the game, but King's father told Atlanta owner Bill Bartholomay that the gesture was unnecessary. For Aaron, focusing on baseball proved a difficult task. He played much of the year as though he were preoccupied. "It was all I could do to try to find a silver lining in this time of sorrow," he said in *Chasing the Dream*.

At least Aaron was healthy—something that could not be said for his fellow Braves. Every week, it seemed, a key player was felled by injury. Johnson and Boyer each went down with a broken hand and combined for a mere 12 home runs and 50 RBIs in the all-important corner spots. Ironman Joe Torre missed 30 games because of assorted aches and pains and was clearly coming to the end of his catching days. On top of Carty's absence, these injuries stretched Atlanta's hitting to the breaking point.

New manager Luman Harris, who had been promoted after leading Richmond to the International League pennant in 1967, simply ran out of ideas. At one point, both Baker and Garr were called up to stop the bleeding. The only thing that allowed Harris to maintain his sanity was his young pitching staff, which actually did quite well with the few runs the offense provided. Those runs came courtesy of Aaron and Felipe Alou, the only consistent bats in the Braves' order. Alou led the league in hits for the second time in three seasons, while Aaron put up 29 home runs and 86 RBIs.

The Braves escaped the second division with an 81–81 record, which landed them in fifth place and gave fans reason to hope for further improvement in 1969. For one thing, the National League was adding two expansion clubs—the Montreal Expos and San Diego Padres—and dividing itself into two six-team divisions. This helped the Braves, who were placed in the NL West, in a couple of ways. First, the juggernaut Cardinals and the fast-rising Cubs and Mets were all in the NL East. Besides the Padres, Atlanta's NL West rivals would be the aging Giants, rebuilding Dodgers, pitching-poor Reds, and hapless Astros. Also, the expansion draft had removed key players from many rosters, but the Braves had lost no one of any real significance. Farmhand Clarence Gaston was the only noteworthy departure, and his star had fallen since stringing together three .300 seasons in the minors.

Aaron's star, meanwhile, seemed almost in a holding pattern. His numbers for the '68 season, though far short of his preseason expectations, were respectable, especially in what has come to be called "The Year of the Pitcher." Still, it was his least productive year at the plate since his first season in 1954. So confounded was Aaron that at one point he tried amphetamines to boost his performance. He quickly realized, however, "it was a stupid thing to do."

His personal highlight came when he blasted the 500th home run of his career, a shot off Mike McCormick of the Giants, the winner of the 1967 Cy Young Award. The Braves honored their record-setting outfielder several nights later in a ceremony at Atlanta

Henry Aaron poses before a 1957 game in Milwaukee. He led the league in homers and RBIs that season, and won his only MVP award. (AP Worldwide Photos, Inc.)

Aaron's 1967 baseball card—the first to actually depict him in an Atlanta uniform. The Braves had moved the previous season, when this photo was taken. (© 1967 Topps Company, Inc.)

Aaron seems pensive on his 1970 Topps card. Many believed his remarkable hitting in the previous year's playoffs was a last hurrah. Instead, it was merely a preview of the amazing things to come. (© 1970 Topps Company, Inc.)

This 1975 card commemorates Aaron's home run record. Though pictured in an Atlanta uniform, he was back playing in Milwaukee when this card was issued. (© 1975 Topps Company, Inc.)

The heart of the Braves' power-packed lineup is featured on this 1958 baseball card. Del Crandall, Ed Mathews, Hank Aaron and Joe Adcock would combine for 98 home runs that year, leading Milwaukee to its one and only championship. (© 1958 Topps Company, Inc.)

DAILY NEWS

NEW YORK'S PICTURE NEWSPAPER ®

Vol. 55, No. 215 New York, N.Y. 10017, Tuesday, April 9, 1974* WEATHER: Rain, windy and cold

715! HENRY DOES IT

Breaks Ruth's Home Run Record

By Dick Young

Atlanta, April 8—Henry Aaron tonight hit the 715th home run of his career, one more than Babe Ruth or anybody else has hit in the majors. He did it in the fourth inning, off Dodger lefty Al Downing. And that's how you will have to say it to avoid arguments; not that Hank Aaron has become the greatest home run hitter that ever lived, because somebody will tell you that Babe Ruth went to bat 8,399 times to Aaron's 11,295.

A capacity crowd of over 50,000 sat through intermittent rains and cheered thunderously at Hank's every move. It also booed thunderously each time the pitcher threw a ball to him — or the umpire called a strike against him.

For once, while circling the bases, Hank's poker face seemed to burst into a bright grin. As he reached home, his teammates, photogs and his parents swarmed onto the field.

Henry's mother, Estella, hugged her

(Continued on page 70)

With every muscle in his lithe body straining, Hank Aaron follows flight of career homer No. 715 in the fourth inning at Atlanta last night. The ball, off a pitch served by Dodger Al Downing, sailed over the left-centerfield fence into baseball immortality. *—Other pics centerfold & back page*

The *New York Daily News* trumpets Aaron's 715th home run.

One of Aaron's rarer cards, which was given away at American Motors dealerships to publicize the television program *Home Run Derby*. (© 1959 American Motors)

The only baseball card depicting Aaron during his Negro League days was issued many years after the fact, in 1976.
(© 1976 R.G. Laughlin)

Among the many corporations to jump on the Aaron bandwagon during his pursuit of the all-time home run record was Magnavox. This membership card was part of an elaborate package given to customers who purchased the company's color televisions. (© 1974 Magnavox)

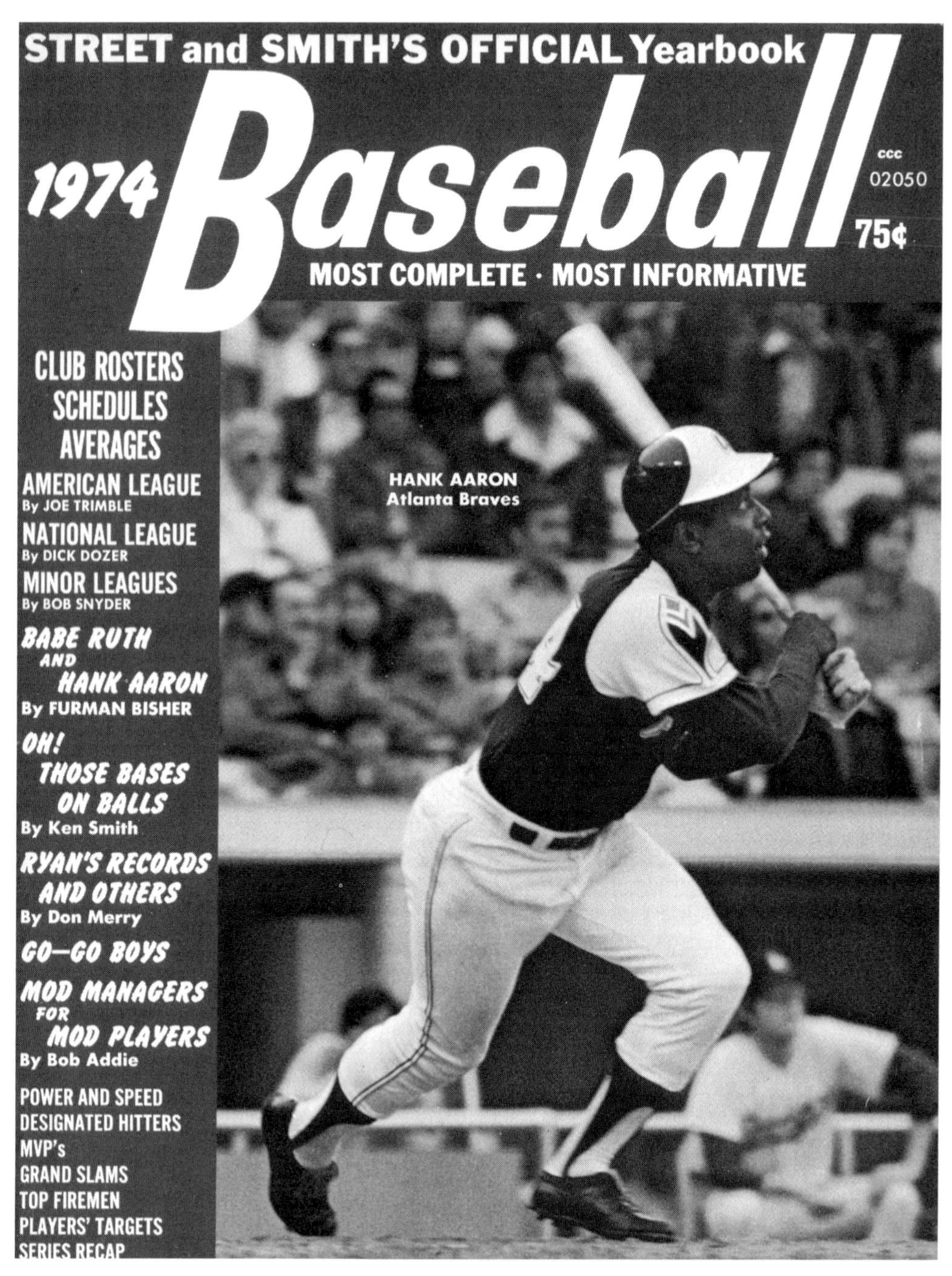

Aaron graced the cover of more than a dozen magazines in the spring of 1974, including the immensely popular *Street & Smith's Official Baseball Yearbook*, which is still published today. (Conde Nast Publications, Inc.)

A great piece of 1970s baseball memorabilia, this *All About Hank Aaron* coloring book sold for a quarter in stationary stores during his pursuit of the Babe. (© 1974)

Ted Turner and Hank Aaron share the cover of the Spring '97 issue of *Braves Fan*, which commemorates the opening of Turner Field. (© 1997 ATCOMM Pubishing)

Stadium. In *I Had a Hammer*, Aaron recalled how nervous he was, harkening to his days as a minor leaguer in Jacksonville. Before his final game there, teammates took up a collection and handed him a bag full of money as a packed house looked on. Aaron promptly spilled the cash all over the field. "This time," he said of the celebration for number 500, "I dropped my hat, and when Bill Bartholomay and I both bent down to pick it up, we bumped and knocked over the microphone."

Aaron's 500th homer carried added significance because Willie Mays was on the field when it happened. The Giant outfielder, claiming it was inappropriate to fraternize with the opposition, refused requests to have his picture taken with Aaron. Mays was in the midst of his second straight off year, and at 37 was finally feeling his age. Perhaps, too, he sensed that Aaron's time in the spotlight was coming.

CHAPTER FOUR:

GOOD VIBRATIONS FOR BAD HENRY

FOR THE MOST PART DURING HIS FIRST 15 SEASONS in the big leagues, Henry Aaron had been denied the full admiration and respect he deserved from fans and the media, partly because he didn't seek headlines and partly because he wasn't great copy. Others—Willie Mays, Mickey Mantle, Sandy Koufax, Frank Robinson, and Roberto Clemente most notable among them—had a knack for attracting the spotlight that Aaron simply did not. But, now, in the unlikeliest of settings, that had begun to change.

When in 1966 the Braves moved to Atlanta—a place where the Confederate flag still waved proudly—it appeared that Aaron's fortunes would never improve. Emboldened by the challenges of his new home, he seemed to only worsen his situation by speaking out about the inequities that plagued baseball and society. Aaron's timing appeared particularly bad, given that he was approaching the twilight of his career. As age increasingly became his enemy, what would become of his legacy? Would Aaron come to be viewed as a bitter old man whose talent and performance on the field were overshadowed by his opinions off it?

Well, a funny thing happed on the way to the old folks home. Like a vintage wine, Aaron got better with age. He enjoyed several remarkable seasons and mounted an assault on some of baseball's most hallowed milestones. Fans and reporters responded in kind, showering him with affection and lauding him with praise. Aaron's rejuvenation focused renewed attention on his steady pursuit of Babe Ruth's record for career home runs. The Atlanta outfielder—and his odds of breaking the Bambino's mark—increasingly became the talk of baseball. Aaron, once a paragon of obscurity, was becoming a national treasure.

Aaron had come to spring training with high hopes before, only to see those hopes dashed by the All-Star break. Yet even he had to see how clear Atlanta's path to the postseason was in 1969. Though still in Aaron's doghouse, Rico Carty seemed good to go. Clete Boyer and Sonny Jackson were healthy, too. But just in case, the Braves had picked up veteran third baseman Bob Aspromonte in a December trade, and longtime Richmond shortstop Gil Garrido was handling himself well at the plate. The pitching staff was set with Phil Niekro, Pat Jarvis, Ron Reed, and Milt Pappas in the rotation. Luman Harris was also feeling good about submarine-baller Cecil Upshaw, and anointed him the team's closer.

The big question mark heading into spring was at first base. Deron Johnson had been sold to the Phillies over the winter, leaving a vacancy the team planned to fill by rotating righties Felipe Alou and Joe Torre with lefties Mike Lum and Tito Francona. A couple of exceptional catching prospects, Bob Didier and Walt Hriniak, gave the Braves the flexibility to go with Torre at first base a couple of times a week and save his aching knees. But a few weeks into spring training, Harris began thinking his young backstops could handle the job full-time.

At about the same time, talks with the Cardinals were heating up. After winning the MVP in 1967, St. Louis first baseman

Orlando Cepeda had limped through the 1968 campaign on aching knees, and his batting average plummeted nearly 80 points. The Cardinals wanted Torre as their new first baseman. The Braves liked Cepeda because he had more power and a winning résumé. Three times in the previous seven seasons, the man called "Cha-Cha" by his teammates and "The Baby Bull" by the press had reached the World Series. And in most other years he was fighting for a pennant well into September. The deal was made on March 19.

Aaron, among others, noticed a difference in the team immediately. "We missed Torre," he said. "Both of them were big-time hitters, but Cepeda was a rah-rah guy who gave us that little push we needed. He was also a great clutch hitter and a major power threat behind me in the batting order, which enabled me to hit forty-four home runs once again that year."

Unbeknownst to Aaron, or anyone else in baseball for that matter, the Cepeda-Torre trade was one of the events that triggered the players' fight for free agency. Despite his drooping numbers in 1968, Cepeda had been a crucial factor in St. Louis's pennant run. As Aaron pointed out, his presence on the field and in the clubhouse could not be measured by mere statistics. Thus when the trade was made, his fellow Cardinals were deeply wounded. "He had symbolized the joyful togetherness of the champion Cardinals," Gold Glove center fielder Curt Flood wrote in his book, *The Way It Is*. "In return for Cha-Cha, the Atlanta Braves sent us Joe Torre, a congenial man and an excellent player. But the glue was gone."

Compounding their depression over the loss of Cepeda was a spring-training speech delivered to them by owner August A. Busch, Jr. Still fuming over his team's seven-game loss to Detroit in the 1968 World Series (like the Braves a decade earlier, St. Louis had led three games to one), he accused his highly paid veterans of becoming flabby and complacent. In Busch's mind, he was simply getting in his retaliatory licks after a winter in which he had to give big raises to Flood, Bob Gibson, Lou Brock, and Tim McCarver. But many of the players, Flood in particular, heard a far different message in the owner's words, and they took it personally.

In his book, Flood portrayed Busch as a man out for blood. He had a point. The owner had called the special meeting at the team's complex in St. Petersburg, where he planned to humiliate his players in front of high-ranking executives from his beer company and selected writers, all of whom had been invited to sit in on the ambush. Busch then launched into a malicious attack on his troops, telling them they were spoiled, pampered, and overpaid. "I can tell you now," he warned, "fans no longer are as sure as they were before about their high regard for the game and the players. Too many fans are saying our players are getting fat—that they only think of money, and less of the game itself."

In a miscalculation of titanic proportions, Busch believed that his vindictive tirade was exactly the motivation the Cardinals needed to claim their third consecutive NL crown. Flood and his mates, however, felt nothing but spite and embarrassment. "The speech demoralized the 1969 Cardinals," he wrote. "Despite two successive pennants, we were still livestock."

Not surprisingly, the Cardinals were never much of a factor during the 1969 season, finishing fourth in the NL East. Then, on October 7, McCarver and Flood were dealt to the Philadelphia Phillies. Flood's now-famous refusal to move his family to what he called "the South's northernmost city" triggered his challenge to baseball's reserve clause, which bound a player to a team essentially for as long as that team desired.

The clause was the linchpin on which every owner's fiscal prosperity hung. A relic of the 1870s—when, ironically, players briefly considered it an honor to be singled out as worthy of being reserved—its legality was upheld in the 1920s when Supreme Court Justice Oliver Wendell Holmes ruled that baseball was immune from antitrust laws. With the help of Marvin Miller, executive director of the Players Association, Flood sued baseball on constitutional grounds.

On June 18, 1972, the high court sided with the owners once again, but just barely. Its opinion was a thinly veiled condemnation of the reserve clause, which not only provided for a moral victory but also lay the groundwork for modern free agency when pitchers Dave McNally, Andy Messersmith, and Catfish Hunter challenged it again a couple of years later.

In the spring of 1969, however, thoughts of free agency were far from the minds of Aaron and Cepeda, who were quickly gaining a mutual respect and trust for each other. Without question, Cepeda's presence on the field and in the clubhouse helped the slugger relax. In June, the two sat down with Fred Katz of *Sport* magazine to "sound off on hitters, spitters and managers they have known." As candid as he had even been, Aaron talked in great depth about a variety of topics.

On the controversial stances he had taken in the past: "I have to tell the truth, and when people ask me what progress the Negroes have made in baseball, I tell them the Negro hasn't made progress on the field. We haven't made any progress in the front office, we haven't made any progress in the commissioner's office. Even with Monte Irvin in there, I still think it's tokenism."

On his future in baseball: "I want to stay in it. But as soon as I can't hit the baseball any more, they're going to move me from the front of the bus to the back again."

On the pace of racial change in the game: "When they keep talking about waiting till the right time, I don't know what is the right time. My grandfather thought it was the right time, and he's dead. They keep telling me to wait till the right time, and I see myself out of baseball and dead, and my kids will be waiting. So I don't know what is the right time."

Though obviously bitter about the injustices that still existed in baseball, Aaron seemed to carry none of his frustrations when he played. It had been years, in fact, since Aaron had had so much fun on the diamond. The 1969 Braves were winning, the team was playing sound baseball, and everyone in the lineup was contributing. The Giants, Reds, Astros, and Dodgers were all playing well, too. For the first time in a decade the Braves were in a fantastic pennant race.

As the "Wild West" careened through the summer, the combatants made on-the-fly adjustments and added spare parts as needed. San Francisco picked up veteran relievers Ron Kline and Don McMahon, the former Brave who was still going strong at 39. The Dodgers grabbed Maury Wills off the Expos' roster and he inspired the inexperienced club with 25 steals and a .297 average. The Reds stood pat despite an injury-riddled mound corps but hit their stride after promoting Wayne Granger—a mop-up man for the 1968 Cardinals—to the closer's role. Astro fans watched in delight as four young starters matured simultaneously and just blew opponents away. Houston later added veterans Jim Bouton and Tommy Davis in a late-season trade with the Seattle Pilots.

The best move of the summer belonged to the Braves. In need of a center fielder with a sound glove and solid bat, they picked up veteran Tony Gonzalez from the San Diego Padres. Gonzalez had not been in a pennant race since 1964, and he instantly rose to the occasion. In 89 games with Atlanta, he batted .294 and was third on the team behind Aaron and Carty with a .447 slugging average.

With much of baseball's attention focused on the NL West, Aaron, who was slugging up a storm, experienced a rebirth of appreciation and popularity. "There is a warm, pleasing undercurrent making its way through the world of baseball," William Leggett wrote in a *Sports Illustrated* article titled "Hank Becomes a Hit." "It flows from the Western Division of the National League, where a stimulating pennant race involving not two clubs, nor three, but five—count 'em!—is adding meaning to every move the players make before the nervous eyes of hopeful fans. The source of this undercurrent is Henry Aaron of the Atlanta Braves, who suddenly this August is attracting the attention his exploits have merited for years."

Aaron began to receive standing ovations in opposing ballparks. Fans clamored outside Atlanta's clubhouse at home and on the road to get an autograph. Now a media darling, Aaron commanded SRO interview sessions at his locker after games. "The mood is changing," added Leggett. "In recent weeks the public—young and old—is beginning to recognize Henry Aaron."

This included criminals, according to a much-circulated story that summer. In late July, burglars broke into the home of Tal Smith, Houston's director of player personnel. Among a slew of sports collectibles, the bandits happened upon two autographed baseballs, one signed by Aaron and the other by Mays. Quickly assessing the value of each, they grabbed the Aaron ball and left the Mays ball behind.

Finally, Aaron was stealing the spotlight from others. Fans everywhere embraced him and celebrated the significance of his accomplishments. They also began to recognize that the slugger was closing in on some impressive milestones, including 3,000 hits. By August he was less than 100 away. Farther on the horizon were the all-time marks for RBIs (2,212), runs (2,245), games (3,033), at bats (11,436), extra-base hits (1,377), and total bases (6,124). All were theoretically within striking range. By even the most generous calculation, however, the 35-year-old Aaron would still need four more years like the one he was enjoying in 1969 to threaten these marks.

Of course, if Aaron did find a way to cheat Father Time and string together four more great years, that would also bring baseball's most hallowed record into his crosshairs: 714 home runs.

Some writers, most notably Atlantan Furman Bisher, had already postulated about Aaron's chances of passing the Babe. The standard response was that the Atlanta outfielder was about to hit that age when the bottom drops out. Mays, the yardstick by which Aaron had been measured for so long, seemed a perfect example of this phenomenon. After smashing 136 homers between the ages of 33 and 35 (and being touted as the generation's biggest threat to reach 714), he totaled just 45 over the next two seasons and was struggling to reach double figures in 1969 at the age of 38. Assuming Aaron followed the same path, he would be lucky to pass 600. Aaron did not necessarily disagree. "I knew the next few years would make all the difference in my final record as a player," he said in *I Had a Hammer*. "I was nearing the traditional age of retirement."

What made Aaron's efforts in 1969 all the more laudable was that he fought through injuries the entire season. Bone chips and calcium deposits in his back caused the most pain. But he was enjoying himself too much to sit down. As the teams headed down the stretch, Aaron was keeping his team in the race for the NL West crown, sometimes almost single-handedly. One could see the pain and exhaustion written on his face, yet he kept hitting homers and driving in runs.

On August 19, the Braves hit their lowest point of the season, dropping to fifth place after Ken Holtzman of the Cubs no-hit them. From then on, however, they played as well as anyone in the majors, winning 27 of 37 games. In the second week of September, the *Sporting News* ran a story on the NL West race, calling it the closest in history. As of September 9, a mere three and one-half games separated the five teams. Aaron was hitting .312 with 39 home runs—just two behind league leader Willie McCovey—causing Bill Bartholomay to gush, "My admiration for him goes beyond description. He's Mr. Brave." Considering that Aaron had long reserved that title for Eddie Mathews, Bartholomay's compliment was particularly meaningful.

Those feelings were underscored later in the month after a crucial sequence of games that separated the pretenders from the contenders in the NL West. In a 24-hour span, three different teams claimed the top spot in the division. "The San Francisco Giants woke up in first, " Mark Mulvoy wrote in *Sports Illustrated*. "By late afternoon, having lost to the Houston Astros, they were out and the Los Angeles Dodgers were in, one one-hundredth of a percentage point ahead of San Francisco and the Atlanta Braves. But that night the Braves beat the Dodgers in 12 innings and they were in first place."

Atlanta's dramatic win came when Aaron stepped to the plate in the top of the 12th to face rookie reliever Ray Lamb. Mulvoy described the ensuing encounter: "Potter Palmer, one of the Braves' owners, studied Lamb when he was warming up in the bullpen and concluded, after one practice pitch flew out of the bullpen and over the head of the Dodger left fielder, that he was wild. He suggested that it might be a good idea if Henry Aaron, the next batter, waited him out. Aaron was thinking that same thing before he saw the third fastball in a row whizzing up to the plate. Never again will Ray Lamb throw three straight fastballs to Henry Aaron. The ball disappeared behind the Dodger bullpen, about 425 feet from the plate, and the Braves were back in first."

But their stay there did not last long. "We were in and out of the lead until a wild game in Houston," Aaron recalled in *I Had a Hammer*. "Norm Miller of the Astros was on third with the tying run in a crucial situation late in the game, with Cecil Upshaw pitching for us and Bob Didier catching. Upshaw threw a pitch that Didier had to reach for, and when he did, his finger guard came off and went flying back toward the screen. Miller thought it was the ball and came tearing for home plate. When he got there, Didier just stepped out as easy as you please and tagged him."

On the emotion of this unlikely victory, the Braves won their next nine in a row, ultimately taking the NL West by three games. And like any club on a winning streak, pitching was key to the team's success. There was Upshaw, whose unorthodox delivery was still baffling opposing batters. Atlanta also purchased Hoyt Wilhelm from the Angels in August, even though the 46-year-old already had a season's worth of innings on his arm. The knuckleballer, however, rose to the pressure of the pennant race. He appeared in eight games down the stretch, surrendering only one run, and in the final week of the season recorded four saves. And then there was Niekro, whose own knuckleball accounted for 23 wins and had earned him a spot on the All-Star squad. Atlanta's poor opponents were lucky if they saw a straight pitch all September long.

Atlanta's NL West crown propelled them into the first-ever National League Championship Series, pitting the team against the storybook New York Mets. The oddsmakers liked the Braves in the best-of-five preliminary to the World Series, mostly because they possessed overwhelming power and had an experienced pitching staff that seemed ideal for a short series. Aaron, however, was not convinced of his club's superiority. The Mets had three live young arms in Tom Seaver, Jerry Koosman, and Gary Gentry. They also played excellent defense and were good clutch hitters. As much as Aaron liked Luman Harris, he also had to give the managing edge to Gil Hodges, who had his team believing they could do anything.

What worried Aaron most was the mood of his own club. He sensed his teammates were not prepared for the intensity of the postseason. The way the Braves players voted on playoff prize money confirmed his suspicions. Rather than basing their shares on a World Series championship, as Aaron suggested, they calculated their take with an NLCS loss in mind. As it turned out, Aaron read the clubhouse correctly.

Leading 5–4 in the eighth inning of Game One with Niekro on the mound, Atlanta fans were already thinking about a sweep. Then Niekro's knuckler stopped dancing. Wayne Garrett doubled, and Cleon Jones and Art Shamsky followed with singles. When Ken Boswell bunted through a Niekro delivery, Jones was caught off second base. Twenty-year-old Bob Didier showed his youth when Jones feinted toward second to draw his throw and then quickly reversed direction and slid safely into third. From there it got really ugly. A missed double play and a wild throw home by Cepeda on an infield grounder enabled Jones to score the go-ahead run. Then pinch hitter J. C. Martin, the proud owner of a .209 average, dinked a ball into the outfield to score three runs.

The carnage continued in Game Two, as the normally anemic Met offense scored eight times before the Braves got on the board. Atlanta came back and drove Koosman from the mound, but fell short by a score of 11–6. Game Three, in New York, saw the Braves get back on track early when Aaron homered (his third in three games) to give Atlanta a 2–0 first-inning lead. Two innings later, the Braves had a chance to blow the game open, when they put men on second and third with none out. Hodges walked to the mound, removed Gentry, and motioned for fireballer Nolan Ryan. The youngster, who was coming off a painful groin injury that had limited him to relief work, proceeded to retire the Braves on two strikeouts and a pop out.

Later in the game, the Mets charged back to take a 3–2 lead, but Cepeda made it 4–3 with a two-run homer off Ryan in the fifth. Hodges then made a critical decision. With Ryan set to lead off the bottom of the inning, the New York manager elected to leave him in the game. The 22-year-old responded with a single. Garrett, the younger brother of Atlanta farmhand Adrian Garrett, came to the plate next. It had been five months to the day since the freckle-faced 21-year-old had hit his last home run. From his post in right field, Aaron watched in disbelief as Garrett lofted the ball down the line and into the seats for a 5–4 lead. Ryan finished off the Braves over the last four innings with his 100 mph heater, and just like that Atlanta's season was done.

There was much finger-pointing in Atlanta after the NLCS disaster, but no one could accuse Aaron of letting down. In three games, he batted .357 with three home runs and seven RBIs. The series capped off a marvelous year in which he hit 44 home runs, knocked in 97 runs, hit an even .300, and slugged .607. After watching the Mets stun the seemingly invincible Orioles in the World Series, Aaron and the Braves turned their thoughts to what promised to be another exciting season.

When Aaron got to spring training in 1970, he found his burgeoning popularity had not subsided. Baseball fans were preparing for his 3,000th hit and wondering how long it would take to reach home run number 600. Aaron used his increasing public acclaim to his advantage. Before the campaign began, he negotiated a new two-year contract worth $125,000 annually. Some questioned the wisdom of paying an aging slugger so handsomely. But Aaron made the front office look like geniuses. On opening night in Atlanta, he slammed a 503-foot homer, becoming the first to reach Atlanta Stadium's upper deck. The Braves commemorated the mammoth blast by painting a gold hammer on the seat where the ball landed.

Aaron remained hot throughout April, smashing seven more long balls before the month ended. His fast break from the gate surprised even him. "I've never had a start like this," he said. "I've hit for a better average early in a season but I've never got as many homers."

Aaron's early power surge caught the eye of all around the game. "Fear of Hank Aaron has been present for most of the past 16 seasons," wrote William Leggett in *Sports Illustrated*. "Now, in his 17th season, that fear is larger than it has ever been."

Don Gullet, who broke into the majors in 1970 with a fastball that topped out on the radar gun at 96 mph, was one of many National League hurlers who pitched with the utmost care to Aaron. Years later, in an interview with George Plimpton, he talked about "Bad Henry" with great reverence. "When the batter gets older, his reflexes are supposed to slow down," he said. "Throw it by them! I could do that with Willie Mays when he was finishing. But Aaron . . . even if you think you have it by him, those great wrists of his flick it out of the catcher's mitt."

The hoopla surrounding Aaron's torrid start earned him a wide lead in the All-Star balloting, which he maintained right into the game. But it also obscured some fundamental problems with the Braves. While the Reds had gotten healthy and the Dodgers more mature, the Braves appeared to have taken a step backward. Once again, they were playing unimaginative station-to-station baseball, with everyone apparently content to wait for Aaron, Cepeda, or Carty to blast a home run. This strategy worked about half the time, which is about how often the Braves won. On the pitching side, Niekro had an off year and was relegated to the bullpen, Reed broke his collarbone, and Upshaw injured a finger and missed the whole season. This sent manager Harris scrambling for replacements. Those he found included former Oakland star Jim Nash and 19-year-old Mike McQueen. The skipper's closers, Wilhelm and journeyman Bob Priddy, looked all of their combined 77 years and pitched like it. Age was also taking its toll on the Atlanta outfield where Aaron, Gonzalez, and Carty allowed a lot of balls to drop in. It was not a pretty picture. Yet as division winners continue to do to this day, the Braves figured the smart move was to stand pat and simply decided to let the players play.

At times, the strategy worked. Whenever Harris was ready to dump his entire staff, someone would come through with a sparkling performance. During 1970, in fact, the Braves' hurlers registered more complete games and shutouts than they had the year before. The problem was stringing those gems together. Aside from one 11-game winning streak, the pitching was inconsistent from April through September. As for the offense, the middle of the lineup was awesome. Carty was on his way to winning the batting title with a .366 average. Cepeda was hitting the ball better than he had since he helped the Giants win the 1962 pennant.

Aaron also was having a spectacular season—precisely the kind the experts said he could not have. On May 17, he singled off Wayne Simpson of the Reds in Cincinnati to become the ninth man in history to accumulate 3,000 base hits. The ball rolled into center field, where Johnny Bench picked it up. (In those days, he often played the outfield to keep his bat in the lineup on days when he was not catching.)

Aaron's 3,000th hit gave him pause to reflect for several reasons. First, he reached the milestone at Crosley Field, where he had begun his major-league career some 17 years earlier. Second, although he made no mention of this fact, Aaron had reached 3,000 before Mays, who joined the club two months later.

Stan Musial, on hand to pay tribute to his friend, jumped on the field to congratulate Aaron as soon as play was halted. The Atlanta outfielder was now the only black player to collect 3,000 hits and the only man of any color to combine 3,000 hits and 500 home runs. An appreciative Aaron hugged Musial and thanked him for showing up. Later in the game, as if to reiterate his feelings, Aaron homered for hit number 3,001, just as Stan the Man had done years earlier. "Go get 'em, Henry," said Musial as he listened to the radio call in his police escort to the airport.

Afterward, when queried about his chances of hitting 714 home runs, Aaron put his accomplishment into perspective. "Sure, catching Ruth would be a thrill, but achieving 3,000 hits is more important because it shows consistency," he said. Several days later,

Aaron also showed that, regardless of his momentous achievements on the field, he had not lost his sense of humor off it. After playing a less than impressive round of golf, Aaron joked, "It took me 17 years to get 3,000 hits, and I did the same thing on an 18-hole golf course."

Maintaining such perspective was important, especially given the dubious treatment Aaron received from baseball's ruling powers. Neither Commissioner Bowie Kuhn nor NL President Chub Feeney bothered to attend the game at Crosley Field when Aaron joined the 3,000-hit club. It would be a long time before the Atlanta outfielder would forget the slight.

Fortunately, baseball fans across the country did not share the disinterest shown by Kuhn and Feeney. Those who witnessed number 3,000 in Cincinnati gave Aaron a thunderous standing ovation. Others sent cards and letters to acknowledge the achievement. "The fans, fortunately, responded to him," offered William Leggett. "Last Saturday evening, after doubling twice to move within one hit of 3,000, Aaron sat in front of his locker in the Braves' clubhouse and said wistfully, 'People have been calling me on the phone and wishing me the best of luck. I appreciate it very much. It's nice to know that people know you are around.'"

All was not happy with Aaron, however. In *I Had a Hammer*, he revealed that by this time he and Barbara had drifted apart. Focusing more attention than ever before on hitting home runs, Aaron found it more difficult to remain on an even keel. "As I drew closer to Willie and Ruth, I fell farther away from Barbara," he said. "We were two people headed in different directions. As a result, I felt more comfortable at the ballpark than I did at home, and the more she objected to my lifestyle, the more I wanted to be away. I felt lonely and angry, and, to a degree, I was taking my domestic problems out on pitchers."

By season's end, Aaron had racked up 38 homers and knocked in 118 runs, his highest RBI total since 1966. But there was little consolation in those numbers. Aaron's marriage continued to crumble. In February of 1971, he and Barbara finalized their divorce.

Now living in an apartment by himself, Aaron was miserable. He missed his children desperately and knew they were suffering more than anyone. He was hardly in the proper frame of mind to prepare for another long summer of baseball. But if there was one thing Aaron prided himself on, it was his ability to block out distractions when he stepped on the diamond.

That legendary capacity to focus was no more apparent than in 1971. Although a sore knee cut his playing time to only 139 games, the fewest since his rookie year—and the Braves found themselves in something of a transitional mode—Aaron knocked more balls out of the park than in any prior season. *Baseball Digest* called his output "one of the best years a 37-year-old player has ever had in organized baseball." It was hard to argue with the magazine's claim. Aaron batted .327, blasted 47 home runs, scored 95 runs, and drove home 118 runs for the second consecutive season. His .669 slugging average not only led the league, it was the highest of his career and the best by a National Leaguer since 1948.

Without Aaron's super season, it is frightening to think where the Braves would have finished. Carty and then Cepeda were felled by knee injuries, forcing Aaron to take over at first base. The team's five starters were an aggregate four games under .500 and Upshaw simply was not the pitcher he was before the injury.

Were it not for a couple of rookies enjoying amazing years, the season would have been over in May. Ralph Garr, who had been impressive during a brief call-up in 1970, broke out with a huge year after taking over for Carty. The "Road Runner" batted .343 with 24 doubles and 30 steals. He was often standing on second base when Aaron came to the plate, and no doubt many of Aaron's 118 RBIs came on singles, which, in other years, would have merely moved men over. Atlanta's other young savior was catcher Earl

Williams. An immense man with a powerful bat, he too had won admirers while enjoying a September "cup of coffee" in 1970. Williams slammed 33 home runs and knocked in 87 runs, won the Rookie of the Year award, and helped protect Aaron in the lineup the way Cepeda had. Williams was not, however, the long-term solution behind the plate; his defense and pitch-calling left a lot to be desired and, given his physique, it was doubtful he would survive the rigors of everyday catching.

More amazing than the breakthroughs of Garr and Williams, however, was Aaron's consistency in 1971. In no month, for instance, did he hit less than seven homers or more than nine. And every week, it seemed, he passed a Hall of Famer or two on one of the all-time lists.

What was the key to Aaron's astonishing success? Baseball experts cited a variety of reasons. "Some believe it has to do with the move he made from right field to first base," reported Kenneth Reich in *Baseball Digest* in January of 1972. "In recent years Aaron has tired and faded slightly toward the end. With less running necessary this year, his own knees held up better and so did his performance."

According to Aaron, however, the answer was much simpler. "It's confidence in what I'm doing, " he said. "I'm either going to scare the pitcher to death by not hitting the ball, or hit it. I just feel I can get a hit."

His biggest hit of the year was his 600th home run, which came on April 27 in Atlanta against the Giants. Aaron's victim, interestingly enough, was Gaylord Perry who had said earlier in the day, "If he gets number 600 off me, he's going to earn it."

Aaron had no reason to doubt this statement. Perry had developed a reputation around the league for throwing a spitter, a pitch that bothered Aaron. Not only did he feel the spitball gave Perry an unfair advantage, he also thought there were too many young pitchers experimenting with it. Aaron feared, among other things, getting plunked in the head by an errant greaser. In his interview with Cepeda for *Sport* two years before, in fact, he had voiced his concerns.

"I feel like most of the pitchers are throwing it," he said. "I really shouldn't name anybody but Perry with the Giants definitely is one. I don't know whether you'd call it a spitball, greaseball, or whatever ball, but it's still an illegal pitch. They're probably going to legalize it. They'd be better off, because then the hitter would know what's coming."

Aaron's homer off Perry helped him finish the year with 639 for his career, putting him seven behind Mays, who had managed only 18 in '71. Now 77 behind Ruth, Aaron knew he needed at least two more healthy seasons to surpass the Babe. "You've got to remember, the older you get the slower you get," Aaron said. "I've seen a lot of players get old . . . if I can have a good season in 1972 and come back with another good one, well, that's different. I might not quit. But two bad ones back to back and staying at home would be written on the wall."

The excitement Aaron's 47-homer performance generated in 1971 carried over into the following season. With Hammerin' Hank less than 80 round-trippers behind Ruth, he was the hottest topic of conversation among fans and sportswriters, who debated endlessly whether the slugger had enough left in his tank to set a new mark. The spotlight shone even brighter after Aaron signed a three-year, $600,000 deal—the most lucrative contract in baseball history—just before the start of spring training. The deal elicited an immediate reaction from the press. It was a feature story on the *CBS News* with Walter Cronkite, and many baseball writers reported that Aaron had finally achieved the recognition he deserved. "It is not only the highest salary ever paid a Brave, it is the highest remuneration ever paid a baseball player," penned Al Thomy of the *Sporting*

News. "At the age of 38, modest Hank Aaron has jumped to the fore of baseball's super stars, ahead of Willie Mays, Carl Yastrzemski, Bob Gibson, Juan Marichal and Harmon Killebrew. At long last, the quiet guy, the one they said lacked color and charisma, whatever that is, had his day in the spotlight."

At the press conference announcing the contract, Aaron responded to questions about the pressure he now faced, especially in light of his pursuit of Ruth. "Pressure, I'm sure there will be pressure," he said. "As I get closer to the record, I'm sure the pressure will get greater. But I have always thought I was at my best under pressure, in tough situations."

Aaron would have to be, because the media onslaught only grew as Opening Day drew nearer. Reporters asked questions about his contract and the home run record on a daily basis. In April, Jesse Outlar of the *Sporting News* described how Aaron's life was changing. "Long the most under-publicized super star in baseball, Aaron seems destined in the next two seasons to become the most publicized player of all time," he wrote. "From here in, Aaron is the No. 1 name in sports. Privacy is out, and fortunately for all concerned, Aaron has as much class off the field as he does at home plate."

Aaron, long distrustful of certain segments of the media, appreciated such sentiments. They helped bolster his confidence with the press, making him more willing to open up and speak honestly about his feelings. That was important, because as Outlar pointed out, "the closer Henry gets to the record, the larger the reportorial platoon will get."

Fortunately, Aaron and the Braves were prepared for this development. Atlanta's front office, which still included Donald Davidson, had already outlined a plan to assist its star attraction. Unlike Roger Maris, who was overwhelmed during his pursuit of the Babe's single-season home run record in 1961, Aaron would not be left by himself to deal with the increasing number of reporters following him. If it was a mob that wanted to get at the Atlanta outfielder, at least it would be a well-behaved one.

For his part, Aaron believed the media glare would be the least of his problems. "They talk to me about the pressure, how it affected Roger Maris when he hit 61 home runs," he said one day to a throng of writers. "Frankly, I am not worried about the pressure of publicity. I'm much more worried about National League pitchers than I am about you guys. The real pressure, in my opinion, comes from the fans when they expect you to hit a home run every time you come to bat."

Aaron reiterated this point years later in *I Had a Hammer*. "I don't know what it is about baseball fans, but many of them just can't stand to see players making big money," he said. "I can appreciate the argument that playing ball is far less important than physics or medicine or public service, but I can't understand why athletes are the only ones who seem to get jabbed with the sharp side of this attitude."

The attitude Aaron spoke of got even sharper on April 1, 1972, when the players staged the first strike in the history of Major League Baseball. Instead of watching Aaron resume his pursuit of Ruth, fans were forced to listen to rhetoric both from the owners and from Players Association executive director Marvin Miller. "At first, it seemed like some April Fool's joke," wrote Phil Pepe in his book *Talkin' Baseball*. "At issue was renegotiation of the players' benefit plan that had been first settled two years ago. While some within the baseball establishment argued that this was hardly a strike issue, others viewed it as gamesmanship on the part of the players, a strategic ploy aimed at attempting to intimidate the owners for the following year when the basic agreement, including the reserve system, was scheduled to be negotiated."

Whatever the motivation behind the walkout, it did not sit well with fans. Livid over the stoppage in play, most sided with the owners. The media fed their anger further by painting the players as greedy and petty. If Aaron thought he and his fellow players suffered from an unfair reputation before, the situation now could only worsen.

On the plus side for Aaron, however, the strike at least shifted focus away from him for a time. For nearly two weeks, the dispute was front-page news, as labor and management engaged in a very public stare down. Then the owners blinked. After 13 days and a total of 86 cancelled games, they acquiesced, consenting to beef up the benefit plan with a $490,000 contribution in 1972 and promising an extra $500,000 the following year. A victorious Miller boasted that the two sides had arrived at "an honorable agreement." But given his distrust of big-league owners, not to mention the fans' growing suspicion of professional athletes in general, Miller's choice of words seemed particularly ironic.

By the time Aaron and the Braves took the field on April 15, it was fair to say that fans viewed them differently. But this was not solely because of Aaron's status as baseball's highest-paid player, or the way the strike influenced public perception. Looking to spark more excitement in the stands and generate bigger profits at the cash register, Atlanta debuted new uniforms for the 1972 campaign. In the words of Wayne Minshew of the *Sporting News*, "The Braves have gone mod."

"Remember those old baseball uniforms where the sleeves extended below the elbow?" asked Minshew. "Or, those pre-war jobs which were so roomy it appeared a family had just moved out? Those guys who wore those uniforms should get a look at the ones unveiled by the Braves the other day. They would rub their eyes in disbelief."

The new uniforms featured perhaps the most flamboyant color combination in baseball: royal blue and white, trimmed with scarlet.

Atlanta's road attire, highlighted by a royal blue jersey with white sleeves and stylized feathers, created the biggest stir. "It looks like they're trying out for a girls' softball team," quipped one fan.

Wayland Moore, the Braves' director of graphics, dismissed such criticism. He believed his design concept had accomplished exactly what he had set out to do. "I'd look out of the stands at one player and I'd say, 'How can I make him appeal more to the fans?" said Moore. "I came up with this uniform."

Luman Harris, who appeared particularly clownlike in the new uniform, tried to be diplomatic. Quoting former Pirate skipper Danny Murtaugh, he said, "Boys, when you're in first place, it doesn't matter what you wear."

The Braves, however, finished nowhere near first place. Cepeda and Carty were hurt again, Boyer retired at 35, and Jarvis was banished to the bullpen. The rebuilding continued, with outfielder Dusty Baker and third baseman Darrell Evans earning full-time jobs—the latter at Aaron's urging—but the youthful enthusiasm that often accompanies such a program just was not there. Perhaps it was the team's pitching staff that sapped its energy. With the exception of Niekro, who went 16–12, the hurlers were horrible. Atlanta's 4.27 ERA was a half-run higher than that of any other team in the majors.

Aaron, the first to admit the Braves played uninspired ball throughout 1972, put up numbers that reflected the malaise. He appeared in only 129 games, batting .265 and driving home just 77 runs. All three marks were his lowest since his rookie season. In addition, his homer total fell to 34. Although the strike could be blamed for many of the season's ills, the fact remained that the Braves only missed eight games. Atlanta finished 70–84, a dismal 25 games behind the first-place Reds.

In Aaron's defense, his body was starting to give out on him. An arthritic condition in his neck hampered him throughout the early part of the campaign. When doctors finally diagnosed the painful problem and prescribed medication, Aaron began to swing the bat with more authority. His surge at the plate included a pair of homers against Bob Gibson during a two-week period in May. "Two off Gibson," he joked. "Man, that's a season against him. Season? It's a career."

As the year wore on, Aaron's knees ached more and more. By season's end there was no longer any question that he was probably best suited to be a full-time first baseman, as he played just 15 games in right field. Yet more taxing on Aaron than the effort involved in getting his 39-year-old body to cooperate was the constant presence of the media. What he initially had dismissed was proving far more intrusive than he ever imagined. And of course it was only going to get worse.

What vexed Aaron most about the unceasing tide of writers and reporters around the Atlanta clubhouse was the effect it was having on the team's younger players, especially Garr and Baker. By this time he was taking his role as elder statesman very seriously, and he did his best to nurture the team's future stars. Indeed, Garr and Baker were rarely seen without Aaron. They shared a row of seats on every flight during road trips. They went out on the town together during home stands. They sat together in the dugout during games. The trio talked about everything, from setting up pitchers to civil rights. When Aaron met Jesse Jackson in the early 1970s, he often asked Garr and Baker to accompany him to dinner with the reverend. The lessons the youngsters learned from their mentor proved invaluable.

"Hank was such a good friend that I just wanted to do things for him," said Garr, who affectionately called Aaron "Supe," short for superstar. "But I could never do as much as he did for me just by taking me under his wing. He gave me the best advice I ever got in the big leagues. He said, 'Whatever God gave you, that's what will keep you here. So whatever you did in the minor leagues to get here, that's what you do when you're here. The coaches will tell you how they want you to hit, and when you're in the batting cage do what they say to do. But when you get to the plate and it's just you and the pitcher, do what got you here. Take advice from everybody, but do what you have to do.' That advice kept me in the big leagues for ten years."

Baker probably cherished his relationship with Aaron even more than Garr. That was partially because the pressure on the youngster to perform was immense. Early in his career, the fans and the media tabbed the outfielder as the successor to Aaron's throne. The youngster could hit for average, showed flashes of power, was a tremendous defensive outfielder, and ran faster than anyone on the team except for Garr. But he was no longer a teen sensation. At 23, he was expected to produce. Baker responded by hitting .321 with 17 homers and 76 RBIs and was voted "Brave of the Year" by the city's writers and broadcasters.

The moment Baker established that he could play at the major-league level, he was set upon by the press already swarming around Aaron. Their first question was usually something like, "How does it feel to be the 'next' Hank Aaron?" For a rookie trying to find his bearings, such questions tend to be mind-boggling, even when the man to whom you've been compared is right there backing you up. Baker played it smart and gave the writers the quotes they wanted. "I can never be a Hank Aaron," he once said to Jim Bukata, a freelancer writing for *All-Star Sports*. "I don't think there will ever be another Hank Aaron. I just want to be the first Dusty Baker and hope the job I do as Dusty Baker will be satisfying to the club and help it win."

No matter how genuine, Baker's humility didn't sell magazines. When *All-Star Sports* hit the newsstands, the cover slug read "Dusty Baker Tells What It's Like to Be Hank Aaron's Heir." Aside from its sensational title, however, the story did paint an accurate picture, stating that Aaron empathized with Baker's dilemma and went out of his way to help him. "Hank was like a father," Baker recalled. "I met Hank when I was eighteen years old and just getting out of high school. At the time, I was trying to decide whether to go to college or sign with the Braves, and when the Braves were in Los Angeles they sent Hank over to talk to me. I asked Hank if I should sign, and he said, 'If you have confidence that you can make it, then sign.' My mother made Hank promise to take care of me, and he promised."

Once the Braves were out of the running in '72, the focus of the season for Aaron became how many home runs he could hit. There was little question he went to the plate looking to hit one out, unless a situation called for something different. He knew what the fans expected and he wanted to please them. Yet as typically happens when a player tries for home runs, they did not always come so easily.

That did not bother the fans. They not only voted Aaron to start in the All-Star Game again, but he repeated as the game's top vote-getter. With the contest scheduled for Atlanta, the stage was set for a dramatic moment. For Aaron, who had eschewed dramatics lo these many years, the pressure to do something great was enormous.

A betting man would not have taken the odds. Aaron had been to every All-Star Game since 1955, and had a miserable .186 average in 59 at bats. His only extra-base hit was a home run he hit off Vida Blue in 1971. "I don't know what it is about All-Star games . . . I just haven't done much in them," he said. "I can't explain it. I wish I could."

Whatever magic Aaron had summoned the previous July he found again as he stepped to the plate against Gaylord Perry—now an American Leaguer with the Indians—in the sixth inning. He picked out a pitch he liked and pulled it over the wall at the 375-foot mark for a home run that brought the house down. "I just floated around the bases," he said. "It left me almost giddy. I was so excited. I knew what Gaylord was going to throw. He's a spitball pitcher. Everybody knows how great he is. If he throws 90 pitches, you know 88 of them will be spitters."

In the top of the seventh, manager Danny Murtaugh (who had come out of retirement to take the reins of the All-Star squad) made sure Aaron fully enjoyed the moment. He sent the slugger out to his post in right field for one more inning. The fans erupted when they spied their hero jogging to his position. "I got an ovation that made me feel more at home there than I ever had," Aaron recalled in *Chasing the Dream*.

Aaron hit two more noteworthy home runs in 1972. The first came on August 6 when he went deep against Wayne Simpson in Cincinnati for the 660th home run of his career, breaking Ruth's mark for the most homers with one team. A month later, Aaron belted two home runs against Philadelphia to surpass Stan Musial's mark for career total bases. "If there is any one record that I think best represents what I was all about as a hitter, that's the one, because, as far as I was concerned, the object of batting was to hit the ball and get as many bases as possible," he said years later. "It also tells me something that the record had been Musial's, because I consider myself to be much more like Musial than Ruth, both as a hitter and as a person."

The day after he hit number 660, Aaron had reason to celebrate again. Atlanta's ownership, tired of watching the Braves stumble along in the NL West, fired Luman Harris and replaced him with Eddie Mathews. Aaron applauded the move, not because he disliked Harris, but because he felt the skipper's relaxed style in the dugout no longer suited the Braves. He knew that Mathews would take a no-nonsense approach to his new job and felt that his longtime friend and former teammate was exactly what Atlanta needed to turn the team around. "I'm sure he will be the same type of manager he was as a player—aggressive," said Aaron. "I expect there will be more discipline, which is one of the most important things you can have."

Even more than the hiring of Mathews, however, Aaron reveled in the news that Atlanta had also relieved Paul Richards of his duties as GM. He had never attempted to hide his intense dislike for the man whom he believed was directly responsible for the Braves' downfall. Though Richards was retained as vice president of baseball operations, his power base was profoundly diminished, and he was subsequently fired that January. While Aaron had yet to meet Richards's successor, Eddie Robinson, he half joked that he "would have welcomed Lester Maddox" if he were replacing Paul Richards.

To their credit, both Mathews and Robinson understood that despite the collection of young talent the Braves had assembled, Aaron remained the heart of the team. When the two were asked if anyone on the roster was exempt from a trade, Mathews responded with the full support of Robinson. "I don't think so, except for Hank Aaron. That's Eddie Robinson's department, but I don't feel there's anybody else who is actually an untouchable."

In a season of change, the final highlight of 1972 offered Aaron a chance at stability. During the summer, he was contacted by Billye Williams, the cohost of a television show called *Today in Georgia*, about a series of profiles she was doing on members of the Braves. Aaron agreed to a live interview, but then failed to show at the station on the day of the booking. Though embarrassed by the incident, Williams refused to give up on the Atlanta star. She rescheduled the interview, and then appeared at Aaron's door on the morning of the taping. Aaron, still sleepy from an extra-inning game the night before, assured her he would not let her down again. The seeds of a relationship were planted. The two began to talk on the telephone regularly. Both found the conversations therapeutic. Aaron was still trying to deal with his divorce, while Williams was coming to terms with the death of her husband.

"She helped bring me into the world of books and ideas and made me conversant in the things I believed in," he said. "My thinking was expanded by being around Billye, but she never tried to change or influence me." Given the pressure and adversity that awaited Aaron over the next 18 months, such support and understanding would be crucial.

CHAPTER FIVE:

FEAR AND LOATHING IN ATLANTA

GOING INTO THE 1973 BASEBALL SEASON, WHAT HAD seemed impossible to almost everyone just a few years earlier was now a fact of life. With 673 home runs to his name, Hank Aaron was within one productive campaign of catching—or even passing—Babe Ruth as the sport's all-time leader in long balls. The magnitude of that feat began to weigh more heavily on Aaron's mind.

Despite his increased popularity, he wondered how people would react. Aaron suspected the media attention would further intensify as he closed in on the most famous record in sports. What about fans in Atlanta and on the road? Aaron knew that a lot of people wanted Ruth's mark to stand forever. More alarming, however, he knew that the most zealous among this wide-ranging group abhorred the thought of a black man breaking it.

If Aaron wondered how baseball itself viewed the breaking of Ruth's record, he had only to look at its treatment of Roger Maris a decade earlier. Although Major League Baseball did not attach an asterisk to Maris's record 61 home runs (as is the popular belief) the commissioner's office sometimes seemed to go out of its way to differentiate what Maris had accomplished in 162 games and what

Ruth had done in 154. In the end, there was only one thing Aaron knew for sure. No one could predict how the '73 season would play out, least of all Aaron himself.

The Braves had some major question marks heading into spring training in 1973. Aaron was still Atlanta's most dangerous hitter, but could Baker and Garr be counted on to repeat their .300 seasons? Would Darrell Evans continue to mature at the plate and become a middle-of-the lineup hitter? And what impact would the three big off-season trades have on the club?

Earl Williams had been dealt to the Orioles for second baseman Dave Johnson, catcher Johnny Oates, and starting pitchers Pat Dobson and Roric Harrison—a quartet of players with World Series experience. Felix Millan and pitcher George Stone had gone to the Mets in exchange for starter Gary Gentry and reliever Danny Frisella. Atlanta had acquired a third starting pitcher, Carl Morton, from the Expos for Pat Jarvis. Morton had actually signed with the Braves out of high school in 1964 and then blossomed into an 18-game winner after being selected from Atlanta in the 1969 expansion draft.

With all these new faces on the club, reporters still swarmed around Aaron during spring training. The question they asked almost hourly was whether he thought he could hit 41 or 42 homers in 1973—and could he do it as an outfielder again. With no one to play right field and hard-hitting Mike Lum languishing on the bench, the Braves had to scrap plans to play Aaron at first. He agreed to assume his old spot in right again with the understanding that he would get plenty of rest.

As the season got under way, Aaron began to see how it was going to shape up. On the field, the Braves were still struggling. Morton and Harrison managed to hold their own in the rotation, but the two Mets pitchers had bad arms. The 30-year-old Johnson had lost much of his range at second base, but made up for it with a swing that was tailor-made for Atlanta Stadium. Oates did fine in his first National League season until he hurt his knee, then backup Paul Casanova filled in. Dobson's time in Atlanta was brief. With a record of 3–7 and an ERA around 5.00 after 10 starts, he was traded to the Yankees for first baseman Frank Tepedino and prospects. As they had since their 1969 division crown, the Braves struggled to win half their games.

Off the field, Aaron's relationship with the city and its fans turned strangely sour. A small but vocal minority was actively rooting against him in his pursuit of history. This group was made up of hard-line baseball traditionalists and plain old rednecks who scorned and ridiculed Aaron whenever possible, claiming he was just pulling on the uniform so he could get the record. Granted, Aaron was no longer the awesome talent who terrorized NL pitchers for so many seasons. He admitted as much, in fact, when writer Al Thomy asked him about his disappointing year in '72. "Let's face it," he responded with great honesty. "I was not a 30-year-old man and the 16 days I missed during the baseball strike hurt me more than it did the younger players. If I had been a man of 30 I could have bounced back. But at my age I had to play my way back into shape and it became a season-long experience."

Still, Aaron was hardly grasping at the threads of his career, as his detractors often painted him. He was a dangerous hitter and a positive force on the team—although you would hardly know it if you lived in Atlanta. No, the sentiments of the anti-Aaron faction were never echoed by the city or its newspapers, but then there was hardly a groundswell of support for Aaron in response. For whatever reason, Atlantans were going to let him fight this battle on his own.

At the same time, the recognition he felt he deserved from the commissioner's office was either slow in coming or never arrived at all. Bowie Kuhn's indifference to his achievements and his plight were at times astonishing. All too often for Aaron's liking, the commissioner acted as though the home run chase meant little to him. While Kuhn always provided a timely excuse for his apathy, Aaron firmly believed his actions spoke louder than his words.

Once he stepped between the white lines, all Aaron could do was play. And love him or hate him, when the Braves arrived in town, fans came out in huge numbers to witness history being made. Before the season, Expo GM Jim Fanning predicted that, as the season progressed and Aaron got closer to 700 homers, "his presence in a park will mean 10,000 more people for a game. People will just want a look at him. They'll be coming out to watch him take batting practice." This was not too far off, except in Atlanta, where fan interest was surprisingly tepid. Early in the season, the Braves were drawing less than 8,000 spectators a game.

For his part, Aaron wanted to hit numbers 714 and 715 as soon as possible, but the idea of a 41-homer season at his age seemed unlikely, even to Aaron himself. In his mind, the record would not come until 1974. "I think I can hit, maybe, 35," Aaron said in an interview with Wayne Minshew for *Baseball Illustrated*. "Forty-one, though, I don't know. Twenty-five or 30 would be a good figure."

For one thing, Aaron was uncertain about how his body would hold up, even in the 120 or so games he and Mathews agreed he would play. The deal was that the manager would pencil Aaron into the lineup unless Aaron told him otherwise. By this stage of his career, he knew how to listen to his body and he fully intended to do what it told him. His psyche was another matter.

In addition to the pressure of the chase, Aaron was carrying the considerable weight of tremendous personal loss. In late October of 1972, his hero and friend, Jackie Robinson, passed away from complications associated with diabetes. A couple of months later, his friend and rival Roberto Clemente died in a private-plane crash while flying relief supplies into earthquake-ravaged Nicaragua. Both deaths caused Aaron to reassess his life and his goals.

Robinson's passing affected Aaron on several levels. The former Brooklyn Dodger had long been his role model, and even as declining health robbed Robinson of his youthful look, Aaron continued to view the Hall of Famer through the eyes of a child. In *I Had a Hammer*, for instance, Aaron used the word "spellbinding" when he recalled Robinson's last public appearance at the 1972 World Series. At a ceremony in his honor prior to Game One, Robinson delivered an impassioned speech in which he stated that until blacks were managing in the big leagues or serving in front-office positions, baseball could not really claim it had achieved any progress in race relations. For Aaron, losing a friend and a mentor who remained so committed to the cause was a painful blow.

It was also hard for him to accept the reaction of his contemporaries to Robinson's death. Aaron stewed at how so few active players attended the funeral, a slight that he took as a personal insult. "It made me more determined than ever to keep Jackie's dream alive," he said, "and the best way I could do that was to become the all-time home run champion in the history of the game that had kept out black people for more than sixty years."

The loss of Clemente helped motivate Aaron as well. Only two years earlier, Clemente had put together a remarkable season, batting .341 during the regular season and then leading the Pirates to the world championship over the Orioles. In 1972, he managed to hit over .300 again, adding an exclamation point by finishing the year with exactly 3,000 hits for his career. Clemente nearly made it to the World Series again—a ninth-inning comeback by the Reds in Game Five of the NLCS robbed him of his chance. No one who watched him trot off the field that day imagined that it was his last moment as a major leaguer. At 38, he still had plenty of baseball left in him.

The only reason Clemente was aboard that airplane on New Year's Eve was because he had heard that the relief supplies he had sent earlier were not being distributed by the Nicaraguan military. Clemente's fame in the Spanish-speaking world was such that he knew no one would dare refuse him if he showed up himself. The cargo must have shifted violently on takeoff, for the plane plunged into the sea just moments after leaving the runway.

Aaron walked around in shock for days upon hearing the news, firmly believing that authorities would find the Pittsburgh outfielder alive and well. But a desperate rescue effort launched by the Puerto Rican Port Authority and U.S. Coast Guard found no sign of survivors. When reports confirmed Clemente's death, Aaron had an epiphany. He realized the good fortune he had enjoyed throughout his career and counted his blessings for meeting Billye Williams. Aaron also reflected on his nearly 20-year friendship with Clemente, one based on equal parts of respect and rivalry. The pair had broken into the majors a year apart and competed against each other from that point on. While Aaron hit with more consistency and power, Clemente's flair for the fantastic always kept fans on the edge of their seats.

Somewhat ironically, however, Clemente had long felt that Aaron had always overshadowed him. For years the debate raged: who was the best right fielder in the National League, Aaron or Clemente? Both took the argument very seriously, and Aaron usually won. But that was of little consolation after Clemente died. Aaron eventually came to the conclusion that the rivalry between the two had been "trivial."

As it turned out, personal loss was not Aaron's only motivating factor going into 1973. He admitted in *I Had a Hammer*, for instance, that the financial windfall the home run record promised to generate was a powerful force. In the early 1970s, Aaron had made a series of bad investments. He now saw a way to recoup those losses through several small deals to license his name and image. His face began popping up everywhere.

"*Time* and *Newsweek* raced to see who could get me on their cover first—*Newsweek* won," he said. "There were five or six ballads written about me and more than a dozen books. I was offered movie parts, and when the soap operas found out that I spent the afternoons watching them—*Days of Our Lives*, *The Edge of Night*, *All My Children*, *The Secret Storm*—I was invited onto their sets. People wanted to put my name on pens and pins and cups . . . one guy even suggested a Hank Aaron Gear Shift Knob."

For advertisers, Aaron was money in the bank. The record was all but assured. The only question was when? Before he was fired by the Braves, Paul Richards projected that Aaron would be in position to pass the Babe before the season ended. "August 31, 1973," he said to Wayne Minshew of the *Sporting News*. "Put that down. He'll break the record or tie it on that date."

Such comments added to the suspense of Aaron's chase. At times, in fact, the unflappable slugger seemed caught up in the excitement himself. At one point, in an interview with Al Thomy, Aaron envisioned his record-breaking at bat. "At that stage, the pitcher will have to be some guy with guts enough to challenge me with his best pitch," he said. "It won't be a rookie and it won't be a border-liner. It will be somebody like Seaver or Jenkins or Gibson or Carlton, somebody not afraid to throw his best pitch."

Thomy used Aaron's quote in an article for *Popular Sports Baseball* that put into perspective the enormity of the task. The story, which included a chart for readers to fill in as they followed Hammerin' Hank through the season, called the pursuit of 715 "a spot unique in all the history of major league sports." Thomy also drew parallels between Aaron and another slugger made infamous by his race against Ruth, Roger Maris.

"Aaron's predicament, and it is a predicament, won't be unlike Maris'," wrote Thomy. "As Maris had pressure, he will have pressure; as people pulled against Maris, there will be people pulling against him; as Maris was pestered by press and fans, he will be pestered; as Maris was reminded of Ruth every day of his season, he will be reminded.

"But Henry Aaron and Roger Maris are cut from different cloths," he continued. "Aaron appears unemotional, a man at peace with himself, a graceful and flawless athlete. He anticipates the pressures."

Here, by the way, was an excellent example of how the media's attitude toward Aaron had evolved into one of respect and at times even reverence. Imagine the adjectives that might have been used a decade earlier to convey the same ideas. Aaron appreciated the media's new take on his demeanor. Indeed, the answers he gave to the increasingly repetitive questions about his pursuit of Ruth were patient and thoughtful. He also was willing to confront the realities of the great chase. He acknowledged to Thomy, for example, that the "odds against me setting the record in 1973 are heavy."

At this time, Aaron also began to mention that he was receiving a lot of mail from fans, both for and against him. "I get letters chastising me for trying to break Ruth's record," he told Thomy. "That's to be expected. But for every letter I get against setting the record, I get four or five for it. Nowadays I think most people want to see all records erased."

For the time being, at least, negative sentiments from fans did not bother Aaron. To the contrary, he was more concerned with the "hidden factors" that would affect him. For instance, Aaron no longer had Williams hitting behind him in the lineup, which meant he might not see as many good pitches to drive. Now protecting him were Johnson, Baker, and Evans, a trio that had produced a grand total of just 41 home runs the year before.

Atlanta's position in the standings was another factor that would play a role in Aaron's approach at the plate. "If we're in a pennant race, a close race, I think I'd have a better chance," he said. "That is the added incentive that brings out the best in an athlete."

Eddie Mathews could not have agreed more with Aaron's assessment, and he instituted several new team policies to hasten Atlanta's return to the top in the West. For one thing, the Braves' manager believed part of the team's recent failures was due to a lack of conditioning. Before spring training in 1973, therefore, he sent a letter to his players instructing each to report to camp at his proper playing weight. Fines of $50 and $100 per pound awaited those who did not. Several days after receiving Mathews' letter, infielder Jim Breazeale joked that he was $1,790 overweight. On Opening Day the joke was on him: Breazeale was in the minors.

Aaron, who had never had any trouble maintaining his weight, was in good shape when the season began. He slammed his first four-bagger of the year, number 674, in Atlanta's second game, against San Diego. He belted another the following day. But homers were all that Aaron could muster. Indeed, while his power stroke went unaffected by the pressure of the chase, his batting average sagged below .200. Of his first nine hits, seven were home runs. Aaron's detractors had a field day.

When the Braves traveled to Los Angeles in May, it appeared that Dodger skipper Walter Alston concurred with the stories of Aaron's demise. In one game, with the score tied in the top of the 10th and Aaron in the on-deck circle, Alston ordered an intentional walk of Evans, a selective young hitter who was just finding his power stroke. The Los Angeles manager believed that Aaron was only interested in home runs and therefore could be retired more easily. Alston was dead wrong. Aaron settled into the batter's box, waited for a pitch he could drive, and calmly singled home the winning run in Atlanta's 3–2 victory. "I don't remember that it ever happened before, although I'm sure it must have," he said with a smile afterward, trying to recall the last time the hitter in front of him had been issued a free pass. "I'm sure Eddie Mathews was walked a few times when I hit behind him in Milwaukee. I'm not about to second-guess Walt Alston, though. That man has been right too many times."

As Aaron heated up and fattened his average, Evans began to see better pitches. Once he learned how to pull the ball, the homers came in bunches. Johnson, who hit behind Aaron, experienced a power surge, too. After joining the club from Baltimore, he and Aaron spoke in great detail about how to be a successful hitter in Atlanta's ballpark. After a few weeks, Johnson also found himself launching balls out of the stadium. "It was the greatest thing that ever happened to me in baseball," Johnson said after the season. "And the big reason was joining Aaron. He helped make me a better hitter.

"Just being able to talk to Hank helped," he added. "I've learned to be more aggressive at the plate, and I don't think it's any coincidence that our whole club is aggressive. The feeling around here, and I think it begins with Aaron, is that we are up there to attack the ball, and having that feeling is half the battle."

For pitchers opposing Atlanta, the Braves' aggressive new approach made the team a troublesome one to face. The middle of the order could go deep at any time. By May 21, in fact, when Aaron clubbed his 12th homer of the season, he, Johnson, and Evans had all reached double figures. For Aaron, this was a tremendous accomplishment, considering that he was playing in only two-thirds of Atlanta's games. True to his word, he took himself out of the lineup whenever he saw fit, typically once during each series, especially when a day game followed a night game. To further rest the aging slugger, Mathews moved him to left field where the throws were easier and runners were less likely to test his arm, which was now below average.

As the season wore on and the mail kept coming in, Aaron began to notice an increase in the volume and viciousness of the negative letters he was receiving. Carla Kolin, the personal secretary the Braves had hired for Aaron, handled as many as 3,000 letters a day, and an alarmingly high percentage could only be described as hate mail. Finally, Aaron did something out of character: he went to the press. "Five years ago, I probably would have walked away from it, and said nothing," Aaron told reporters. "But now I just feel I've taken all I can."

Though he had made mention of hate mail in his interview with Al Thomy, it was not until the 1973 season was in progress that the media ran with the story. It quickly made headlines across the country.

No one could blame Aaron for venting his frustrations. As demonstrated in *I Had a Hammer*, the racist taunts and threats offered by some fans were of a most vile nature. The book provides one example after another of letters that called Aaron a "nigger" or a "jungle bunny." While most of the missives denigrated the slugger only, some attacked his family, too. "I didn't realize how many sick Americans we had," he said in *Hank Aaron . . . 714 and Beyond!* "I'm amazed that the post office would even deliver some of the filthy stuff written on open postcards."

Reading every piece of mail would have been impossible, but Aaron asked Kolin to keep all of the correspondence on file nonetheless—at least the ones she did not have to turn over to authorities. The letters, including their almost comical spelling and grammatical errors, served as important reminders not only of the challenge before Aaron on the field, but also of the battle for equality that so many others before him had waged. "Well, I'm not going to stop because of this," he said. "Put it this way: The more they push me, the more I want the record."

Aaron reiterated those feelings after the season in an interview with the *Sporting News*. "I decided that the best way to shut up the kind of people who wrote those letters was to have a good year," he said. "The letters, I would say, inspired me."

Finding inspiration in the rude way Braves fans treated him in Atlanta was a more difficult task. As Wayne Minshew described in the *Sporting News*, the personal attacks that rained down on Aaron in Atlanta Stadium were just as savage as the hate mail. "Most of the abuse at the park comes from the right field stands," he wrote before Aaron switched to left. "He hears the old, sick cry of 'Nigger!' He hears, 'You are not as good as Babe Ruth.' And he hears somebody calling him an S.O.B. Aaron gives the initials when he says it, for he isn't ready to join his taunters in the gutter—yet."

As far as Aaron was concerned, the lack of support he received in Atlanta was more hurtful than any nasty letters from faceless, and often nameless, fans. "I didn't expect the fans to give me a standing ovation every time I stepped on the field, but I thought a few of them might come over to my side as I approached Ruth," he said in *I Had a Hammer*. "At the very least, I felt I had earned the right not to be verbally abused and racially ravaged in my home ballpark. I felt I had earned the right to be treated like a human being in the city that was supposed to be too busy to hate. The way I saw it, the only thing Atlanta was too busy for was baseball. It didn't seem to give a damn about the Braves, and it seemed the only thing that mattered about the home run record was that a nigger was about to step out of line and break it."

Just as displeasing were the embarrassingly small crowds that showed up each night at Atlanta Stadium. Aaron interpreted the sparse attendance as a sign of how little the people in Atlanta truly cared for him. Feeling more and more abandoned, he suggested in the *Sporting News* that his days with the Braves might be numbered. "I try to pass it off as ignorance, but the more it continues it gets to the point that you say, 'What's the use?" said a clearly distraught Aaron. "I've enjoyed playing in Atlanta. . . . I've loved playing here, but when you get this hatred and resentment . . ."

Fans around the rest of the country must have been stunned by Atlanta's disregard for its superstar. Aaron received standing ovations everywhere he appeared during road trips. In Houston, Astro management posted a message of support on the scoreboard: Mr. Aaron . . . for every one of those bad letters you receive, there are thousands pulling for you. Good luck in your homer quest . . . after you leave the Astrodome.

Aaron appreciated such gestures. Luck, however, was one thing the slugger did not need in 1973 to hit home runs. Whether swinging for the fences or not, he found himself in a nice groove. On June 9, Aaron slammed two homers, numbers 687 and 688, which put him very near the pace necessary to overtake Ruth by season's end. Several weeks later, in a wonderful bit of foreshadowing, Aaron hit the 693rd long ball of his career off the Dodgers' Al Downing in Atlanta. And he did this all in what was not exactly a "homer-happy" season. On the contrary, aside from Aaron, Evans, and Johnson, the only National Leaguers putting up big numbers were Willie Stargell, Bobby Bonds, and Greg Luzinski.

By then, speculation about when and how Aaron would break Ruth's record was running rampant. And according to Bowie Kuhn, it had gone far enough. The commissioner arrived at this decision in June after the Associated Press conducted a survey of NL pitchers asking how they would react with Aaron at bat and the record on the line. For the most part, each answered honestly, which did not bother Kuhn. What irritated the commissioner was how many indicated they would have no misgivings about surrendering the historic blast. Some went as far to say they would welcome the opportunity. "I'd throw a medium fastball right down the pike," said Reggie Cleveland of the Cardinals. "If he's going to get it off somebody, it might as well be me."

Larry Dierker of the Astros and Andy Messersmith and Pete Richert of the Dodgers echoed those sentiments. So did Phil Hennigan of the Mets, who said, "I'd almost tell him what's coming . . . a half-speed fastball right down the middle . . . just like batting practice. I'd be a fool not to if I wanted people to remember my name."

To some pitchers, including Hennigan's teammate Tom Seaver, such comments bordered on blasphemy. As one player squarely in Kuhn's corner, Seaver called it a "disservice" to intentionally lay one down Main Street for Aaron. "He worked to hit all of his other homers, and I knew he wanted to hit the one that broke the record the same way he hit all the others," Seaver wrote in 1974. "Besides, the pitcher giving up the record-breaking homer is insignificant. The whole meaning of the event is right there at home plate."

As soon as the AP story hit the papers, Kuhn acted to quell the reaction to it. On June 18, he fired off a letter to all NL clubs airing his feelings on the matter and setting policy for how he would handle any ensuing disciplinary situations:

> *I am greatly disturbed by press stories quoting some of our pitchers as saying or implying that they would be willing to groove a pitch to Henry Aaron to help him in his pursuit of the record for total home runs.*
>
> *While I recognize the possibility of misquotation, I must remind you that any such conduct would violate the requirements of Major League Rule 21 that every player must give his best efforts toward the winning of any baseball game in which he is involved.*
>
> *To do otherwise will result in a long-term suspension.*
>
> *Since the possibility of a misunderstanding of Rule 21 may exist in both leagues, all clubs are*

> *hereby directed to review this subject with all your team personnel immediately and to warn them that suspension will follow where anyone intentionally fails to give his best efforts.*
>
> *You should know that each of the pitchers so quoted in the press is being individually warned. I might add that nothing will be permitted which would tarnish the achievements of a truly great player such as Henry Aaron.*

Not surprisingly, Kuhn only added to the controversy. His letter was picked up by a number of national publications, which drew even more attention to the pitchers in question. Aaron, for one, believed Kuhn mishandled the situation. "I've thought about this, and I think what the commissioner should have done was consult each one privately," he said. "I'm sure they were just talking."

Several days later, Aaron did some "talking" of his own, poking fun at Kuhn after a game against the Mets in which he launched two homers. "Neither pitch was a strike," he told reporters. "The first was hit off a low, change-up curveball. The second was off a fastball, wide. I hope Commissioner Kuhn was watching. Neither one of those pitches was down the middle."

An interesting side note to the controversy was that several pitchers uttered similar comments some six months earlier and no one seemed to notice. During the off-season, Aaron had hosted a bowling tournament in Atlanta to raise funds for research for sickle-cell anemia. Among those who attended were pitchers Claude Osteen of the Dodgers and Danny Frisella whom the Braves had just acquired from the Mets.

When asked if he would mind giving up number 714, Osteen cracked, "It might be the only way I'll be remembered. When people think about Hank Aaron breaking Babe Ruth's record, they'll think of me at the same time." For the record, at the time the Dodger hurler had served up more gopher balls to Aaron than any other active player.

Frisella answered the same question with equal amounts of humor. "My only disappointment is," he said about joining the Braves, "I wanted to be the guy who threw Aaron's 714th home run."

Aaron's sarcasm toward the commissioner provided further evidence of the growing rift between the two. The slugger had never forgotten Kuhn's seeming indifference when he registered his 3,000th hit in Cincinnati back in 1971. In the ensuing months and years, Aaron found it more and more difficult to hide his bitterness. From his perspective, his quickly deteriorating relationship with Kuhn made little sense. Here was the game's biggest name, about to set the game's most significant record, and he could barely summon the composure to act civilly to the game's head man. Amazingly, the situation would only worsen.

Going into a home series against Philadelphia in mid-July, Aaron stood one home run away from 700. Obviously, no one but Ruth had ever reached this milestone (Willie Mays, playing in his final season, would hit six more round-trippers to finish with a total of 660). Consequently, as Aaron approached his 700th, the excitement surrounding the event rose to a fevered pitch. The Braves, for example, planned on commemorating the blast in grand style. The team announced that, in return for the ball, it would present the fan that caught the historic shot with 700 silver dollars. Every homer slammed by Aaron in Atlanta thereafter would fetch its corresponding sum. Additionally, all fans in attendance for number 700 would receive a special scroll and medallion verifying their presence in Atlanta Stadium.

Not everyone, however, shared the team's enthusiasm for the momentous occasion. Those opposed to Aaron voiced their opinions as loudly as ever. The phone lines on radio shows lit up like a scoreboard in a slugfest, with callers belittling Aaron and detailing why he was less of a player than the Babe. Bumper stickers disparaging Aaron were also very popular. The top-seller read, "Aaron is Ruth-less."

By now, Aaron had learned to ignore such rebukes. Dealing with Kuhn, however, was an entirely different matter. The closer Aaron got to number 700, the more distance the commissioner put between them. Therefore, it came as no surprise that Kuhn was nowhere to be found on July 21 when Aaron turned on a 1–1 fastball from Phillies' left-hander Ken Brett and drove the pitch out of the park for the 700th home run of his career.

The 2,000 or so fans in Atlanta Stadium who watched Aaron round the bases saw the stoic slugger flash a quick smile. A University of North Carolina sophomore named Robert Winborne, who had purchased a ticket in the left field bleachers, emerged from the scuffle with ball in hand. The $700 no doubt came in handy at school (but he'd probably like to have that ball back today). Aaron received a standing ovation, which did not end until his second curtain call.

After the game, a frustrated Aaron hardly felt like celebrating. He expected to receive personal congratulations from both Kuhn and President Nixon. Instead, he heard nary a word from either. "President Nixon and Commissioner Kuhn sort of let me down," Aaron said. "I thought they both should have sent me telegrams of congratulations. The president has often called football coaches after they've won a big game. But not many people hit 700 home runs. And I think Bowie Kuhn, as Commissioner of Baseball, had an obligation too."

The aftermath of number 700 left Aaron torn. He felt equal amounts of excitement and relief knowing that he was now on "Ruth's street, turning into his driveway." But Kuhn's reaction bothered him. Granted, the commissioner offered an excuse, saying he had planned all along on congratulating Aaron in person at the All-Star Game, which was only a few weeks away. But his absence from the historic occasion in Atlanta was conspicuous nonetheless, and it was one of the reasons that Aaron refused to turn the home run ball over to the Hall of Fame. Even more telling of Aaron's mind-set, however, was that for one of the few times in his career, he allowed his feelings off the field to affect his performance on it. "The whole situation took something out of me," he said in *I Had a Hammer*. "I think I let up a little while after that, and suddenly I stopped hitting home runs. It was ten days before I hit my 701st and more than two weeks after that before I hit number 702."

The pressure of the chase had officially begun to bother Aaron. Fans wanted a piece of him everywhere he went. In Houston, autograph seekers and well-wishers learned his hotel room number and spent two days knocking on his door before he fled to the trainer's room at the Astrodome where he was able to get some rest. Eventually, it became so commonplace for the slugger to steal some shut-eye at the ballpark that the Braves made sure a cot was always available for Aaron at home and on the road.

The media pursued the slugger just as aggressively as the fans. In *I Had a Hammer*, Aaron recalled being trailed by three boats of reporters and photographers during a fishing trip in Mobile. Another time, Tom Brokaw and a camera crew from NBC followed him for three weeks straight. Afterward, Aaron joked that during that time period he saw more of Brokaw than of Eddie Mathews.

Of all the consequences of the increased attention, Aaron lamented the loss of camaraderie in the Atlanta clubhouse as much as any. Teammates quite naturally shied away from him, either not wanting to intrude on his spotlight or hoping not to get sucked into the media vortex. Aaron understood their behavior and hardly blamed them for it. But that did not mean that he wished any less for his life to return to normal. "I missed my teammates," he stated despondently.

Roger Maris knew exactly what Aaron was going through. He found facing scores of reporters day in and day out to be pure torture during the 1961 season. He literally lost his hair in clumps, developed bags under his eyes, and began snapping at reporters whom he had once treated with cordiality. They responded by raking him over the coals, questioning his character, and twisting his innocent jokes into tasty column fodder. Now, as Aaron approached the Babe's all-time homer mark, he was reliving Maris's nightmare. Retired to a quiet life in Gainesville, Florida, where he owned a beer distributorship, Maris answered questions almost every day from writers working on stories about Aaron. Older and wiser, he handled the situation with great aplomb, demonstrating the grace and charm he had been unable to muster 12 years earlier. "I'll be glad when he does it," he said of Aaron. "The girls in the office are taking calls from the press and it requires a lot of their time."

At one point, when asked if he ever reflected on the '61 campaign by reading old clippings, Maris responded, "Once was enough. Maybe when I'm old and senile, I'll go back and look at them." This time around, his deadpan sense of humor played much better in the newspapers.

Clearly, if only to restore peace in his life, Maris was rooting for Aaron and showed his support for the slugger by attending a Braves game in July. For Maris, who retired after the 1968 season, it was the first time he had set foot in a big-league ballpark that year. The two met before the contest, sharing a brief conversation. The meeting provided a wonderful photo opportunity, but no earth-shattering revelations. "I don't think Hank needs any advice," said Maris. "He's a big boy and knows how to care for himself."

Actually, Aaron might have accepted counsel on how to reverse his sudden power outage. For 15 straight days beginning in August, he failed to go deep. His slump between homers 700 and 701 had lasted more than 30 at bats, which seemed like an eternity to him. Now he pressed even more at the plate. The Braves were back on the road and playing in front of packed houses every day. Aaron hated to disappoint the thousands of fans who came to the ballpark only to see him. Finally, on August 16 in Chicago, he snapped out of it, belting number 702 over the ivy-covered wall at Wrigley Field. A 15-year-old boy in the bleachers grabbed the shot and headed to Atlanta's locker room after the game for an autograph. Though Aaron wanted the ball for his own collection, he signed it for the youngster and sent him on his way. "I would have liked to have it for myself," he said. "But I don't blame the kid for keeping it."

In Montreal the following day, Aaron blasted number 703, which tied him with Stan Musial for the all-time lead in extra-base hits. Aaron appeared less than enthusiastic afterward, however, at a loss to explain his offensive inconsistency. "I wish I could find the answer to tell you why I go two weeks without hitting a homer and then hit two in two days," Aaron told a group of reporters. "I just don't know why these things happen. It's nothing that I'm doing or not doing."

After the series against the Expos, the Braves returned to Atlanta where attendance inexplicably continued to be low. Crowds rarely surpassed 10,000, and all too often no more than a few thousand came through the turnstiles at Atlanta Stadium. Those who showed up at games usually did so with either fishnets or baseball gloves. Each home run hit by Aaron was worth more than 700 silver dollars. To many, making a quick buck was a bigger draw than watching Hammerin' Hank make history.

"Oh, you're disappointed at the small crowds, but being a professional, you have to go out and play whether you have 1,300 or 52,000," said Aaron. "I feel 1,300 are entitled to see you play, if that's all there are, just as hard as you always play."

Aaron publicly brushed aside the paltry attendance figures. But privately, he felt insulted. Local high school football games were drawing bigger crowds than the Braves. That said it all to baseball's soon-to-be home run champ.

Besides the opportunity to see Aaron during his historic pursuit, fans in Atlanta missed several other memorable moments by staying away from the ballpark in 1973. On August 5 against the Padres, for example, Phil Niekro tossed the first no-hitter in the history of Atlanta Stadium. Only 8,748 witnessed the gem. The knuckleballer, who dedicated the effort to his ailing father, surrendered only one hard-hit shot, a two hopper off the bat of rookie Dave Winfield in the eighth inning. Second baseman Chuck Goggin, subbing for Dave Johnson, fielded the chance cleanly and threw on to first baseman Frank Tepedino for the out. "I never had a no-hitter, except once in a sandlot game," said Niekro afterward. "I like the feeling."

The feeling around baseball entering September was that Aaron had a realistic shot at tying or passing the Babe before season's end. With 706 homers, the Atlanta slugger needed eight to pull even with Ruth. No one doubted he could pump out that many in a month, despite his recent struggles at the plate (and that he was not playing every day). In the *Sporting News*, however, Aaron kidded that he might have other things on his mind. Now hitting .290, Aaron had seen his average steadily climb to respectability after his slow start. "Maybe I'll go to my choker swing and bat .300," he said. "Forget the home runs."

No one of course, especially fans in opposing stadiums, could forget the home runs. In early September, the Braves embarked on their final road trip of the season. It was yet another cross-country journey to the West Coast (an occupational hazard for the Braves, an eastern team playing in the NL West), which the players hated. Competing in the same division as Los Angeles, San Francisco, and San Diego, the team logged more flight time than any other squad in the league. The travel tended to wear down players, including the aging Aaron. Going back to that first train ride he took as a teenager to join the Indianapolis Clowns in North Carolina, he had never enjoyed this part of baseball. In his estimation, the advent of air travel had done nothing to improve the situation. After slamming number 710 in the last game of the San Francisco series off Don Carrithers, for instance, Aaron could not summon the energy to play the following day when the Braves opened a three-gamer in L.A.

At home, his absence from the lineup would have rankled only a few thousand. On the road, Aaron had to answer to packed stadiums. "More than 40,000 people came to Dodger Stadium in Los Angeles hoping to see him get closer to Ruth's mark," wrote Jerry Brondfield in *Hank Aaron . . . 714 and Beyond!* "They saw Henry Aaron step up to home plate, but it was before the game when, as Captain of the Braves, it was his duty to hand a lineup card to the umpire.

"The lineup card did not carry his name that night. Henry hoped the fans would understand. 'You can do just so much with a 39-year-old body,' he explained by way of apology to the fans."

By the time the Braves had landed in Los Angeles, procedures were in place to ensure that each baseball used when Aaron came to bat could be officially identified. This was because every long ball he hit from here on in promised to fetch a high price on the open market, and Kuhn wanted to guard against the likelihood of fraud. Indeed, the commissioner knew that fans would go to just about any lengths to profit from Aaron's chase. Donald Davidson, in fact, had been dealing with such deceptions all year. In recent weeks, for instance, he had received scores of baseballs from fans asking for Aaron's signature. Many of the autograph seekers claimed that Babe Ruth had already signed the ball in question and that Aaron's John Hancock would put the finishing touches on a cherished memento. But Davidson was not so gullible. A batboy for the Braves during Ruth's final year in Boston, he had seen the slugger's autograph up close on countless occasions. "Only thing, some aren't authentic," he said of the supposed signatures. "I know how Babe signed his name."

To ensure the authenticity of every ball Aaron hit out of the park after number 710, each time the slugger stepped into the box, the home plate umpire introduced into play balls encoded with an indelible mark visible only under a special light. The first time Dodger pitcher Charlie Hough picked one up, he looked at it inquisitively and joked, "I thought it would be so different that maybe it would have a heartbeat." The knuckleballer was not quite so cheerful later when he was roundly booed by his hometown faithful after walking Aaron on four fluttering pitches.

The keeper of the Aaron baseballs was Atlanta batboy Gary Stensland. The 16-year-old high school student carried several dozen with him every game, placing his bounty in a bag identified with a piece of white tape that read "Aaron." Whenever the slugger strode to plate, Stensland ran four or five balls out to the home plate umpire. A short delay always ensued, adding to the drama of Aaron's impending at bat.

On September 22, against southpaw Dave Roberts of the Astros, Aaron belted a deep fly over Bob Watson's head in left. The drive soared over the fence, caromed off an obstruction in the Astrodome stands, and bounced directly back to the Houston outfielder. Watson picked up the ball and tossed it into the Braves' bullpen as Aaron circled the bases for the 712th time in his career.

Atlanta finally returned home in late September with Aaron stuck on 712. When the team landed at Hartsfield International Airport, for the first time in a long while, Aaron actually felt welcome. During the road trip, Mayor Sam Massell and Chamber of Commerce President-Elect Bradley Currey Jr. had kicked off a citywide campaign called "Atlanta Salutes Hank Aaron." According to Currey, the city hoped to accomplish three goals: "to commemorate Hank's actual breaking of the record, to honor Hank in a perpetuating manner and, finally, to let people all over the world know how proud Atlantans are of Hank Aaron."

The campaign put Aaron front and center all over the city. At the airport, an "Aaron Home-Run Countdown" barometer replaced the lighted sign that read "Welcome to Atlanta." The slugger's visage adorned a 12-by-25-foot billboard outside Atlanta Stadium, as well as on billboards in 20 other locations around the city. The Hank Aaron Scholarship Committee was created, announcing its plan to raise $100,000 for deserving, college-bound students. The chamber of commerce commissioned special artwork, which was promoted by local radio and television stations. Atlanta newspapers agreed to publish an insert saluting Aaron the following spring.

At the press conference launching the campaign, the mayor declared Aaron a "civic asset" and referred to him as the city's "greatest hero." Like many politicians of the early 1970s, however, Massell's words rang hollow. Atlanta, in fact, could not muster a sellout for any of the Braves' remaining home games.

The final home stand proved frustrating for Aaron. Though he needed only two homers to match Ruth's career total, his bat went silent. Aaron knew that drawing even with the Babe or setting the record outright would make the off-season much quieter and more pleasurable. Coming up one or two home runs short, on the other hand, would give the pressure that many more months to build. But long balls were hard to come by until Houston visited Atlanta on the last weekend of the season. On Saturday, September 28, lefty Jerry Reuss hung a breaking pitch to Aaron, which he promptly deposited in the left field seats. The homer gave the slugger an even 40 for the season, and with Johnson and Evans already above that total, they became the first trio of teammates in big-league history to each belt 40 or more.

Aaron joined Johnson and Evans after the game to talk with the media. Ever mindful of his teammates, he cut the interview session short when every question was directed at him. "Look, I wanted to share this with these guys," Aaron told the throng of reporters gathered before him. "If nobody is interested in that, then the press conference is over."

Interestingly, before his home run against Dave Roberts in the Astrodome, Aaron had hit 11 consecutive off righties. Now, with his homer off Reuss, he had gone deep twice in a row off left-handers. Many thought that bode well for Aaron, since Atlanta was scheduled to face Roberts again on Sunday, September 29, the last day of the regular season. But Aaron saw things differently. Sunday's forecast was cool and wet—weather that did not usually produce long balls. On top of that, Roberts was the type of pitcher who gave Aaron fits. Not a particularly hard thrower, the southpaw rarely challenged a hitter, preferring to nibble around the corners of the plate. Patience was the key against Roberts, and Aaron had become a notoriously impatient batter.

Another distraction for Aaron was his batting average, which was just a few points from .300. He admitted later, in fact, how tempting it was to concentrate only on eclipsing this plateau. Fans had grumbled all season that he was washed up. The criticism reached its apex in June when Aaron's average was still in the mid-.200s. Now he had the opportunity to silence his critics. "If I'd had to choose on Sunday between getting one more home run and hitting .300, it would have been a tough call," Aaron conceded in *I Had a Hammer*. "The best plan was to hit the ball where nobody could catch it, the best place being the other side of the left field fence."

Getting the ball out of the infield, however, proved to be difficult enough. Aaron beat out a dribbler his first at bat and then blooped a single into shallow center field his next time up. Standing in against Roberts once again in the sixth, the slugger hit a bounder through the box that sneaked through for another single. The third hit put Aaron far enough above .300 that he could look for a pitch to hit out of the park in what would likely be his final plate appearance in the eighth inning. The only problem was that fireballer Don Wilson had replaced Roberts. Though Aaron loved to hit against hard throwers, he had never felt comfortable in the box facing Wilson. The right-hander threw a cut fastball with late movement that Aaron had never been able to handle. Usually against Wilson, he found himself walking back to the dugout and shaking his head after recording yet another weak out. Much to Aaron's displeasure, history repeated itself on this dreary afternoon in Atlanta when Wilson induced him to pop out to second baseman Tommy Helms. His season over, Aaron headed out to his position in left for the top of the ninth.

But there was one more twist to the drama of the 1973 campaign. As Aaron emerged from the dugout, the fans in Atlanta rose to their feet in thunderous applause. It was the last thing the slugger expected to hear, and he has never forgotten the gesture. "There have been a lot of standing ovations for a lot of baseball players, but this was one for the ages as far as I was concerned," he said. "I couldn't believe that I was Hank Aaron and this was Atlanta, Georgia. I thought I'd never see the day."

Aaron's teammates and family were just as moved. "It gave everyone in the ballpark chills," said Johnson. "It showed the immense respect they had for the man."

Aaron's father, Herbert, who was seated in a special box seat next to the Braves' dugout, was near tears. "It made me feel so good to see all those people standing," he said. "It was like he'd hit a home run. To do what they did after he popped up was a great, great honor."

The greatest honor of all, however, breaking Ruth's record, still awaited. But Aaron would have to endure six more months of torturous anticipation before that opportunity would come.

CHAPTER SIX:

NOWHERE TO HIDE

IN 1973, BY THE TIME THE DOG DAYS OF THE SUMMER had given way to the cooler temperatures of the fall, few stories were powerful enough to bump Henry Aaron from the spotlight. On September 20 in Houston, for instance, Billie Jean King struck a blow for women everywhere with her emasculating defeat of Bobby Riggs in the "Battle of the Sexes." But two days later, when Aaron put on his own show in the Astrodome, hitting number 712 off Dave Roberts, the media quickly refocused its attention on the home run chase.

This pattern repeated itself over and over again in the ensuing weeks and months. Even Jack Benny, who called himself the world's most famous 39-year-old, weighed in on Aaron, who possessed a birth certificate that proved conclusively that his next birthday was his 40th. "That guy is number one right now," said the beloved comedian. "I'm really pulling for him."

For so many to be caught up in Aaron's race to catch Ruth was truly amazing, especially because the final months of 1973 produced some of the biggest headlines in recent years. On October 16, OPEC instituted an oil embargo against the U.S. and other Western industrialized countries. Over the course of the next four months, the price of crude oil would triple, causing some of the greatest consumer unrest in the history of America.

A week after OPEC's crippling move, the noose around Richard Nixon's neck began to tighten. First, the Court of Appeals ordered him to turn over the Watergate tapes. Then, days before the House introduced eight impeachment resolutions, public scorn against Nixon increased further when he dismissed Archibald Cox during the villainous "Saturday Night Massacre." Next, adding insult to perjury, Spiro Agnew was forced to resign as vice president. Finally, while on a trip to Disney World, the president made his infamous "I'm not a crook" speech, telling 400 newspaper editors at an AP convention that he welcomed the intrusive examination of his office.

The world of sports journalism was not hurting for stories either. Willie Mays announced he would retire. Charles O. Finley, irate over defensive replacement Mike Andrews's two errors in Game Two of the World Series, "fired" his second baseman, only to be ordered by Bowie Kuhn to reinstate the infielder. Weeks later, the great Secretariat ran his final race. In mid-December, O. J. Simpson surpassed 2,000 yards, becoming the first running back in NFL history to eclipse the magic mark. The year ended with Houston outfielder Cesar Cedeno being jailed in the Dominican Republic on involuntary manslaughter charges.

Despite it all, Aaron remained a fixture in the headlines. And, as he admitted in *Chasing the Dream*, the pressure became almost too much for him to handle. "I think I was kind of numb to it all," he said. "It wasn't about being sad or happy. It was about surviving."

Survival was made somewhat easier by the support of Billye Williams, who became Billye Aaron in November. The couple sneaked down to Jamaica for what they thought would be a private ceremony. But after granting exclusive photo rights to *Jet* magazine, word of the wedding location leaked to the rest of the media. Aaron's quiet honeymoon quickly exploded into a frenzy of cameras and reporters.

As cohost of *Today in Georgia*, however, Billye was accustomed to such intrusions, which was a comfort to Aaron. He called her a "godsend" in *I Had a Hammer* and said she was fully prepared for the demands of her new life in *Chasing the Dream*. The newlyweds worked as a team, trying to keep their lives as normal as possible. Their attempts were mostly futile. The chase was all anyone cared about when they spoke to Aaron.

"I have hopes of having the same type of year in 1974 that I had this year," he said at one point. "I'm disappointed I didn't make it, but I have all winter to go home and rest up."

But deep down, Aaron knew rest would be virtually impossible to come by. Reporters and fans hounded him everywhere he went. Endorsement opportunities came flooding in. Hollywood and television wanted a piece of him. Rest in the off-season? Hardly.

If Aaron had clung to any notions about ducking the media, they had been crushed immediately upon entering the clubhouse after Atlanta's final game of the season. No less than 100 reporters laid in wait for him. "Well, it's over," he said as he sat down to answer questions.

"I feel good and my legs feel good," Aaron continued. "As long as my legs feel good, I can do the job. At the beginning of the season, I had 10 homers and was hitting about .250. People said I was swinging for homers, which was untrue. I felt I was in shape, but I really wasn't when we broke spring camp.

"About the middle of the season, my legs got stronger and I felt a lot better. To be very frank, I'm pleased about this season. I felt like I contributed something to the ball club rather than having people say I'm thinking only about myself."

Besides the obvious questions, reporters also asked Aaron about Houston pitcher Larry Dierker, who had claimed earlier in the year that he would groove one to Aaron with Ruth's mark on the line. The two had faced each other on the last Saturday of the year, in the same game that Aaron belted his 713th against Jerry Reuss. "I'll say this, Dierker was one of the pitchers who made the statement about throwing the ball down the middle if I get to 713," said Aaron. "Well, you could see for yourself he was throwing harder to me than anybody else, so there's no truth in that at all."

There was truth, however, in the belief that for one of the few times in his baseball life, Aaron suffered from horrible timing. Indeed, finishing the season on number 713 set the stage for an off-season of constant disruptions and media hype. More than ever, Aaron would rely on his bodyguard, Calvin Wardlaw, who had been hired by the Braves to watch over him. The idea of employing outside security was proposed midway through the 1973 season. Ever protective of his privacy, Aaron hesitated initially, but ultimately relented. Though he shrugged off many of the threats mailed to him, he felt he could not take any chances. "Once in a while, I'd think about what an easy target I was if someone wanted to do something crazy," Aaron said.

There was also the fear of what might happen to his family. Aaron stayed away from his children for weeks on end, afraid that they would become ensnared in the turmoil. When he did see them, having Wardlaw nearby provided a comforting safety net. In other instances, he asked Barbara to make sure the kids did not stray from the front of the house when they played outside. He had his reasons. At one point, in fact, Aaron's oldest daughter, Gaile, became the target of a kidnapping plot. She was informed of the threat by federal agents in Nashville, where she attended Fisk University. When Aaron learned of the news, his emotions ranged from shock to dismay to relief.

Wardlaw, a major in the Atlanta police department, acted as Aaron's shadow and tried to keep him on an even keel. During games he sat in the stands, either behind the dugout or home plate, keeping a vigilant eye on any fan who looked the least bit suspicious. As the season progressed and the pressure intensified, Wardlaw stuck even closer to Aaron, accompanying him to and from the stadium. Always at the officer's side were a pair of high-powered binoculars and a .38-caliber snub-nose.

Also among Wardlaw's duties was sifting through Aaron's hate mail, particularly the death threats. Most of the letters he turned over to the FBI. But years later, Wardlaw admitted he kept some for himself. "One of them, which I still have, was written on toilet paper," he said in an interview in the *Sporting News*. "It had a picture of an ape or gorilla on it and said 'Nigger, you'll never be as great as the Babe,' something to that effect. It was half a paragraph.

"Another one ironically was threatening to kill Hank if they didn't release Patty Hearst. But most of them were 'nigger' and stuff, saying he couldn't fill the Babe's shoes."

Though Aaron appreciated the feeling of security provided by a bodyguard, he hated being watched around the clock. It was not that he disliked Wardlaw. On the contrary, the two men, both thoughtful and soft spoken, got along very well. But Aaron was a proud man who seldom relied on those around him.

"The most miserable thing in the world is to walk around with somebody having to monitor everything you do," he once observed. "It wasn't so much making adjustments; it was always having someone shadowing you. Personally, I'm a loner. It was a little bit difficult for me."

When it was his choice, Aaron did not mind having the eyes of the nation fixed upon him. Sometimes, in fact, it seemed that he truly enjoyed his status as a national celebrity. Before Game One of the 1973 World Series between the Mets and A's, he became the first active player to throw out the first pitch. He embarked on a cross-country banquet tour that saw him honored in cities from

Denver to Chicago to Boston. Georgia Governor Jimmy Carter made him an official admiral in Georgia's unofficial navy. He flew to Mobile for "Henry Aaron Day" and to Hollywood to visit Sammy Davis Jr., who wanted to discuss a movie based on Aaron's life. During their meeting, the entertainer offered to pay $25,000 for the home run ball that broke Ruth's record. Aaron declined.

The slugger, on the other hand, rarely turned down an opportunity to appear on television. He worked the entire talk-show circuit, sitting down to chat with some of the biggest stars of the day, including David Frost, Merv Griffin, and Mike Douglas.

One of his funniest moments occurred on *The Flip Wilson Show*. Looking happy and relaxed, Aaron clowned his way through a skit that had Wilson playing the proprietor of a sporting goods store and him a customer looking to purchase a bat, ball, and glove for his nephew. When the total for the equipment came to $7.14, Aaron found himself a penny short. "Would you settle for 7.13?" he asked with a wide smile. "No way," responded Wilson, "Would you?" Aaron and the comedian then burst into laughter.

Aaron also seemed at ease when he and Billye appeared together on *The Dinah Shore Show*. At the urging of Shore, the couple actually broke into song, crooning, "And stars fell on Alabama last night." Aaron showcased a surprisingly harmonious singing voice.

Along with Aaron's increased visibility came the promise of even more lucrative endorsement opportunities. For several years, he had been attempting to cash in on his fame. A few years earlier, he got his first national ad campaign when he starred in an Oh Henry! candy bar commercial. Most memorable was his Wheaties television commercial. "Henry, you didn't get your Wheaties," went the catchy refrain as canned clips of Aaron showed him moving sluggishly in the field and at the plate. Other endorsers included Hillerich & Bradsby Co., maker of Louisville Slugger, and The

Equitable. Both companies featured Aaron in print ads that ran in the *Sporting News*, among other publications.

But those deals were small potatoes compared to what awaited Aaron. Poised to become baseball's all-time home run king, Aaron was a hotter commodity than ever. In December of 1973, he announced that he had signed with the William Morris Agency, the nation's preeminent representation firm. Already the company had lured Mark Spitz and Secretariat into its clutches. Now it pledged to make Aaron more money in his next couple of seasons than he had earned in the previous 20 years. William Morris lived up to its claim almost immediately when Aaron inked a deal for $1 million to endorse televisions for Magnavox.

Most people around the country, including those in the media, cheered Aaron, acknowledging that the spoils of his success were overdue. "It pleases me that Henry is finally getting the kind of recognition from the sports press that he has long deserved," wrote Tom Seaver in *How I Would Pitch to Babe Ruth*.

But some, most notably Pat Conroy, winced at the prospect of Aaron becoming a corporate shill. In an article in *Sport*, the writer questioned whether the William Morris Agency would strip Aaron of all his humor and heart.

"You suspect that the William Morris people search for small pieces of personality in their clients and like bone fragments have them surgically stripped away," he wrote. "You can only cling to the hope that after Hank has been packaged, programmed, ticketed and punched, a little of Mobile, Alabama, will linger along with a lot of the quiet, decent man who played this game so patiently and so well for so long. But even if Hank does undergo a William Morris lobotomy, the agency does a splendid job of making their clients very unlike you and me. At a winter press conference, Hank announced that he had sold himself lock, stock and jockstrap to Magnavox Corporation for one million dollars. After the consummation of the deal, no one except William Morris . . . knows how much Hank Aaron is actually worth, but rumor has it that he had entered secret negotiations to buy England."

The publishers of the annual guide books certainly knew the value of Aaron's picture. Shots of him appeared on the covers of *Major League Baseball 1974* and *Baseball Stars of 1974*, both of which offered special features on Aaron. The first asked the question, "Can Anyone Top Hank?" The answer was about as deep as an owner's pockets at the arbitration table: "It took quite a man to top the record left on the books by Babe Ruth. And it's going to take quite a man to top the one that will be left on the books by Hank Aaron."

The modest Aaron, however, seemed convinced he would eventually be nothing more than a footnote in the annals of baseball history. "The legend of Babe Ruth is indestructible," he said in the same story. "It won't matter whether I hit 800 homers—there will never be another Babe Ruth as far as the baseball public is concerned. And some day, some young guy will come along and hit 850 homers and I'll just be a fellow who hit 750 or whatever total I finish with."

Dan Schlossberg's article in *Baseball Stars of 1974* regurgitated most of what had already been written of Aaron. So did Tommy Kay's *Big Book of Baseball*, though the publication made one interesting observation: "Because of the immense publicity accompanying the Aaron home run department, Atlanta became the first team to our knowledge to ever prepare a special publicity brochure covering the activity of one individual player."

It was not surprising at all that sportswriters had begun to repeat one another when covering Aaron. What more was there to say? Every question imaginable had been asked of Aaron and he had answered them all. The home run record was the only thing on the mind of any baseball fan with a pulse. "We felt sorry for him," remembered teammate Tom House. "He had 35, 40 people following him everywhere he went."

As Aaron readied himself for spring training, he too could not help but think about the upcoming season, specifically his first at bats of the year. On the beach in Jamaica during his honeymoon, he envisioned facing Don Gullett or Jack Billingham of the Reds, the team Atlanta was scheduled to play on Opening Day in Cincinnati. After the 1973 campaign had ended, in fact, reporters had pressed Eddie Mathews on whether Aaron would be in the lineup in the first series, or wait to set the record in front of the fans in Atlanta. The Braves' manager thought he had smartly hedged his bets, suggesting Aaron would play Opening Day and then sit until the Braves returned home. "That gives both places a fair shake," he said. "If he hits two the first day, that's life."

Mathews's comments, however, had raised some eyebrows around baseball, most notably those in the commissioner's office. Inadvertently, the Atlanta skipper had stirred up one more storm of controversy. This one pitted Bowie Kuhn against Braves' owner Bill Bartholomay, who floated the idea that Aaron ride the bench for all three games of the opening series in Cincinnati. Once again, Aaron would find himself in the eye of a tempest.

CHAPTER SEVEN:

GENTLEMAN AL, CINCINNATI JACK, AND THE CURIOUS WORLD OF COMMISSIONER KUHN

AS THE FINAL DAYS OF FEBRUARY PEELED off the calendar in 1974, the world was becoming an increasingly complicated place. The American Cancer Society struck fear into the hearts and bowels of red-meat eaters with the announcement that it had found a link between beef consumption and colon cancer. Thanks to the Symbionese Liberation Army, kidnapping was now the preferred business practice among fanatical groups in America. Richard Nixon was bracing for the inevitable, as Chief U.S. District Court Judge John Sirica prepared to hand down indictments of administration bigwigs John Ehrlichman, H. R. Haldeman, Charles Colson, and John Mitchell for their roles in the Watergate coverup. And every night, television viewers were treated to at least one story about the energy crisis, complete with footage of endless gas lines and sound bytes from irate drivers.

It was getting so that the average person was afraid to turn on the tube.

Hank Aaron's world was no less complicated. At the end of February, he reported to spring training knowing full well what he would encounter there. From the moment he set foot in camp, the media swirl that had enveloped him all winter spun further out of control. How does it feel to surpass the Babe? When will you do it? Where will you do it? What's your favorite flavor of ice cream? Aaron was still willing to answer any question, no matter how inane or absurd. What irritated him was that there was little he could do to control the media circus forming around him. He knew it would continue to grow until he hit his two homers, and that would not be possible until the regular season began. Needless to say, Aaron could hardly wait.

Among other things, Aaron was disturbed by the effect his celebrity had on the Braves. It was one thing to watch it build over the course of a season, as it had during 1973. But spring training was neither the time nor the place for such a monumental distraction. This is a time for players to focus themselves on the season ahead. The younger men on the team need to sharpen their skills and determine how and where they fit into the mix; the veterans need to take stock of their careers and make the little adjustments required to hold their jobs for another year. This is when a team starts to establish chemistry, both on the field and in the locker room. Obviously, a certain amount of intimacy is required for this to happen. Players need to feel comfortable in the clubhouse. They need a place where they can be themselves—a place to form friendships, air their differences, tell dirty jokes and, of course, revel in all the disgusting habits—cursing, belching, and passing gas—of grown men playing a kids' game. And they need to do all this without worrying it will end up on the six o'clock news. In the spring of 1974, the Brave clubhouse was not this kind of place.

The players were used to having a handful of reporters around, but the newsmen were almost always people they knew and could trust. Now dozens of unfamiliar intruders were milling about with notepads, tape recorders, and television cameras. When reporters were unable to get to Aaron and ask him about breaking Ruth's record, they would ask the other players about it. When you are a 23-year-old rookie trying to make the team, how do you answer a question like that? The whole scene was overwhelming.

As reporters followed his every move and pressed around him whenever he stopped to sit down, Aaron realized that one of the things he loved most about his job had been taken away. He was no longer part of the easy fraternity of the clubhouse. Few outside of the game realized it, but he was an entirely different person in baseball's inner sanctum. Although Aaron was never the life of the party, he had become quick with a punch line. Through all the madness of 1973, in fact, he displayed a wry, keen sense of humor with his teammates, and he was either in on, or aware of, most of the Braves' off-the-field shenanigans. Now many players were subtly evading him. The process had started. The more in demand Aaron became, the more he was actually alone.

"Poor guy," wrote longtime *Atlanta Journal* columnist Furman Bisher on March 13, "there's nothing private for him anymore. He must feel like a streaker in slow motion down here. He's being guarded like a threatened heiress."

In *I Had a Hammer*, Aaron talked about the importance of having close friends on the Braves, including those in management, during the 1973 campaign. As the season wore on and the slugger inched closer to the record, he embraced allies in the clubhouse who helped deflect the growing pressure. "You find out who your real friends are during times like that," Aaron stated.

Outfielders Ralph Garr and Dusty Baker and catcher Paul Casanova were his closest friends. They always seemed able to see the humor in Aaron's pursuit of the Babe. Lew Burdette, now a coach with the team, surprised Aaron with his compassion. He and Aaron never had much to say to each other as teammates. In general, Burdette was more ornery than most pitchers, and specifically, as a born-and-bred West Virginian, he was not exactly enlightened when it came to dealing with the team's black players. Now he offered heartfelt support to Aaron without hesitation.

Bob Hope, Atlanta's head of public relations, handled the media with great poise and imagination, and for this he earned Aaron's eternal gratitude. He once stood in for Aaron when a dozen Japanese writers showed up unannounced at the ballpark. They left the session 30 minutes later with pages and pages of notes from one of the best interviews they had ever conducted.

On the other hand, Eddie Mathews, who shared a unique relationship with Aaron, found it impossible to maintain the same level of intimacy with his former teammate. He had to step out of the picture, or his team would have been a mess. There were simply too many people looking for a piece of Aaron, and too many people following his every move.

Commissioner Bowie Kuhn was among those keenly interested in Aaron's daily activities. On March 4, Kuhn met with Bill Bartholomay to discuss what was now a full-fledged controversy: would Aaron appear in any of the first three games of the season that were scheduled to be played in Cincinnati?

Public opinion was divided. Many supported Kuhn's somewhat dramatic position that the integrity of the game hung in the balance. Using "the best interests of baseball" as his rationale, the commissioner claimed it was Aaron's duty to hit in his customary third slot in the batting order and take his position in left field. Kuhn believed the good name of America's pastime depended on it.

It was an easy cause to champion, and old-line scribes from the Midwest to the East Coast to New England joined the fray on the commissioner's side. They were particularly abrasive in New York. Larry Merchant called the idea of benching Aaron an "insidious fix." Dick Young went even further, "Baseball has gone crooked. There is no delicate way of putting it."

In Atlanta, however, Furman Bisher skewered Kuhn, stating he was "trying to play baseball commissioner again." To some, Kuhn had earned the reputation as a leader in absentia—one who carefully picked his spots to get involved with the game and then did so with perfectly awful timing. "This is unadulterated meddling," Bisher wrote. "Is Sinatra ordered to play Wichita Falls? Does Jack Nicklaus have to play the Sertoma Classic? Did the Jockey Club order Secretariat to run at Latonia Park?"

Mathews was not all that crazy about Kuhn's interference either. Atlanta's skipper was a throwback, steadfast in his belief that the manager, and only the manager, called the shots on the field. He did not appreciate being told which names to scribble on his lineup card. Mathews swung away at Kuhn, blasting the commissioner whenever he got the opportunity.

To his credit, Kuhn proved adept at avoiding the verbal brushbacks hurled in his direction, most of the time refusing to acknowledge the public attacks. In a letter to Bartholomay dated March 18, he warned the Braves of "very serious consequences" if Aaron was not in the lineup on Opening Day. Kuhn detailed the severity of the penalties that awaited Atlanta if the team disregarded his order, including the dreaded Rule 50, which allowed for suspensions. He concluded the letter with an ominous reminder, telling Bartholomay that the "reputation of the game is in your hands."

Given Kuhn's unwavering stance, did Bartholomay really have a choice other than to order Mathews to start Aaron? Actually, it seems he did. Though Kuhn's letter reaffirmed his position that Aaron was to play against the Reds, it also provided the Braves with an escape clause. "As I advised you on the telephone last week," the commissioner wrote to Atlanta's owner, "I will expect you to use Henry Aaron in the opening series in Cincinnati in accordance with the pattern of his use in 1973 when he started approximately two of every three Braves' games. Of course, this would be barring disability." Kuhn admitted in his book, *Hardball: The Education of a Baseball Commissioner*, that he would have been helpless if the Braves had claimed that Aaron was injured.

Speaking of hardball, another controversy erupted in the spring of 1974 that, fortunately for Aaron and the Braves, had nothing to do with the home run record. This one concerned the introduction of cowhide baseballs to the big leagues. In every year since the game's inception, major leaguers had thrown, hit, and fielded horsehide baseballs. After the 1973 campaign, however, a switch was made to cowhide. The change came about partly because of the eating habits of Americans. Thanks to the proliferation of fast-food restaurants taking place in the early 1970s, people were consuming more beef than ever. As more cattle were sent to slaughter, the price of their hides plummeted. Major League owners, always looking to save a buck, saw an easy way to cut expenses on baseballs. Believing that no fundamental differences existed between the two hides, the owners opted for the cheaper material. Kuhn authorized the change in the winter of 1973, and Rawlings began manufacturing the new cowhide baseball in huge quantities.

The players, however, weren't concerned with economics—at least not when it came to baseballs. They complained that the new ball, though identical in appearance to the old one, did not act like the old one. William Leggett detailed their beefs in the 1974 baseball preview issue of *Sports Illustrated*. "It rolls funny at times, comes apart on occasion and goes lopsided," he wrote. "Sometimes hits that start out with line-drive purpose hang in the air and die. Everybody knew that this year's models were going to be made of cowhide but few suspected that they would behave in such queer ways."

With so many players grousing about the new ball, one who had little patience for such whining was Al Downing. That was not the 33-year-old left-hander's style. Intelligent, humble, and soft-spoken, Downing was in camp with the Los Angeles Dodgers, gearing up for his fourth year with the team. Like Aaron, the veteran pitcher had earned the respect of players around the league for his quiet, workmanlike approach to the game.

Actually, Downing and Aaron had a number of traits in common. Both men felt that learning the weaknesses and tendencies of opposing teams was key to beating them. Ted Williams once said that no one knew more about pitchers in the National League than Aaron. The Atlanta outfielder often sat in the dugout holding his cap across his face. Using the vent holes in the hat like the eyepiece of a microscope, he isolated the man on the mound and studied his every movement. When Aaron stepped to the plate, he had a clear picture of how that pitcher would attempt to retire him.

Downing had his own methods of getting inside the mind of the opposition. He once told George Plimpton during an interview for *Sports Illustrated* that it helps to be "exposed to the enemy camp." For several years he roomed with Maury Wills, who himself knew something about chasing legends. He had eclipsed Ty Cobb's stolen base record in 1962. Downing learned a lot from the veteran shortstop, including the art of holding runners on base.

Ultimately, both Aaron and Downing believed baseball was a game of feel. All the knowledge they accumulated helped them develop an instinct for every situation a game presented. In Downing's case, Dodger catchers Joe Ferguson and Steve Yeager expected him to wave off their signs as many as 25 times a game. He simply would not throw a pitch if he did not feel right about it.

Downing and Aaron were also alike in that their careers were winding down. Unfortunately for Downing, that is where the similarities ended. On the brink of breaking baseball's greatest record,

Aaron was sure to leave the game on his own terms. Downing, on the other hand, was coming off his second consecutive 9–9 season, and could not be certain how many more spring training trips remained in his future. Even though the preseason guides in 1974 had him listed as the Dodgers' fourth or fifth starter, there were no longer any guarantees for him. No matter how much respect he commanded in the clubhouse, Downing was beginning to relinquish control of his baseball life.

The man known to his teammates as "Gentleman Al" hardly resembled the fireballing phenom who had made his debut with the New York Yankees in July of 1961. Once called the "black Sandy Koufax," Downing by 1974 had lost his fastball and was relying on a deep supply of guile and guts whenever he took the mound. Indeed, the spindly southpaw had acquired the dreaded "crafty" label, a euphemism for a pitcher who can no longer rear back and burn one past a hitter.

Actually, Downing had not always been so calculating in his approach to the game. In fact, the journey that would ultimately bring him to his historic meeting with Aaron was a textbook case of the arduous, and often cruel, maturation of a major-league pitcher. When New York skipper Ralph Houk handed the ball to Downing 13 years earlier to pitch the second game of a doubleheader against the Washington Senators, the 21-year-old relied mostly on pure heat. His debut was as much the result of necessity on the manager's part as Downing's hard work and good fortune. "Ordinarily I'd put you in the bullpen for a few weeks," Houk told him after his call-up from Class-AA ball, "but I'm so short of pitching that I'll have to start you soon."

The 1961 Yankees are remembered for their hitting. Few recall the fact that by midseason, the team's usually reliable stable of veteran starting pitchers was wearing thin. New York was in a tight race and needed help, and it looked to Downing who had pitched beautifully during three months with the club's minor-league affiliate in Binghamton. His record stood at 9–1, and he was among the Eastern League leaders in several statistical categories. But what most impressed the Yankee brass was Downing's outstanding velocity. Though he liked to mix in a sweeping curve and an occasional changeup to keep batters off balance, the lefty was blessed with a fastball that batters often heard more clearly than they saw.

Downing fanned two of the first three batters he faced as a major leaguer. But the second inning of his debut was a disaster. Washington players picked up on Downing's inexperience, and danced all over the base paths to unnerve him. By the time the Yankees recorded the third out of the frame, the Senators had plated seven runs.

Downing, who appeared in only four more games in 1961, spent the rest of the season watching from the dugout. But that certainly was not a waste of his time. He received the equivalent of a baseball PhD from the tutelage of professorial masters such as Johnny Sain, Whitey Ford, Yogi Berra, Luis Arroyo, and catcher Elston Howard, the only other African American player on the team. Besides, the chance to start even one game in Yankee Stadium—the most hallowed of baseball shrines—had been Downing's overriding pursuit since he first got the baseball bug on the streets and sandlots of Trenton, New Jersey.

His neighborhood had all kinds—Italians, Jews, and blacks. There were no divisions, especially on the baseball diamond. "A bunch of us kids on our street would get together and challenge kids from other streets or the nearby project houses," Downing recalled in a 1963 interview in *Baseball Digest*. "We played on sandlots or in the school playground, or wherever we could stake out a diamond. We kids played together, visited each other, went to the movies and seashore together, and never mentioned any differences in race, religion or color."

From the time he was eight years old, it was clear that Downing had magic in his left arm. By his 16th birthday he had developed his curve and changeup, making other kids his age helpless against him at the plate. In the summer of 1957, Downing led his local team to the Babe Ruth World Series, where he won the first and last games of the tournament, including a shutout in the clincher. This is when he realized that pitching in the big leagues was more than a pipe dream.

Three years later Downing received one of the most important lessons of his life. The star hurler on a semipro club he had organized himself, Downing pitched against Satchel Paige in a national tournament in Wichita, Kansas. Afterward, the legendary Paige gladly revealed his mound philosophy. "[I] throw the ball hard but keep it down around the knees," he told an awestruck Downing. "Then when I get men on base I just throw the old snakey and make 'em hit it on the ground."

That advice did not seem to really sink in until 1971, after Downing's skills had begun to erode. He had enjoyed several good seasons with the Yankees in the mid-'60s, leading the American League in strikeouts in 1964 and posting double-digit victory totals for five straight years. But his best season was 1967, when he began sacrificing strikeouts for better control. Downing baffled hitters all summer long, ending the season with 14 wins and a 2.63 ERA. Considering the Yankees finished a miserable ninth in the 10-team American League, his record was all the more remarkable.

The following season, however, Downing began experiencing arm trouble. Two years later, New York shipped him to Oakland. The A's then moved him to Milwaukee, where Downing lost 10 games and won only two with the Brewers. The silver lining around this dark cloud was that he made 16 starts over the last half of the 1970 campaign. The Los Angeles Dodgers, in need of pitching help, acquired Downing prior to spring training in 1971, sending outfielder Andy Kosco—a former teammate of Downing's on the Yankees—to Milwaukee.

It was a brilliant move. In his first year in a Dodger uniform Downing became a 20-game winner—the only time in his career he did so—and led the National League with five shutouts. During the next two seasons, however, hitters began to catch on to Downing's tempting mix of well-placed off-speed pitches, forcing him to be perfect in order to win. No longer the ace of the Los Angeles staff, he produced two solid, yet unspectacular .500 seasons.

Now, in perhaps his last spring training stint, Downing viewed his future in baseball objectively and without any hint of self-pity. That included the prospect of facing Aaron early in the season. "If I throw 715 I'm not going to run and hide," he told Plimpton. "There's no disgrace in that. On the other hand, I'm not going to run to the plate to congratulate him. It's a big home run for him, for the game, for the country, but not for me!"

Once it was decided that Aaron would be in the lineup on Opening Day, attention shifted to the pitching staff of the Cincinnati Reds, particularly their starter, Jack Billingham. A distant relative of Hall of Fame hurler Christy Mathewson, Billingham would be the first pitcher on the hot seat against Aaron. Indeed, Billingham had known from the start of spring training that he, not Don Gullett, would get the call in the season's first game. That not only meant he could serve up number 714, but number 715 as well. For Aaron, hitting two home runs against the Reds was not out of the question. Entering the 1974 campaign, he had belted more long balls off Cincinnati pitchers than any others in his career.

Billingham, a throw-in in the 1971 deal with the Houston Astros that brought Joe Morgan to the Reds, had developed into one of the toughest starters in the National League. In fact, many felt that he, and not Tom Seaver of the New York Mets, deserved the

Cy Young Award in 1973. Billingham had won 19 games that season, and led the league in innings pitched and shutouts. "No one would suggest that Billingham is a better pitcher than Seaver," contended an editorial in the book *Major League Baseball 1974*, "but the fact is that the results the Reds got with him pitching were just as good as the Mets got with Seaver on the mound."

Billingham was never the type of pitcher whom anyone would describe as a "hard thrower." One was more likely, in fact, to see the adjective "gentle" before his name. He spent seven long years in the Los Angeles Dodgers' minor-league system before being called up in 1968 at the age of 25. Though Billingham preferred to start games, Los Angeles felt he would be most effective as a reliever and used him in that role for half a season. The gangly right-hander went 3–0 with a 2.17 ERA, but the Dodgers decided not to protect him in the October expansion draft, and he was selected by the Montreal Expos. A short time later, Montreal packaged Jesus Alou (Felipe's brother) and Donn Clendenon (a veteran first baseman drafted from the Pirates) to the Houston Astros for All-Star outfielder Rusty Staub. Clendenon threatened to retire if shipped to Houston, so the Expos sent Billingham in his place, along with prospect Skip Guinn and cash. With the Astros, Billingham got the chance to start. His best year came in 1970, when he posted a 13–9 record. But the following season, despite lowering his ERA to 3.39, he finished 10–16 and was deemed expendable.

Houston moved him to Cincinnati before the 1972 campaign as part of a seven-player trade. To fans of the Reds, Billingham was an afterthought. In their minds the key to the deal was Morgan, an All-Star second baseman with speed and power, and former Atlanta shortstop Denis Menke, who would move over to third. Add to that the fact that Billingham had recently had surgery to remove varicose veins from his legs, and it is understandable why his name generated little excitement. As William G. Holder observed rather bluntly in an issue of *Baseball Digest*, "Since varicose veins are normally associated with old age, this didn't help a whole lot with Billingham's introduction to Cincinnati."

Billingham performed well in his first season with the Reds, though he showed no signs of developing into the team's top pitcher. He posted a 12–12 record, logging more than 200 innings, and kept his ERA at a very respectable 3.18. Billingham was a perfect complement to control artist Gary Nolan and the wall-to-wall heat of Don Gullett.

Ironically, without the pressure to be the team's ace, that is exactly what Billingham became. Unlike some starters, he flourished under the command of manager Sparky Anderson who was known as "Captain Hook" for his habit of yanking starting pitchers early in ball games. In six years with Cincinnati, Billingham won 87 games, including back-to-back 19-win seasons in 1973 and 1974. Some would argue, in fact, that the "Big Red Machine" was more like the "Little Engine That Could" until Billingham showed up. He was the guy Anderson looked to in a big spot, and Billingham rarely disappointed.

For steely professionals like Downing and Billingham, the prospect of facing Aaron with so much on the line would not be the source of any sleepless nights. And although their fates would soon be intertwined, each was eager in his own way for the season to begin. In the meantime, the controversy and expectations surrounding Aaron's inevitable ascension to baseball's home run throne continued to build.

By the middle of March, Aaron's quest to eclipse the Babe was a staple of almost every evening news broadcast, and daily reports of his progress filled thousands of column inches in hundreds of newspapers. Nothing, it seemed, could hold back the confluence of so many powerful forces, for in Aaron's story the media had all the elements of a best-selling novel or big-screen blockbuster: history, politics, race, heroism, cowardice, and good, old-fashioned drama.

Finally, as spring training ended, it was all ready to play itself out.

CHAPTER EIGHT:

715

IF HENRY AARON'S JOURNEY THROUGH THE BASEBALL world was about gaining respect, then he was soon to meet his destiny—if only briefly. For 20 years, Aaron had played the game as well as anyone who had ever put on a uniform. His résumé included a World Series championship, two batting titles, four home run crowns, an MVP award, and an unbroken string of All-Star appearances dating from 1955. His peers had already acknowledged his talent and heart. Now, the fans and the media, although somewhat grudgingly, were doing the same.

For a nation in turmoil, Aaron's ascension to baseball's home run throne could not have come at a better time. The country found itself at a critical juncture, a period when so much seemed so wrong. "Americans had lost faith in their government, in the White House, because of Watergate and the tragedy of the war in Vietnam," said former President Gerald Ford in *Chasing the Dream*.

Aaron's pursuit of Ruth's career mark provided a sorely needed diversion. It demonstrated the potential of human achievement, rather than the depths to which society could sink. It proved once and for all that African Americans held a significant place in America's pastime, a sport with a history as rich as the nation that gave birth to it.

But unlike other extraordinary events of the game's epic past, no one doubted the outcome of this drama. Barring some unimaginable tragedy, Aaron would hit 715. It might take one swing or one hundred. Sooner or later, though, it was going to happen. This gave Americans time to ponder the meaning of Aaron's accomplishment. It also enabled them to root for someone who was absolutely certain to reach his goal. In the old days, Americans expected to win—in war, in business, in sports—but their self-confidence was now at a low ebb. Aaron became a symbol of national achievement, a guaranteed winner.

The irony of the man who struggles against everything that is bad in the system, only to become its flag bearer, is both sad and sweet. In Aaron's case, he assumed this role with some reluctance, of course. But he meant to relish this moment; he had earned that much. And America, in turn, relished Aaron.

Of all the summing-up that was done in the weeks prior to Opening Day, no one did a better job than Frank Hyland of the *Atlanta Journal*. "I will remember the incredible dignity of the man," he wrote. "A proud, black man who endured pressures others would never endure. A man ignored most of his professional career who could have struck back at those who had snubbed, but who didn't. The word is class. When it comes to class, Hank Aaron never has been No. 2 to Babe Ruth. Or anyone else, for that matter."

Finally, it was time to crown the king.

As Hank Aaron stepped to plate on Opening Day of 1974 for his first at bat of the season, who could have blamed him if his mind was elsewhere? Flying into Cincinnati the day before, he was as shocked as anyone by the wreckage below him. Catastrophic tornadoes had just ripped through Ohio. From the air, the region resembled a war zone.

"The devastation was awesome," reported Joe Falls in the *Sporting News*. "I couldn't believe my eyes. As our plane started down toward the Cincinnati airport, somebody said, 'Look at all that damage down there.' Everyone began getting out of their seats, even with the seatbelt sign on, and looking out the right side of the plane."

The scene made it easy for Aaron to forget about the spectacle that awaited him at Riverfront Stadium. He admitted as much in *I Had a Hammer*, saying "Suddenly, I didn't feel like the center of the world anymore."

To those close to Aaron, it was absurd to think that he had ever considered himself "the center of the world." Aaron was simply too modest. "His hat size never has changed," said Donald Davidson.

"The thing I'll always remember about Hank is the way he handles himself," echoed Darrell Evans during a conversation with Wayne Minshew of the *Sporting News*. "That's the biggest thing. Nobody else could go through this kind of pressure—nobody. He is amazing. And you know something else? None of this has changed him as a person."

What may have been news to Evans was how important he and his teammates were to Aaron. They helped him stay loose. When he arrived at the ballpark for the opener in Cincinnati, for instance, veteran Ron Reed had taped a can of Raid to Aaron's locker. The good-humored hurler told his teammate it was the best way to keep the pesky press off his back. An appreciative Aaron laughed at the joke with everyone else in the clubhouse.

Still, just hours before the Braves were to take the field, Aaron felt a bit unsettled. Deep down, he admitted in *Chasing the Dream*, this Opening Day seemed different from any before. He tried to relax during batting practice, even knocking two over the fence, but the buzz around the stadium had an effect on him. Maybe it was that so many people were pulling for him. For the first time in Aaron's career, public sentiment was almost completely in his corner.

The excitement that pulsed through Riverfront Stadium on April 4 created an atmosphere unlike any other opener in baseball history. Vice President Gerald Ford, attending in place of his beleaguered boss, was on hand to throw out the first pitch. Bowie Kuhn, making a rare appearance at a big-league game that included Aaron in the lineup, sat next to Ford along the first base line. At least 250 writers assembled in the press box and at other spots around the park. The crowd, some 52,000 strong, rippled with anticipation. "If there's an empty seat in the house," Reds' play-by-play man Marty Brennaman told viewers at home, "I can't find it."

The playoff-like environment had everyone on edge. Surprisingly, it appeared to bother Jack Billingham the most. From the outset, the normally unflappable Cincinnati starter struggled to find the strike zone. Billingham issued a base on balls to free-swinging Ralph Garr to begin the game. Then Mike Lum laced a hard single to advance Garr to second. When Billingham retired Evans, the third-place hitter, for the first out of the inning, he took a deep breath and prepared to face history.

Aaron, still wearing the eye-straining road uniform introduced two seasons earlier, left the on-deck circle and headed toward the batter's box. Billingham was already under pressure to throw strikes to Aaron. The prospect of walking the bases loaded to start the season only added to his predicament. Understanding the hurler's dilemma, the crafty Aaron knew he could look for a pitch to drive. He also knew not to tip his hand. Aaron walked to the plate as calmly as ever. "I realize that the only way I can play the game is to do things my way," he would say later. "I can't get tense and tight. Fortunately, when I'm on the field, I am able to shut out everything else. And when I'm hitting, I can concentrate fully on the pitcher."

Billingham was not as lucky on this day. He threw four pitches, one a strike, and Aaron took them all. Now he needed to make a perfect pitch. The hometown fans let Billingham know in no uncertain terms that, staff ace or not, he was not to pitch around Aaron. "I had just won 19 games the previous year," he recalled in *Chasing the Dream*. "I go three-and-one on Hank and people start booing me!"

On the fifth pitch of the at bat, Billingham threw his specialty—a fastball designed to tail down and in on righties just enough to make them beat it into the ground. But adrenaline got the better of him. The offering stayed up in the zone and Aaron, taking his first swing of the season, jumped all over it. Almost everyone in the park rose to their feet instantly. The high line drive soared toward left center field and cleared the wall above the 375-feet sign. Afterward, Billingham called the pitch a mistake. He then stated the obvious, noting that Aaron "hits mistakes."

Aaron jogged around the bases as he always did, deliberately and without a hint of ego. His statement told nothing of the significance of the homer. The uninitiated fan might actually believe the blast only mattered because it was the first of the cowhide era.

Aaron's teammates knew better. "The dugout response was something," said reliever Tom House. "When he hit the ball, I heard someone go, 'Holy shit, there it goes,' then it was pandemonium."

"I got goose bumps," said Jack Aker, an off-season acquisition by the Braves, who, in stints with the A's and Yankees, had already witnessed some of baseball's most meaningful moments. "For the third time in my career, I got goose bumps. I got them when Catfish Hunter pitched a perfect game. I got them when they had Mickey Mantle Day in New York and now I got them again."

House and Aker spilled out of the dugout with the rest of the Braves to greet Aaron at home plate. Johnny Bench waited there also, offering a heartfelt handshake. Once again, the Cincinnati catcher had been fooled by Aaron's nonchalant approach at the plate. "You think he's still a little bit rusty, and he's not ready for anything," Bench said years later. "Didn't make a difference."

In the *Sporting News*, Minshew noted Bench's sportsmanship: "There was an unspoken tribute when Aaron hit his 714th homer in Cincinnati. It showed up in a picture which moved around the country the following morning.

"The picture showed Aaron about to step on home plate following his momentous trot to history. There waiting were a couple of Braves and Reds' catcher Johnny Bench. All three had their hands extended, ready to congratulate Aaron. It revealed the respect opposing players have for the current home run king. Aaron's blow put the Reds behind, 3–0, yet Bench was ready to congratulate his opponent."

As soon as Aaron touched the plate, the game was stopped. He found his wife and his father in the stands and embraced them. Ford and Kuhn then walked on the field together to offer their congratulations. With microphone in hand, the vice president publicly voiced his compliments. "This is a great day for you and a great day for baseball," Ford said. "Good luck for 715 and a good many more."

Taking the microphone from the vice president, Aaron thanked Ford and then admitted he was glad the chase was drawing to a close. As it turned out, the brief respite from the game proved to be one of the few instances of peace he enjoyed all day long. Though he received a telegram from President Nixon, Aaron was upset after the contest because the Braves had lost in extra innings, 7–6, blowing a lead with two out in the ninth. His day had ended after the seventh, with Atlanta up by five. Now, watching from the clubhouse, Aaron groaned as a wild pitch from Buzz Capra allowed Pete Rose (whose double had knotted the score in the ninth) to score from second with the winning run.

"I got a thrill out of the home run that won the pennant, and when I hit No. 500, and I thought this would mean something extra special to me," Aaron said. "I felt good all day long, until Rose tied the game. Losing just took the edge off of it. It's just another home run."

Aaron's comments came immediately after the game when the ache of Atlanta's loss stung most sharply. The Reds had set up a small interview room beneath the stadium where first Aaron and then Billingham answered questions from the media. Initially, Aaron's "just another home run" remark confounded reporters. They wanted a good quote for tomorrow's papers. The Atlanta outfielder eventually obliged them once he had a little more time to reflect. "Yeah, I feel like I'm sharing it," Aaron said of number 714. "It's a great moment for me, for black kids, for every kid in America."

The slugger responded to all sorts of questions during the session, not budging until everyone in the room was satisfied. But when he got up to leave, he found he had one more query to answer. Ironically, it did not come from a member of the media. Exiting the interview room, Aaron passed Billingham, who was about to take the hot seat. The two exchanged a friendly greeting before the pitcher asked, "Why did you have to do it on me?" Aaron smiled and kept on walking.

If Aaron seemed somewhat subdued about his accomplishment, the mood in the Reds' clubhouse was completely opposite. "Hank Aaron had done the biggest thing in baseball here," crowed Cincinnati's manager, Sparky Anderson. "And it couldn't have happened to a better man, a finer gentleman. That man has been a credit to the game, never a problem, never talking against it, always showing a lot of class. He's an amazing man."

"The best thing you can say about him is when you walk on the field and you're playing against Hank Aaron, you are in the big leagues," added Rose.

Despite all the good tidings, Aaron still felt somewhat angry about the day. Garr had reminded him before the contest that it was the anniversary of Martin Luther King's death. Knowing that Kuhn was in the ballpark, Aaron quickly politicked for a moment of silence, but his request was denied. He spoke bitterly afterward, questioning why such a simple plea could not be accommodated. When the writers pressed him on the subject, Billye stepped in to defend her husband (a move she later regretted). "They were coming after him," she recalled. "It was an instinctive reaction. Looking back, I think that incident planted the seed of suspicion that maybe I was putting ideas into Henry's head."

But no one was going to tell Aaron what to say or how to act, especially when it came to racial issues. His attitude irked some in the media, including Joe Falls, who believed Aaron had, in his finest hour, displayed a measured lack of class. "No, no, Henry, I thought—not now," he wrote, wondering why the victims of the recent tornadoes did not deserve recognition as well. "Be graceful. Be dignified. Be a man."

In retrospect, Falls's comments seemed misguided, if not hypocritical. It is worth noting, for example, that the columnist, who had never even been introduced to Aaron, had asked him for his autograph before the game. Aaron, of course, signed.

Included among those who respected Aaron's right to speak out was Furman Bisher. In fact, his take on the day had nothing to do with politics. He saw it simply as splendid vindication for Aaron and his team. The afternoon's events also provided the southern scribe a perfect opportunity to take a swipe at his brethren in the North.

"Here, in the final result of opening day, we find something for the boys from New York," he typed. "All those who singed the Braves for their original intention of benching their idol to save his historic moments for Atlanta. Those who loudly contended that the Braves without Aaron were not the Braves with their best foot forward.

"Please, no honor to those adolescent bellows of 'fix' and 'rig.' They were as much out of the park as 714."

Drawing even with Ruth took a great deal of pressure off Aaron. Until he passed the Babe, however, the media onslaught would continue. Aaron now looked forward to setting the record and then fading into the background.

"I will be glad to get all this behind me," Aaron said. "I like the exposure, naturally. I get a kick out of it, but I don't like the way it is overshadowing the performances of such fine players as Dusty Baker, Ralph Garr, Dave Johnson and Darrell Evans. They had fine seasons last year, with outstanding accomplishments, but no one seemed to notice."

The next chance Aaron would have at 715 came on Sunday, April 7. Friday was an off day for both teams, and Aaron sat out on Saturday. Though Eddie Mathews would have preferred to hold out his star one more day, he had no choice in the matter. Kuhn called the Atlanta manager on Saturday night to make sure Aaron would start the following day. The edict from the commissioner was clear: Aaron was to play at least two of the games in Cincinnati. In effect, it was Kuhn who penciled the slugger's name onto the lineup card, not the Atlanta manager.

"On the day off Friday, I said to him, 'Damn, Hank, if you don't break the record in Cincinnati, we've got an 11-game home stand coming up, and we can put a lot of people in the stands,'" recalled Mathews, who more than a decade later was still annoyed by Kuhn's interference. "So I said I wasn't going to play him anymore in Cincinnati, and that's when the commissioner got pissed. And I mean pissed. He was gonna suspend me, suspend the owners, the integrity of baseball was at stake, blah-blah-blah. So I had to play him Sunday."

Aaron agreed with Mathews's position, though he did not feel as strongly. More than anything, he appreciated the way his skipper stuck up for him. "It's not often that a manager is such a loyal friend of a player," he said in *I Had a Hammer*.

While Aaron believed he owed his hometown fans a shot at the record breaker, he stated plainly that such feelings would not influence him or his performance on the field. "I'm certainly going to play the game the way it's supposed to be played," Aaron said, "and if I get a pitch to hit, I'll try to dispose of it."

As it turned out, he never got that pitch, and Sunday proved a day of rest anyway. The Reds' starter was Clay Kirby who, while not the most fearsome pitcher in the league, did possess a nasty slider that gave Aaron fits when it was working. And, on this day, it was working every time the slugger stepped to the plate. In three times at bat, Aaron grounded out once and went down looking twice. Unfortunately for Kirby, the rest of the Atlanta lineup had no problem figuring him out. The Braves built a comfortable lead and once again Mathews pulled Aaron from the game in the seventh inning.

In the press conference afterward, some writers suggested that Aaron may have dogged it to better his chances at hitting 715 in Atlanta. In columns the next day, several went as far to call him a "disgrace to the game." The situation infuriated Aaron. His angered reply was that never in his career had he given less than 100 percent and that he certainly was not going to jeopardize his reputation now.

He reiterated the point in *I Had a Hammer*: "I believed in the integrity of the game as strongly as anybody, and it irked me to have my own integrity assaulted. The fact is, on both strikeouts I was called out by John McSherry, and one of them was a bad call that I argued. Even Kirby said he thought the pitch was a ball."

With the media's unwarranted criticism fresh in his mind, Aaron was in a foul mood when he flew back with the team to Atlanta for the Braves' home opener against the Dodgers. No matter what he did on the field, it seemed, someone in the press box had a problem with him. His disposition did not improve when he walked off the plane. Hundreds of fans awaited him, as did several television cameras, which instantly began to roll. Aaron found his mother, whom he had advised to stay at home, and made his way through the maze of people.

Sleeping in his own bed helped Aaron relax, and he woke up Monday morning feeling refreshed. The atmosphere at Atlanta Stadium later that evening promised to be a circus. Even so, Aaron did not change his game-day routine. First he tuned into his soap operas. Then, at one o'clock on the nose, he took his ritualistic two-hour nap. When he awoke, he made the one-hour drive to Atlanta Stadium.

At about the same time, some 800 miles away in New York City, Mrs. Babe Ruth was just returning from a long day of shopping with her daughter. The home run chase was of little interest to baseball's most famous widow. Nine months earlier, in fact, she had admitted to Ken Nigro of the *Sporting News* that she hardly ever thought about it.

It was not that Mrs. Ruth disliked baseball. Indeed, she had stayed involved in the game over the years, but only on the outside edges as it pertained to her late husband. She served as a donor and volunteer to the Babe Ruth Shrine and Baseball Museum, which had opened its doors the previous summer. She also personally answered each piece of mail addressed to the Babe, including those that were delivered to Yankee Stadium or to the Hall of Fame in Cooperstown and then passed on to her. "I receive about 12 to 14 letters a day," she said. "It keeps me pretty busy since I answer all the letters myself. It's impossible to get any help in New York."

There was no doubt that Ruth's legacy was in good hands, even if Mrs. Ruth was unconcerned that he was about to drop to second on baseball's career home run list. She had no plans to watch the game on Monday evening.

When Aaron pulled into the players' parking lot at Atlanta Stadium, he looked calm and eager to play, secure in the knowledge that the Braves had closed the clubhouse to reporters. The team had made the decision earlier in the day, hoping to keep the pressure off its star. Ever since home run number 700, in fact, Atlanta's front office had done all it could to keep the media at bay. The team's most effective move was scheduling pregame press conferences before every home contest. Instead of allowing reporters to jump Aaron as soon as he arrived at the ballpark, the Braves ran tidy Q&A sessions where writers were compelled to ask questions in an orderly fashion. Consequently, the time Aaron had to spend before the media was limited, and he did not have to answer the same questions over and over again.

With his personal press conference set to begin in an hour or so, Aaron took a seat in the trainer's room. There, clubhouse manager Bill Acree ordered some food for him from the Stadium Club before tending to his most important duty of the day. Acree now was in charge of safeguarding the specially marked baseballs to be used each time Aaron stepped to the plate.

After finishing his afternoon snack, Aaron met with the press, took batting practice, and then retired to the clubhouse. The mood was more solemn than usual. The players seemed to sense they soon would become a part of history. Aaron added to the intensity of the moment by issuing a forecast to his teammates. "I'm gonna get it out of the way tonight, boys" is the way House recalled the prediction. No one doubted Aaron's words.

The scene outside hardly resembled the serene atmosphere in the clubhouse. Joseph Durso described the mayhem the following day in the *New York Times*: "The stadium was packed with its largest crowd since the Braves left Milwaukee and brought major league baseball to the Deep South nine years ago . . . the Jonesboro High School band marched; balloons and fireworks filled the overcast sky before the game; Aaron's life was dramatized on a huge color map of the United States painted across the outfield grass, and Bad Henry was serenaded by the Atlanta Boys Choir, which now included girls."

Remembering the game 10 years later in a story for *Baseball Digest*, Glenn Sheeley elaborated further: "There are 5,000 balloons. A red, white and blue United States map—140 feet by 84 feet—is painted on the outfield grass. In a 'this-is-your-life Hank Aaron' presentation, his parents represent Mobile (where Aaron was born) on the map, John Mullen represents Indianapolis (where he signed Aaron), Braves executive Donald Davidson represents Boston (where the team was located when Aaron signed), and Charlie Grimm represents Milwaukee (where he managed Aaron as a rookie), among others. Eight-foot letters around the fence proclaim: 'Atlanta Salutes Hank Aaron.'"

The whirlwind of activity on the field made Joe Shirley's job all the more difficult. The director of security at the Stadium, he was responsible for keeping Aaron safe in the event he broke the record. That meant Shirley had to maintain close contact with Calvin Wardlaw, who was seated with Aaron's wife and parents. As usual, Wardlaw was armed and ready to act, the threat of a sniper's bullet with Aaron's name on it more serious than ever. "I tried to always approach it as a possibility," Wardlaw said in *Chasing the Dream*.

Shirley also had to make sure the ensuing scuffle for home run 715 did not erupt into a riot. Sixty-three patrolmen—three times as many as the Braves usually employed for a game—were placed strategically around the ballpark. Paying particular attention to the resting place of many of Aaron's homers, Shirley dispatched six police officers, four security guards, and eight extra ushers to the left field stands. "I had visions of some little old lady getting stomped by a Georgia Tech football player," joked House.

That was not going to happen if Bill Buckner had anything to say about it. Before the game, the Los Angeles left fielder practiced climbing the outfield wall in front of the Atlanta bullpen. Making like Spider Man, Buckner got a feel for how high and how long he could perch himself on the fence.

Buckner's odd-looking pregame exercise caught the eye of those who had showed up early to watch batting practice. Atlanta Stadium had been constructed to hold 52,769, but nearly a thousand more fans elbowed their way in on April 8. Of those 53,775 (a record gate for the Braves, which broke the mark set when Sandy Koufax dueled Denny LeMaster on August 9, 1966) there were more than a few dignitaries. Pearl Bailey landed the gig to sing "The Star-Spangled Banner." Aaron's father, Herbert, was chosen to throw out the first pitch. Sammy Davis Jr. settled into a prime seat, as did Governor Jimmy Carter. Earlier in the evening, Davis had paraded through the clubhouse offering as much as $30,000 to the bullpen occupant who snagged number 715.

As expected, there was also a large and impressive delegation chosen to represent baseball, including NL President Chub Feeney. Conspicuously absent, however, was Bowie Kuhn. Claiming he had a prior commitment in Cleveland, the commissioner sent Monte Irvin in his stead. Not surprisingly, he incurred widespread criticism in the hours and days that followed. "The commissioner was wrong tonight in not being here," wrote Dave Anderson in the *New York Times* the following day, rehashing the controversy of the past several weeks. "He had stood up gallantly, but suddenly sat down again. Henry Aaron should have ordered the commissioner to be here."

David Scott, married to Aaron's sister Alfredia, and a member of Jimmy Carter's staff, was even more outspoken. "Where was Commissioner Bowie Kuhn, and did the New York press tell him not to come?" he wondered. "Hank's a great gentleman and completed a great era here tonight. I feel like Atlanta, the Braves and Hank have been insulted by his absence."

It was the fans, however, who perhaps felt most cheated by the commissioner's failure to show. Many came to the stadium with signs chiding Kuhn, boasting slogans such as "Phooey on Bowie" and "Send Kuhn to the Moon." They wanted to tell the commissioner exactly what they thought of his policies concerning Aaron. Now their opportunity was lost.

Since Kuhn was a no-show, the Braves had to scratch him from the pregame festivities, a dog and pony show that made the contest feel like a Super Bowl. When Aaron was announced, for example, he entered the field through a double line of girls raising bats. Unaccustomed to such extravagance, he asked whether he should run or walk. Aaron was only half kidding.

The hoopla was fine as far as NBC was concerned. The network had acquired the rights to broadcast the games, and the potential ratings bonanza promised to be a TV executive's dream—especially if Aaron did not hit one out that night. With the promise of an enormous primetime audience, advertisers were lined up for spots. If it took Aaron three or four games to reach 715, NBC stood to mop up.

Ironically, the game was almost blacked out in Atlanta. According to baseball regulations, if a game was not sold out 72 hours in advance, it could not be aired in the home team's viewing region. When the cutoff came on the preceding Friday, Aaron had already hit 714. Enough people thought he would reach 715 over the weekend so there were still tickets available for the Monday night contest. Only a special ruling by the league office—announced by Bartholomay an hour or so before game time—kept the Braves (who did sell out after all) on the air.

For Al Downing, ratings points and ad dollars were of little interest. But when the Los Angeles starting pitcher claimed that this was just any other game (and that he was unconcerned about yielding the record breaker to Aaron) there were few believers in the ballpark. As Downing took his warm-up tosses in the bullpen, he seemed distracted. Later he would admit that he probably was not "mentally prepared" to take the mound.

Despite his butterflies, Downing retired the Braves in order in the first inning. As Aaron walked to the plate to lead off the second, the crowd rose to its feet. House, peering in from the left field bullpen, characterized the feeling around the park as "a kid anticipating Christmas." But the first gift opened turned out to be no more exciting than a pair of socks. Aaron walked on a 3–1 pitch. He did make a bit of history moments later, however, when he scored on Dusty Baker's double. Not that anyone really cared, but the run marked the 2,063rd of his career, breaking the National League record held by Willie Mays.

Two innings later, Aaron prepared for his next plate appearance. A light rain (tears from the Babe, some claimed) had begun to fall, making the chilly evening seem a bit colder. Evans led off with a ground ball up the middle. Shortstop Bill Russell failed to field it cleanly, and his throw to first was too late. The scoreboard flashed *E-6*.

Up stepped Aaron and again the crowd was on its feet. Downing's first pitch was low for a ball. Boos cascaded onto the field from impatient fans. Aaron was expecting Downing to throw him a lot of screwballs, which would fade outside as they reached the hitting zone. Downing was smart enough to know that Aaron, eager to hit 715, would try to yank anything that looked good over the wall in left. Pulling a dying screwball was a recipe for groundouts. Aaron, thinking one more step ahead, decided to set up a couple of inches closer to the plate, just in case one of Downing's screwballs didn't screw. This meant leaving himself vulnerable to inside pitches, but he doubted Downing would try to pitch him there. The game within the game had been played. Now it was time for Downing's second pitch.

Catcher Joe Ferguson called for a fastball down and away. Downing, throwing from the stretch, rocked and delivered. The pitch headed for the outside corner, but it was not low enough. Aaron, still a great "bad ball" hitter, started his swing. "I think it would have been a ball," home plate umpire Dave "Satch" Davidson said years later.

Aaron snapped his wrists, coming around the ball and getting under it. It rocketed off his bat and rose toward Buckner in left. Aaron did not get all of the Downing pitch, popping it higher than he would have liked. No one in the stadium was sure it had enough to leave the yard, least of all Aaron. He normally did not watch his home runs, but this time he made an exception. His eyes widened as the ball started its descent and Buckner began feeling for the fence. It had a chance.

In the on-deck circle, Dusty Baker stood up and raised his fist. He said later that he was certain the ball was gone. In the radio booth, Milo Hamilton said nothing. Like almost everyone else, he was not sure.

At the wall, a simple chain-link fence, denizens of the Braves bullpen sprinted to their predetermined spots. To keep from killing one another, they had agreed to divide the pen into 10-yard patches. In this apportionment process, House, a left-handed reliever drafted out of USC in 1967, received a less-than-prime piece of real estate. It was as far from the left field line as you could get and still be in the bullpen. House had two nicknames. One was "Green," a moniker bestowed upon him by Ron Reed, who claimed he knew nothing about baseball (later House would become a highly respected pitching coach). The other nickname was "Puma," which he earned for the cat-quick reflexes he exhibited in pepper games. As the ball curled and dropped, House waited several yards behind the fence, in front of a BankAmericard sign that read Think of It as Money. He was as certain as Baker that the ball was a home run. "As soon as it left the bat," claimed House after the game, "I knew it was coming right to me."

On the field, Buckner stuck a cleat in the fence, steadied himself with his left hand, and started his climb. He could not know it, but he was about to make the most-replayed unsuccessful fielding attempt of all time (the second probably being his fielding gaffe against the Mets a dozen years later). Buckner waved futilely at Aaron's blast as it burrowed through the cool, wet night and carried over the fence, a few feet over his glove.

As the ball sailed toward the corner of the bullpen where House was stationed, pitcher Buzz Capra who had just joined the team, forgot himself and drifted under it. He banged into House who held his balance and gloved the ball (encoded as #12–12–2–2) on the fly. "Everybody said 'Nice catch,' but if I didn't lift my glove up, it would have hit me in the forehead," he told Bill Koenig of *Baseball Weekly* 25 years later.

At precisely 9:07 p.m., just as the ball found House's glove, Atlanta Stadium erupted in delirious celebration. Fireworks exploded above the field, lighting up the sky. In numerals six feet tall, the scoreboard flashed "715" over and over again. Atlanta's bench emptied onto the field, players jumping around like Little Leaguers.

Behind the dugout, the Aaron family burst into tears. President Nixon called, though Donald Davidson unintentionally hung up on him and the commander in chief had to dial back later in the evening. And Hamilton delivered his famous call, "There's a new home run champion of all time and it's Henry Aaron!"

At the center of the pandemonium, Aaron circled the bases, trying desperately to contain his emotions. It became more and more difficult with each 90-foot segment he covered. At first base, he shook the hand of Steve Garvey. At second, Davey Lopes offered his congratulations.

Then, in a flash, two young men raced onto the field and were at Aaron's back. Britt Gaston and Cliff Courtenay, who had spotted that the security guards stationed nearby them were as distracted as everyone else in the ballpark, jumped from the stands and sprinted toward Aaron as he rounded second. Calvin Wardlaw froze for an agonizing instant as he eyeballed the intruders. Instinct told him the long-haired duo meant no harm. Aaron certainly did not seem threatened by them. Concentrating so intensely on touching each base, he barely noticed their presence as they shouted plaudits and patted him on the back before disappearing into the clutches of stadium security. Later on, in fact, Aaron worked behind the scenes to have the criminal charges against the two dropped. As Aaron rounded third, he could no longer control himself. A wide smile broke across his face. The grin spoke volumes. "I purposefully never smiled as I ran the bases after a home run, but I suppose I couldn't help it that time," he said in *Chasing the Dream*.

Aaron's teammates mobbed him when he reached home plate. Garr, the first in line, made sure Aaron touched the dish. The team then tried to lift Aaron onto its shoulders, a scene similar to the one that followed his homer against the Cardinals in 1957 that won the pennant for Milwaukee. But he slid back to the ground.

His mom and dad were waiting. Estella proceeded to give her son the most emphatic hug in the history of mother-son embraces. "She wasn't letting go 'til she was sure her boy was safe, even if it meant hanging on all night," he said in *Chasing the Dream*. Aaron had no idea his mother possessed so much strength.

By this time, House had come in from the outfield, holding the ball above his head in his glove as he ran to join the celebration. He was overcome with emotion—"nuclear" was the word he used to describe his reaction. When he reached Aaron, who was still clutching his mother, House handed him the baseball. In a scene right out of a Hollywood movie, Aaron simply said, "Thanks, kid," and held the ball up for all to see.

"What made it worthwhile was what I saw when I ran in with the ball," House revealed to George Plimpton in 1974. "I saw what many people had never been able to see in him—deep emotion. I'd never seen that before. He has such cool. He never gets excited. He's so stable. And I looked, and he had tears hanging on his lids. I could hardly believe it."

To this day, House proudly states that he will never forget the moment. "That catch was the highlight of my pitching career," says the pitcher who won 29 games and saved 33 others during his otherwise unspectacular eight-year stint as a major leaguer. "It's how I'm introduced at every dinner or clinic. It got me in the Hall of Fame. It got me a card in Trivial Pursuit. Is that immortality or what?"

The rest of the moment progressed predictably. A ceremony followed immediately after the home run to honor Aaron. Bartholomay presented him with a plaque. Irvin gave him a wristwatch valued at $3,000. When the commissioner's emissary stepped to the podium, the fans booed him lustily. Irvin, knowing the catcalls were really directed at Kuhn, did not seem overly upset. Aaron, on the other hand, got a kick out of the crowd response. "I was smiling from the boos," he said when questioned about the incident afterward. Irvin then introduced the new home run king, referring to him as "the greatest ballplayer, the finest gentleman," a sentiment that quickly turned the stadium in his favor.

Looking more relieved than excited, Aaron paused for a moment. When the ovation finally died down, he told the crowd, "I would just like to say to all the fans here this evening that I just thank God it's all over with . . . thank you very much."

With that, the ceremony ended, play resumed, and the fans began to leave. Aaron's homer had knotted the score at 3–3, but no one seemed at all concerned about the outcome. When Aaron came up to bat again, the crowd had thinned by a good 20,000. By the top of the ninth, with the Braves enjoying a 7–4 lead (thanks to six errors committed by the dumbstruck Dodgers), no more than 10,000 remained in the stands. "I think the fans showed poor taste," said Mathews after the game. "It was a helluva tribute to Hank, but there are 24 other guys on the team. I think they should have stayed for the game."

Capra, the man who literally shoved House into the spotlight, was somewhat more philosophical. "It was no shock to see them leave," he said. "They came to see a home run by Hank first, and the game second."

The comments by Mathews and Capra did not come until a while after the game. That was because the Atlanta manager had closed the clubhouse for a private celebration. Toasting his friend with a glass of champagne, he called Aaron "the best baseball player ever to put on a pair of spikes." Mathews cared little that the media was cursing his name outside. As he said in *I Had a Hammer*, "At that point, I didn't give a damn about the sportswriters."

In the meantime, others kept the press busy. "As a fan and club owner, this is the greatest moment of all," gushed Bartholomay. "I'm fortunate to be involved. And it's much more than just baseball. It's a happy event in a country that needs good news."

Pearl Bailey also talked of the home run in terms of its impact on society. "This is proof we can lose those god-dog labels," she said. "People here tonight came and saw a man. Catholic, Jew, black, purple . . . I don't give a darn if he's a green man. So, as it happens he's a man of color—marvelous. Even though Hank Aaron doesn't base anything on that, he happens to be. It ain't gonna get nobody off welfare or nobody in the King's palace, but it sure proves a man can be a man."

Speaking of being a man, Al Downing faced the music like a true pro. His postgame remarks were thoughtful and dignified. "It was a fastball, right down the middle of the upper part of the plate," he said. "I was trying to get it down to him, but I didn't and he hit it good—as I knew he would.

"When he first hit it, I didn't think it might be going. But like a great hitter, when he picks his pitch, chances are he's going to hit it pretty good."

The media finally got its chance to meet with Aaron after Mathews's clubhouse celebration ended. When the new home run king entered the press conference, the roomful of reporters rose to their feet and applauded. It was hard to tell who was more shocked by the unprecedented and altogether sincere ovation, Aaron or the press.

Then, showing the patience and class that typified him throughout his career, Aaron again answered every question put to him. Before he left, however, he wanted to set the record straight one more time about whether he had mailed it in in Cincinnati. "I have never gone out on a ball field and given less than my level best," Aaron said. "When I hit it tonight, all I thought about was that I wanted to touch all the bases."

More than a quarter of a century later, when people go back to that April evening in Atlanta, one of their most vivid memories is Milo Hamilton's call of Aaron's historic shot. "It was completely spontaneous," he says. "George Plimpton tried all winter to get me to tell him what I was going to say. But I honestly didn't know. Spontaneity was my strong suit. I didn't want to make it sound contrived."

Contrived or not, Hamilton's words were heard by only a fraction of the viewers who remember seeing the game live. Most were treated to Vin Scully's call. He was doing the national game for NBC. His decades of experience offered a wonderful perspective on the drama unfolding on the field before him. "And for the first time in a long time, that poker face of Aaron's shows the tremendous relief," reported Scully in his dulcet voice. "What a marvelous moment for baseball. What a marvelous moment for Atlanta and the state of Georgia. What a marvelous moment for the country and the whole world. A black man is getting a standing ovation in the Deep South for breaking a record of an all-time baseball great. And it's a great moment for all of us, and particularly for Henry Aaron."

Indeed it was. Hammerin' Hank had touched 'em all, giving the media fodder for headlines, sound bytes, and highlight clips to last the rest of his life—and the nation, at least for this brief moment, the savior it so desperately needed.

CHAPTER NINE:

LONG LIVE THE KING

AS WITH ALL STAR-CROSSED ROMANCES, THE AFFAIR that climaxed on the evening of April 8, 1974, soon fizzled out. The lovefest between Henry Aaron and the city of Atlanta came crashing back to reality two nights later, when 6,000 or so showed up for the final game of the Dodger series. For any Atlantan harboring dreams of a divisional crown, Los Angeles represented one of the hurdles that would have to be overcome. The young Dodgers were coming together nicely, and they would in fact go on to win the National League pennant that season. The Braves finished a respectable third, with a record of 88–74, but were out of the running by September.

Aaron played in 112 games, though he started fewer than 90. In 340 at bats, he hit 20 home runs and posted an average of .268. For the first season in his professional baseball life, he failed to produce 100 hits. It seemed clear that the Braves were easing him out of the lineup. Consider that he did not make a single appearance at first base, which was manned by Mike Lum, Frank Tepedino, and Dave Johnson, who at 31 was losing both his range and power stroke. For Aaron, whose speed and reflexes were no longer good enough to qualify him as even an average outfielder, first would have been a natural spot.

Aaron shared left field with Rowland Office, an impossibly skinny 21-year-old who played his position with tremendous enthusiasm, if not always the highest regard for his body. (A year later, in 1975, he would leap entirely over Atlanta Stadium's seven-foot outfield wall to make what is still regarded as the greatest catch ever by a Brave.) The 1974 season would be Aaron's last in Atlanta. The team had come to this inescapable conclusion after taking a long, hard look in the mirror.

Like the Braves, the nation was reassessing its priorities. The House Judiciary Committee voted to issue a subpoena ordering President Nixon to turn over the Watergate tapes. The national outrage over kidnapped heiress Patricia Hearst took a sudden and unexpected turn after a security video caught her brandishing a machine gun during a bank heist perpetrated by her captors. In Denver, a judge ordered the integration of the city's public schools. Meanwhile, the Supreme Court ruled that the parents of the students gunned down at Kent State could sue state officials and the National Guard. Small wonder Aaron all but disappeared from the national consciousness after April.

For a man who savored the peace and quiet of life away from the media glare, these developments were the reward for nearly two years of nonstop insanity. What did bother Aaron, however, were the three words—Home Run King—that now preceded his name every time he was written or talked about. Ironically, the record had obscured his glorious career even further. Arguably baseball's greatest five-tool player, Aaron was now reduced to one dimension for the purposes of public consumption.

Although he went through the 1974 season with the look of a man comfortable with the idea of retirement, Aaron found baseball's grip to be stronger than he anticipated. That November, while in Japan for a home run contest against Sadaharu Oh, he received an early-morning call from Bud Selig, a friend from his old days with the Braves and now the owner of the Milwaukee Brewers. Selig had taken control of the expansion Seattle Pilots prior to the 1970 season and moved the bankrupt franchise to Milwaukee. He informed Aaron that the Brewers and Braves had reached agreement on a trade that would enable Aaron to return to his old stomping grounds. The news invigorated the aging slugger. He was going home again.

The trade itself was a token deal. The Brewers sent Atlanta a minor-league pitcher and Dave May, a 31-year-old outfielder who had enjoyed a remarkable "career year" in 1973 when he led the American League in total bases. Milwaukee had a pair of hot, young outfielders—Sixto Lezcano and Gorman Thomas—and needed to clear space for them to play. Aaron, Selig explained, would be the team's designated hitter. The Brewers were still a few seasons away from competing with the likes of the Orioles and Yankees, so Aaron was a good fit, both as a team leader and from a publicity standpoint.

Some questioned Aaron's decision to play another season, feeling he was just hanging on to the vestiges of his once-superb career. But he knew he had made the right choice when he took the field for Milwaukee's home opener. A crowd of 48,610, a record for County Stadium, serenaded him with a rendition of "Hello, Henry," sung to the tune of the Broadway hit *Hello, Dolly!* "I've always felt a special place in my heart for Milwaukee," he told the packed house. "I hope we can write a new chapter in the hearts of so many wonderful fans."

Actually, Aaron ended up playing two seasons for the Brewers. While he no longer frightened pitchers, he did have enough left in the tank to produce a total of 22 home runs and 95 RBIs. His average, however, sank well below .250, and the highlights were few and far between. Perhaps his most satisfying moment came against the Texas Rangers in 1976, when he hit a game-winning homer in the 10th inning and circled the bases as Milwaukee fans cheered wildly. "I'd had others that won ball games, but at the age of forty-two, every home run took on a little extra meaning to me," he said in *I Had a Hammer*. "And it meant even more to hear the fans chanting my name one last time."

It was at about this time that Aaron decided he would hang up his spikes for good at year's end. The remainder of the season turned into an unofficial farewell tour. Fans at home and on the road came in large numbers to witness Aaron in one last game. For many American League fans, it was the first time they actually got to see him play. Aaron hit his final homer, number 755, off reliever Dick Drago of the Angels in Milwaukee. He had said two years earlier that his last trip around the bases would mean the most to him. "I won't hang around for records," he added. "It will be a sad day when I have to take off the uniform for the last time, but it's something every player has to face sometime."

His playing days over, Aaron headed back to Atlanta. Media mogul Ted Turner, the new owner of the Braves, had asked him to take over as the team's director of player development. The decision to leave Milwaukee was difficult. Aaron had rediscovered the charms of the city and the enthusiasm of the fans. The temptation to stay and make a life there must have been strong. But given his Alabama roots, Aaron considered himself a southerner at heart, and Billye ached to be back among family and friends. He also embraced the idea of working in a front-office position. A year earlier, Frank Robinson had become the first black manager in baseball history. Aaron now saw a chance to make similar inroads in upper management.

His outlook would change over the years.

Aaron found that others viewed him as a figurehead without any real power or knowledge of the business of baseball. This bothered him greatly. After all he had seen and accomplished as a player, Aaron felt he had earned the respect of everyone in the game. In his mind, discrimination was once again holding him down, and he often reacted with hostility. As the years wore on, Aaron increasingly used his position as a pulpit on racial issues. And he pulled no punches when he did. Such was the case during a 1993 interview with William Ladson for *Sport* magazine. "I hate the way baseball has treated minorities," Aaron railed. "It has the worst track record in sports."

When asked whether he thought he would be considered to fill the recently vacated commissioner's job, he responded indignantly. "There's no chance in hell that I'll convince the owners that I'm qualified to be commissioner," Aaron said. "Let's face it, I'm a black man."

In Aaron's mind, that fact seemed to shadow him in other arenas as well, including sports memorabilia. During Aaron's retirement years, collectors helped keep alive the comparisons between him, Mantle, Mays, and Clemente. Spurred in part by Aaron's own fame, the baseball card and autograph market grew dramatically in the 1970s and 1980s. After a brief decline in the early 1990s, it evolved into a semiorganized commodities exchange. A retired athlete's "worth" could now be measured in dollars and cents.

For many years following his record-breaking home run, Aaron was the number one name among collectors. But with time, issues of race appeared to creep into the sports memorabilia market, as he lost ground to Mantle and Joe DiMaggio, and even Sandy Koufax—three white athletes whose mythology blossomed more with each passing year. Since white collectors and dealers control an enormous percentage of the dollars spent on memorabilia, this was hardly a surprise. The demand for Aaron items, however, often lagged behind that for cards and souvenirs of Mays and Clemente as well, a fact that obviously had nothing to do with race.

Needless to say, this was a battle Aaron could not fight. But that is not to say that it did not have an impact on him. Aaron's appearance fees were substantially lower than those for Mantle and DiMaggio who became their own memorabilia industries, and for Koufax whose reclusive nature and connection to the New York and Los Angeles markets always made him a hot ticket. Mays's fees ran roughly equal to Aaron's, mainly because of his constant availability. To his credit, Aaron took whatever slights were implicit in these facts with a grain of salt. Impressing baseball card show promoters and sports collectors was low on his list of priorities.

Aaron was more concerned with the charitable organizations he helped establish, which focused on helping young people. He continued to work for Turner, playing a vital role in the magnate's television empire. In 1991, he penned his autobiography with Lonnie Wheeler. Also, when the situation dictated, Aaron was able to put aside his feelings and act with great diplomacy. His 1982 induction into the Hall of Fame was a perfect example. Though Bowie Kuhn, still the baseball commissioner, introduced him at the ceremony in Cooperstown, Aaron chose to overlook the obvious irony of the situation and delivered a heartfelt speech that reflected on his long career in the big leagues and acknowledged family and friends as well as former teammates and managers. "I never dreamed this high honor would come to me," he said. "For it was not fame I sought, but rather [to be] the best baseball player I could possibly be."

Although the neglect and abuse he experienced at the hands of the game he loved was hard to forget, on April 8, 1999—exactly 25 years after he had donned the all-time home run crown—Aaron found a way to forgive. In a grandiose display, baseball celebrated his career during a pregame ceremony at Turner Field. Days earlier, Bud Selig, then commissioner of Major League Baseball, had announced the creation of the Hank Aaron Award, to be given annually to the top hitter in each league. "It's an award that embodies everything," said Selig. "It's clearly the person in either league who's been the best all-around hitter, not just the [best] power hitter. That's what makes it so unique."

The first winners were sluggers Sammy Sosa in the NL and Manny Ramirez in the AL. Winners in the years since include Alex Rodriguez, Barry Bonds and Albert Pujols.

The sellout crowd that shook the stadium on that Thursday evening in 1999 displayed equal amounts of love and admiration. Fans cheered the slugger as though he had just hit number 715 again. Players and coaches in both dugouts stood for a full 30 minutes, applauding throughout the ceremony. Aaron, whose amazing composure had distinguished him during his career, had tears in his eyes.

"Look at him, will you," said Frank Robinson, on hand for the festivities. "Look how happy he is. These past few months, I've never seen Henry so happy. I think it's the happiest he's been since he left the game of baseball.

"Ten years ago, I don't think this could have happened. He wasn't ready to forgive. There was still too much bitterness . . . the timing now is perfect."

Looking joyful rather than relieved, Aaron agreed. "It's been a long time coming, but I'm happy," he said. "I am so happy. I am at peace with the game.

"I had scars on me from those letters and all the other things. It chipped away at me a little bit. . . .Time has ways of healing some things."

Or does it? Less than a month after the celebration in Atlanta, Aaron sat down for a very frank interview with his old friend William Ladson, who had become an associate editor for the *Sporting News*. At one point, Ladson asked Aaron if he was happy.

"I think I am," he said. "That's for other people to decide."

EPILOGUE

THE LAYERED COMPLEXITY OF HENRY AARON'S LIFE and career has continued to grow since that warm spring evening in April of 1999, when he was honored by Major League Baseball at Turner Field. In fact, events in the game—most notably the "steroid scandal"—have further complicated his legacy. This seemed the most logical place to end our examination of baseball's home run king.

As mentioned in this book's foreword, attempts were made to contact Aaron during the initial research for *Hammering Hank*, and after the initial manuscript was completed. Neither effort resulted in an interview. Lonnie Wheeler, who worked with Aaron on *I Had a Hammer*, did not seem surprised. He confirmed the fact that Aaron had developed a wariness of the media early in his career—when he was portrayed "almost like a field hand"—and that he admitted to Wheeler during their work together that he was very slow to trust anyone in general.

Wheeler was obviously intrigued enough by the approach of *Hammering Hank* to talk with us. Indeed, he too had formed his initial opinion of Aaron based entirely on his portrayal in the media. Needless to say, the writer got to know a very different person. Aaron, he observed, evolved from a kid too scared to speak into an elder statesman who stands for what he says. "He is one of the first calls a reporter makes when an important issue surfaces in baseball," Wheeler said.

The irony, Wheeler added, is that he has been espousing the same beliefs for many years. "The shaping of his image has come with time, and the times."

Time, and the times, of course, also brought to light revelations that baseball's modern-day record-breakers may have been "juiced." So too came the realization that Aaron's home run record was suddenly and surprisingly reachable. The game's balance of power appeared to have shifted dramatically to the sluggers, who were launching home runs at a pace that served to diminish much of what Aaron had spent a baseball lifetime quietly building and then protecting.

Records being what they are, fans began preparing themselves for the inevitability that someone would crank out enough four-baggers to supplant Aaron at the top of the all-time home run list. Baseball itself seemed to be gearing up for this historic moment, in that wonderfully self-conscious way it has of celebrating the fall of a major record. The fact that Barry Bonds emerged as the man most likely to pass Aaron provided an even more compelling story line. Bonds and Aaron were cut from the same cloth in so many ways. Their late-career power surges were the stuff of baseball mythology. They shared an unhealthy disdain for the media—one clearly expressed, the other largely unexpressed. They even knew and liked each other. What better way to pass the torch?

As Bonds powered his way ever closer toward the blessed event, Aaron, quiet as usual, seemed to sense what the San Francisco slugger would soon be facing. Early in the 2004 season, Bonds crashed his 661st lifetime home run to pass Willie Mays, Barry's godfather and Aaron's historical alter ego. With the record now as close as two seasons away, scrutiny and criticism of Bonds intensified. Those extraordinary seasons seemed a little too extraordinary;

as soon as Aaron's mark was in his sights, Bonds found himself in the crosshairs, too.

The numbers suggested that something was amiss. It was not the fact that Bonds hit 73 homers at the age of 37. Within the context of baseball's overall power surge, this was a plausible number. After all, Aaron himself had rediscovered his power at about the same age, so why not Bonds? Besides, fans could absorb the occasional statistical anomaly, especially when cartoon heroes like Mark McGwire and Sammy Sosa were doing the record-breaking. It was the other numbers that raised the game's collective eyebrow.

There has always been a certain elegance to the math of baseball, and the statistics that Bonds was compiling were strikingly inelegant. Batting in a ballpark that did not offer any extreme advantages, supported by a lineup composed of ordinary hitters, and lumbering gracelessly around left field, Bonds was nevertheless producing godlike results. His power numbers, his average, his on-base percentage—all suggested that he was playing a different game on a higher plane than everyone else. Yes, Bonds was an extremely intelligent and disciplined hitter. Yes, he was a madman when it came to conditioning. And yes, he was the best player in baseball before he became something even better than that. Still, in the culture of baseball, what Bonds was doing simply did not compute.

After a decade of nervously celebrating the sport's new era, baseball pulled its head out of the sand and began to look into rumors of rampant steroid abuse. It did not take long for a smoking gun (BALCO) to appear, and it came as no surprise when Bonds seemed to be a central figure in the scandal. And because Bonds was in it up to his treetrunk-like neck, the man he was chasing—Henry Aaron—became part of this sensational story, too. Steroids were not just an affront to baseball, they now directly threatened Aaron's legacy.

Aaron's response was nothing if not revealing. In many respects, it mirrored his evolution as a media figure. Initially, he took what one might characterize as the high road: he refused to pile on when Bonds was publicly vilified. Perhaps Aaron recalled those hellish weeks and months before he eclipsed the Babe. "I've had that record a long time," he told Tom Haudricourt of the *Milwaukee Journal-Sentinel* after the 2003 season. "But I've always said, records are made to be broken."

"I think it would be good for baseball," Aaron said of Bonds's usurping his home run record. "I really do."

When asked about the steroid allegations with which Bonds was being confronted, Aaron was equally diplomatic: "My assumption is he's innocent until proven guilty. Until then, you can't say anything other than he's a very good player. One of the best ever."

This sounded like the Henry Aaron of the 1950s—unsure of his footing and distrustful of the media. When pressed on the issue the following spring by a *New York Times* reporter, Aaron held fast. "I admire Barry Bonds," he said. "Steroids or no steroids, he would have had a Hall of Fame career."

By November of 2004, when Bonds reportedly admitted to a grand jury that he had taken steroids—albeit unknowingly, he claimed—Aaron was beginning to change his tune. He had always assumed his place in history would be defined by shattering Ruth's home run record. In the thirty summers that had passed, however, he had come to understand that owning the record—being baseball's all-time home run king—was an even more important part of who he was and, ultimately, how he would be remembered. Clearly, this was on his mind when he told the *Atlanta Journal-Constitution*, "Any way you look at [Bonds's use of steroids], it's wrong."

"At that age," Aaron said, "you have to ask, 'Did he accomplish all of this by rejuvenating his strength day to day with those substances?'"

Aaron had moved into the mainstream regarding the steroid issue, echoing the feeling of many players, most fans, and virtually every retired star. As had been the case late in his playing career, he felt compelled to speak out on what he viewed as injustice. One could argue that, as the man who stood to lose the most if steroid use continued unchecked, Aaron had put the final stamp on the call to clean up baseball. If "Hammerin' Hank" was actually pissed off and willing to say so publicly, well, something definitely had to be done.

A few months later, some of the game's most storied sluggers were called to Washington, where they were subjected to a very public grilling by grandstanding senators. The players—backtracking on previous statements, shedding crocodile tears, bad-mouthing one another and hoping to veil attempts at self-promotion—actually made the *politicians* look good. Bud Selig, baseball's commissioner and a longtime friend of Aaron's, was raked over the coals, as were his underlings. The game's powers that be claimed they had no power at all, insisting that they were held hostage by the fine print in the collective bargaining agreement.

Aaron no doubt watched these hearings with intense interest. Steroids were not only threatening to knock him off his perch as the all-time home run king, they were threatening the very integrity of the game he loved. It was time to get involved. Aaron joined four fellow Hall of Famers—Lou Brock, Phil Niekro, Robin Roberts and Ryne Sandberg—who accompanied Selig to subsequent Senate appearances that were aimed at creating a more effective drug policy. Aaron's presence changed the entire mood of the hearings. The tone of the questions became respectful, almost deferential.

Aaron said he was saddened by the beating baseball was taking, and disturbed by the lack of an effective drug policy. It was not about home runs anymore. It was about something even more important to him. Aaron's message was crystal clear: "Whatever we do, we have to make sure we clean up baseball."

Interestingly, Aaron was asked during his testimony whether pre-steroid records should retain some sort of special status. He knew as well as anyone that baseball has never worked this way, yet nevertheless fashioned an intriguing response. "That's going to be left up to the commissioner and the rules committee," he said. "They will probably go back and look at some of those things that happened at those times."

Although his name was not invoked, everyone in the room knew Virginia Senator George Allen was referring to Barry Bonds when he said, "Forget an asterisk—there probably ought to be an Rx beside it if a certain player breaks Mr. Aaron's record."

Mr. Aaron, looking stately and dignified—and all of his 71 years—did not have to respond.

BIBLIOGRAPHY

BOOKS

Aaron, Henry. *Aaron, r.f.* With Furman Bisher. Cleveland: World Publishing Company, 1968.

———. *I Had a Hammer: The Hank Aaron Story*. With Lonnie Wheeler. New York: HarperCollins, 1991.

———. *Home Run: My Life in Pictures*. With Dick Schaap. New York: Total Sports, 1999.

Associated Press Sports Staff. *The Sports Immortals*. Englewood Cliffs, NJ: Prentice Hall, 1972.

Baseball Stars of 1959. New York: Pyramid Books, 1959.

Baseball Stars of 1960. New York: Pyramid Books, 1960.

Baseball Stars of 1961. New York: Pyramid Books, 1961.

Baseball Stars of 1963. New York: Pyramid Books, 1963.

Baseball Stars of 1974. New York: Pyramid Books, 1974.

Baseball Research Journal. Society for American Baseball Research, 1977.

Bisher, Furman. *The Furman Bisher Collection*. Dallas, TX: Taylor Publishing, 1989.

Brondfield, Jerry. *Hank Aaron . . . 714 and Beyond!* New York: Scholastic Book Services, 1974.

Brown, Gene, ed. *The New York Times Book of Baseball History*. New York: Quadrangle/New York Times Book Company, 1975.

Cohen, Eliot, ed. *My Greatest Day in Baseball*. New York: Little Simon, 1991.

Cohen, Joel. *Hammerin' Hank of the Braves*. New York: Scholastic Book Services, 1971.

Dickey, Glenn. *The History of National League Baseball*. New York: Stein and Day, 1979.

Flood, Curt, with Richards Carter. *The Way It Is*, New York: Trident Press, 1971.

Gutman, Bill. *Henry Aaron*. New York: Tempo Books, 1974.

James, Bill. *The Bill James Historical Baseball Abstract*. New York: Villard Books, 1986.

Johnson, Lloyd, and Brenda Ward. *Who's Who in Baseball History*. Greenwich, CT: Brompton Books, 1994.

Kay, Tommy. *Tommy Kay's Big Book of Baseball*. Scottsdale, AZ: Jalart House, 1974.

Kuhn, Bowie. *Hardball: The Education of a Baseball Commissioner*. New York: Times Books, 1987.

Major League Baseball 1974. New York: Pocket Books, 1974.

Musick, Phil. *Henry Aaron: The Man Who Beat the Babe*. New York: Popular Library, 1974.

Pepe, Phil. *Talkin' Baseball: An Oral History of Baseball in the 1970s*. New York: Ballantine, 1998.

Rodgers, William Warren, et al. *Alabama: The History of a Deep South State*. Tuscaloosa: University of Alabama Press, 1994.

Rust, Art, Jr. *Get That Nigger Off the Field: The Oral History of Black Ballplayers from the Negro Leagues to the Present*. Reprint, Brooklyn, NY: Book Mail Services, 1992.

Seaver, Tom. *How I Would Pitch to Babe Ruth: Seaver vs. the Sluggers*. With Norman Lewis Smith. Chicago: Playboy Press, 1974.

Shapiro, Milton, J. *The Hank Aaron Story*. New York: J. Messner, 1961.

Shatzkin, Mike, ed. *The Ballplayers: Baseball's Ultimate Biographical Reference*. New York: Arbor House/William Morrow, 1990.

Summerall, Pat, and Jim Moskovitz. *Pat Summerall's Sports in America: 32 Celebrated Sports Personalities Talk About Their Most Memorable Moments In and Out of the Sports Arena*. With Craig Kubey. New York: HarperCollins, 1996.

MAGAZINES

ALL-STAR SPORTS

Bukata, Jim. "Dusty Baker Tells What It's Like to Be Hank Aaron's Heir." May, 1974.

BASEBALL DIGEST

Bisher, Furman. "Hank Aaron Tells a Secret." November, 1971.

Brown, William T. "The Pursuit Resumes." April, 1974.

Chapman, Lou. "Hank Aaron Talks About Changes in the Game." December, 1981.

Dexter, Charles. "The Changes in Henry Aaron." August, 1966.

———. "Kid with K Arm." October–November, 1963.

Finch, Frank. "How They Pitch to Aaron." October, 1959.

Fraley, Gerry. "Players Recall Diamond Deeds of Henry Aaron." November, 1966.

Grady, Sandy. "2,500 Hits—and Aaron Hit Every One Wrong." September, 1967.

Heling, Joe. "It Was Embarrassing." February, 1968.

Hertzel, Bob. "Aaron Recalls Major League Debut." December, 1974.

Holder, William G. "Jack Billingham: From 'Throw-In' to Stardom." October, 1973.

Holway, John. "Aaron's Silent Home Run Handicap."
September, 1973.

Johnson, Chuck. "Hank Aaron Talks About Hitting." July, 1975.

Reich, Kenneth. "Hank Aaron in Countdown on Ruth Mark."
January, 1971.

Sheeley, Glenn. "The Night Hank Aaron Hit His Record-Breaking
Homer." August, 1984.

Walfoort, Cleon. "How They Pitch to Aaron." October, 1959.

———. "Natural Comeback." October–November, 1958.

———. "The Second Aaron May Be First." July, 1962.

Baseball Illustrated 1973

Minshew, Wayne. "Hank Aaron 42 And Counting."

Baseball Sports Stars of 1972

Olan, Ben. "Letters to Hank Aaron Plead 'Don't Break Babe Ruth's Record.'" Spring.

Black Sports

Andrews, Samuel A. "Bad Henry." May-June, 1972.

Cord Sportfacts Baseball Report

Down, Fred. "Can Anyone Top Hank?" 1974.

Popular Sports Baseball 1973

Thomy, Al. "Hank Aaron's Pursuit of the Babe." May.

Saturday Evening Post

Bisher, Furman. "Born to Play Baseball." August 25, 1956.

Sport

Conroy, Pat. "Henry Aaron and the Magic Number." May, 1974.

Holtzman, Jerome. "I Could Do the Job." October, 1965.
Kahn, Roger. "Hank Aaron's Success Story." September, 1959.
Katz, Fred. "Aaron and Cepeda Sound Off on Hitters, Spitters and Mangers They Have Known." September, 1969.
Ladson, William. "Hank Aaron, Q&A." February, 1993.
O'Brien, Jim. "Hank Aaron: What It's Like to Be a Neglected Superstar." July, 1968.

Sports Today

Allen, Maury. "The Day the Braves Almost Gave Up on Hank Aaron." 1972.

Sporting News

Bisher, Furman. "Joy—And Gloom—for Aaron." April 20, 1974.
Blair, Sam. "Mantle, Aaron Agree: They Hate 1B." April 7, 1973.
Falls, Joe. "A Great Diversion." April 20, 1974.
Kindred, Dave. "A Face to Remember." June 14, 1999.
Ladson, William. "Still Hammerin' Away." April 26, 1999.
Lieb, Frederick G. "Babe Thought 714 HRs Would Stand Forever." June 3, 1972.

Minshew, Wayne. "Aaron Giving Sherman Tips on How to Capture Atlanta." September 29, 1973.
———. "Aaron Has Sore Neck; Hurlers Doubt It." May 22, 1972.
———. "Aaron Slurred as He Assaults Ruth's Mark." May 26, 1973.
———. "Aaron Zeroed In on HR Mark by Sticking to His Guns." October 13, 1973.
———. "All-Star Aaron . . . 20-Year Memories." July 29, 1972.
———. "Braves Get Their Orders: Shed Weight." December 30, 1972.
———. "Hate Mail Was Inspiration to Aaron." November 3, 1973.
———. "Hectic Week for Deals—68 Players Are Traded."

December 16, 1972.
———. "In Midst of Uproar, Aaron Just Plays It Cool." July 14, 1973.
———. "Johnson Credits HR Binge to Aaron's Presence." November 10, 1973.
———. "Keystoner Dave Gets Key Atlanta Hits." June 30, 1973.
———. "Kuhn Warning on Aaron Bid." June 30, 1973.
———. "Maris Pulling for Aaron to Top Ruth." July 21, 1973.
———. "Mathews Applies Acid Test to Braves." August 26, 1972.
———. "Mod Braves Will Dress in Royal Blue and White." February 26, 1972.
———. "Once upon a Time, Aaron Worried." April 15, 1972.
———. "Richards Picks Aug. 31, 1973, Date When Hank Beats Babe." January 1, 1972.
———. "Touch of Class—HR Slugger Hank Aaron." April 20, 1974.
Mizell, Hubert. "Aaron at 19: Shy, Clumsy Sally League Rookie." April 20, 1974.
Nigro, Ken. "Mrs. Ruth 'Hasn't Thought Too Much' About Record." June 23, 1973.
Outlar, Jesse. "Aaron Calm under Pressure of Assault on 714." April 8, 1972.
Spander, Art. "A Sticky Situation." April 20, 1974.
Thomy, Al. "$600,000 Cushion to Aid Aaron's Bid for Ruth Mark." March 18, 1972.

Sporting News 1982 Baseball Yearbook
Hyland, Frank. "No. 44 a Quiet Man with a Big Bat."

Sport Scene
Jacobsen, Steve. "Aaron Mays Ruth—The Great Home Run Record Farce." July, 1971.

Sports Illustrated
Capuzzo, Mike. "A Prisoner of Memory." December 7, 1992.
Flood, Curt, and Richard Carter. "My Rebellion." February 1, 1971.
Horn, Huston. "Bravura Battle for the Braves." November 2, 1964.
Keith, Larry. "Back Where He belongs." April 20, 1975.
Leggett, William. "Hank Becomes a Hit." August 18, 1969.
———. "Henry Raps One for History." May 25, 1970.
———. "Leave Us Eddie Mattress." April 26, 1965.
———. "Poised for the Golden Moment." April 8, 1974.
Mann, Jack. "Danger with a Double A." August 1, 1966.
Mulvoy, Mark. "Knockdown Time in the Wild, Wild West." September 29, 1969.
Plimpton, George. "Final Twist of the Drama." April 22, 1974.
Terrell, Roy. "Murder with a Blunt Instrument." August 12, 1957.

Sports Quarterly Presents . . . Baseball
Hirshey, Dave. "Bittersweetness to His Reflections." Spring, 1974.
Schlossberg, Dan. "Where Does 'Bad Henry' Rate?" Spring, 1974.

Street & Smith's Official Baseball Yearbook
Bisher, Furman. "Babe Ruth and Hank Aaron." 1974.

USA Today Baseball Weekly
Koenig, Bill. "715: 25 Years Later." April 7–13, 1999.

NEWSPAPERS

AAP Sports News (Australia)
"US homerun king Aaron blasts Bonds over steroids." December 7, 2004.

Agence France Presse English
"Aaron backs tougher doping plan as Bonds' record quest questioned." September 28, 2005.

AP Online

"Steroids Won't Affect Aaron View on Bonds." April 7, 2004.

Atlanta Constitution

Minshew, Wayne. "Aaron Hammers No. 715 and Moves Ahead of Ruth." April 9, 1974.

Roberts, Charlie. "Aaron Family Relieved, Satisfied." April 9, 1974.

———. "Braves Family Overwhelmed by 715." April 9, 1974.

Atlanta Journal

Bisher, Furman. "Rerun of Ol' 693." April 9, 1974.

Hyland, Frank. "One Game Season." April 9, 1974.

———. "On the Aaron Watch." April 9, 1974.

McKenzie, Mike. "Kuhn Gets Stadium Boos: It's 'Phooey on Bowie.'" April 9, 1974.

———. "Ted Williams Was a Prophet: Braves Were to Profit." April 9, 1974.

Atlanta Journal-Constitution

Bisher, Furman. "Aaron Played Game Right." April 4, 1999.

Hudspeth, Ron. "The Loudest Shot." April 4, 1999.

Rogers, Carroll. "MLB Creates Hank Aaron Award." April 4, 1999.

Stinson, Thomas, and Gita M. Smith. "MLB Creates Hank Aaron Award." April 4, 1999.

Milwaukee Journal Sentinel

Haudricourt, Tom. "Aaron says he expects home-run record to fall soon." October 30, 2003.

New York Times

Anderson, Dave. "The Sound of 715." April 9, 1974.

Chass, Murray. "At Long Last, Aaron Basks and the Fans Just Love It." April 9, 1994.
Durso, Joseph. "Aaron Hits 715th, Passes Babe Ruth." April 9, 1974.
Shearer, Ed. "Slugger Would Like to Do It in Atlanta." April 4, 1974.

The Washington Times
Loverro, Thom. "Senate demands stricter testing; Fehr defends union's stance." September 29, 2005.

VIDEOCASSETTE
Hank Aaron: Chasing the Dream. Written and directed by Mike Tollin. Studio City, CA: TBS Productions, 1995.

GENERAL REFERENCE
The following books, magazines, and newspapers were used for general reference and fact checking:

Atlanta Journal-Constitution
Bill James Historical Baseball Abstract
MacMillan Baseball Encyclopedia
New York Times
Sporting News
Sporting News Baseball Guide
Sporting News Baseball Register
Sports Encyclopedia: Baseball
Sports Illustrated
Street & Smith Baseball Yearbook
Total Baseball
USA Today Baseball Weekly

INDEX

B

I

J

K

N

Y